Bioarchaeology of Native American Adaptation
in the Spanish Borderlands

The Ripley P. Bullen Series
Florida Museum of Natural History

Florida Museum of Natural History
The Ripley P. Bullen Series
Jerald T. Milanich, General Editor

Tacachale: Essays on the Indians of Florida and Southeastern Georgia during the Historic Period, edited by Jerald T. Milanich and Samuel Proctor (1978).

Aboriginal Subsistence Technology on the Southeastern Coastal Plain during the Late Prehistoric Period, by Lewis H. Larson (1980).

Cemochechobee: Archaeology of a Mississippian Ceremonial Center on the Chattahoochee River, by Frank T. Schnell, Vernon J. Knight, Jr., and Gail S. Schnell (1981).

Fort Center: An Archaeological Site in the Lake Okeechobee Basin, by William H. Sears, with contributions by Elsie O'R. Sears and Karl T. Steinen (1982).

Perspectives on Gulf Coast Prehistory, edited by Dave D. Davis (1984).

Archaeology of Aboriginal Culture Change in the Interior Southeast: Depopulation during the Early Historic Period, by Marvin T. Smith (1987).

Apalachee: The Land between the Rivers, by John H. Hann (1988).

Key Marco's Buried Treasure: Archaeology and Adventure in the Nineteenth Century, by Marion Spjut Gilliland (1989).

First Encounters: Spanish Explorations in the Caribbean and the United States, 1492–1570, edited by Jerald T. Milanich and Susan Milbrath (1989).

Missions to the Calusa, edited and translated by John H. Hann, with an Introduction by William H. Marquardt (1991).

Excavations on the Franciscan Frontier: Archaeology at the Fig Springs Mission, by Brent Richards Weisman (1992).

The People Who Discovered Columbus: The Prehistory of the Bahamas, by William F. Keegan (1992).

Hernando de Soto and the Indians of Florida, by Jerald T. Milanich and Charles Hudson (1993).

Foraging and Farming in the Eastern Woodlands, edited by C. Margaret Scarry (1993).

Fort Center: An Archaeological Site in the Lake Okeechobee Basin, edited by William H. Sears, with contributions by Elsie O'R. Sears and Karl T. Steinen (first paperback edition, 1994).

Tacachale: Essays on the Indians of Florida and Southeastern Georgia during the Historic Period, edited by Jerald T. Milanich and Samuel Proctor (first paperback edition, 1994).

Puerto Real: The Archaeology of a Sixteenth-Century Spanish Town in Hispaniola, edited by Kathleen Deagan (1995).

A History of the Timucua Indians and Missions, by John H. Hann (1996).

Bioarchaeology of Native American Adaptation in the Spanish Borderlands, edited by Brenda J. Baker and Lisa Kealhofer (1996).

Bioarchaeology of Native American Adaptation in the Spanish Borderlands

EDITED BY
BRENDA J. BAKER
AND
LISA KEALHOFER

UNIVERSITY PRESS OF FLORIDA

*Gainesville/Tallahassee/Tampa/Boca Raton
Pensacola/Orlando/Miami/Jacksonville*

01 00 99 98 97 96 6 5 4 3 2 1

Library of Congress Cataloging-in-Publication Data

Bioarchaeology of Native American adaptation in the Spanish borderlands / edited by Brenda J. Baker and Lisa Kealhofer.
    p.   cm.—(The Ripley P. Bullen series)
    Includes bibliographical references and index.
    ISBN 0-8130-1464-6 (alk. paper)
    1. Indians of North America—Southern States—Anthropometry. 2. Indians of North America—Southwest, New—Anthropometry. 3. Indians of North America—Southern States—Population. 4. Indians of North America—Southwest, New—Population. 5. Ethnoarchaeology—Southern States. 6. Ethnoarchaeology—Southwest, New. 7. Southern States—Antiquities. 8. Southwest, New—Antiquities. I. Baker, Brenda J. II. Kealhofer, Lisa. III. Series.
    E78.S65B56 1996
    975.01—dc 20 96-24085

The University Press of Florida is the scholarly publishing agency for the State University System of Florida, comprised of Florida A & M University, Florida Atlantic University, Florida International University, Florida State University, University of Central Florida, University of Florida, University of North Florida, University of South Florida, and University of West Florida.

University Press of Florida
15 Northwest 15th Street
Gainesville, FL 32611

Contents

LIST OF FIGURES

List of Tables

Acknowledgments

We would like to thank the contributors to this volume for their patience and generous assistance. Marie Ellsworth deserves special thanks for her work on the index. In addition, we are grateful to the reviewers of the manuscript at the University Press of Florida, whose comments and advice were much appreciated.

FOREWORD

The Columbian Exchange, the meeting of East and West that began with the initial voyage of Christopher Columbus, brought great changes to the world. One aspect of that exchange was the European colonization of the Americas, a process that took place in the context of a hemispheric-wide demographic collapse: for in the several centuries following 1492, Native American populations suffered precipitous reductions. Some native groups ceased to exist, while others adapted to the new world that was taking shape around them and of which they were a part.

This volume is composed of a group of essays that focus on the nature of that demographic collapse. The contention is that such a catastrophe indeed did take place. But the process was much more variable than that proposed by those scholars who believe the collapse resulted from disease-caused pandemics that swept across North and South America. This latter model holds that in only a few short years a single epidemic could have spread from the Great Lakes to Tierra del Fuego, devastating the native groups who had no immunities to smallpox, measles, and other diseases introduced into the Americas by European explorers and early colonists.

Editors Brenda Baker and Lisa Kealhofer argue that in contrast to this pandemic model are data showing that the responses by Native Americans to the presence of people from Europe were not uniform. Many groups did adapt to conditions of the post-Columbian era, and those adaptations varied by culture and circumstance. Epidemics were circumscribed, affecting different populations in different ways. And different cultural factors—such as population densities and the nature of European contact situations—led to different epidemiological and demographic outcomes. As a result, some Native American groups disappeared within several decades after 1492, while others were relatively unaffected for several centuries. From examining the cultural and biological contexts of specific contact situations, a more accurate model explaining the impact of that contact can be developed.

This perspective on population collapse in the Americas is illustrated with case studies taken from the region that today is the southern United States:

the area from Florida and Georgia through Alabama, Mississippi, and Texas into New Mexico and California. Taken together, these well-documented investigations convincingly support the contention that archaeological and bioanthropological research are powerful tools for interpreting the variable cultural and biological factors affecting Native American groups in the post-Columbian world.

JERALD T. MILANICH
FLORIDA MUSEUM OF NATURAL HISTORY

Chapter 1

Assessing the Impact of European Contact on Aboriginal Populations

BRENDA J. BAKER AND LISA KEALHOFER

The effects of European contact on New World populations have been the subject of a proliferating body of literature in recent years (e.g., Axtell 1981, 1985, 1992; Crosby 1972; Denevan 1992; Dobyns 1966, 1983; Jennings 1975; Johansson 1982; Larsen and Milner 1994; Ramenofsky 1987; Reff 1991; Rouse 1992; Sale 1990; Salisbury 1982; Stannard 1992; Steele 1994; Thomas 1989, 1990, 1991; Thornton 1987; Trigger 1985; Verano and Ubelaker 1992; Viola and Margolis 1991). Many investigators focus on the impact of European-introduced epidemic disease and subsequent demographic "collapse" of indigenous populations. In many groups, however, population decline did not occur in a matter of a generation or two but took place over several centuries. This gradual depopulation resulted from the interaction of many factors, only one of which was introduced disease. As the chapters in this volume demonstrate, biocultural responses to European contact were not uniform, ranging from rapid cultural and demographic collapse to adaptation and resilience.

To assess the magnitude of demographic collapse, scholars have devoted considerable effort to reconstructing the size of precontact and protohistoric Native American populations. Less attention has been paid to rigorous definition of the parameters of demographic collapse. How long does this "collapse" take? Is it caused by one major pandemic? Does it take five years or fifty?

We suggest that demographic collapse—or an *"abrupt and catastrophic decline"* (as defined by Ramenofsky [1987, 22], emphasis in original)—is a special, short-term case of depopulation, which is a gradual process of population reduction. Recent uses of the term *collapse* have included population loss over long periods (e.g., Dobyns 1983; Ramenofsky 1987; Thornton 1987). There is no question that most indigenous groups experienced depopulation during the historic period. What is at issue here is the nature and magnitude of this decline, and the extent to which it is correlated with epidemic disease. The question of demographic collapse has been inexorably tied to demographic reconstruction and the epidemiology of diseases introduced to previously unexposed populations.

Invariably, epidemics are cited as having resulted in cataclysmic population reduction throughout the Americas (e.g., Ashburn 1947; Crosby 1972; Dobyns 1966, 1983; Duffy 1953; Reff 1991; Smith 1987; Stannard 1992; Stearn and Stearn 1945; Thornton 1987), thereby allowing Europeans to gain a foothold on the continent. Epidemiological models (e.g., Milner 1980; Thornton et al. 1991; Upham 1986; Zubrow 1990), and a spate of historical references used to document epidemic episodes (e.g., Ashburn 1947; Crosby 1972; Dobyns 1983; Reff 1987, 1991), have been employed to calculate ratios of population decline. What is markedly lacking in most discussions is a biocultural perspective on the process of depopulation; typically, the data derived from physical remains and historical documents are divorced from their cultural context.

The goal of this introduction is to evaluate the perspective currently dominating the literature and suggest an alternative approach to investigating the impact of European contact on Native American populations—an approach exemplified by the essays in this volume.

Depopulation: Theoretical and Historical Background

Previous determinations of the extent of postcontact demographic change hinge on the size of the precontact population. In a circular chain of reasoning, aboriginal population is extrapolated from depopulation ratios that assume high epidemic mortality; these projections then become the basis for concluding that epidemics caused demographic collapse.

Early investigators, such as Mooney and Kroeber, distrusted the first European accounts of Native American populations (see discussions in Denevan, ed., 1992; Dobyns 1966; Ramenofsky 1987). They assumed Spanish observers exaggerated the size of indigenous populations and, to mitigate this bias, they discounted such estimates in reconstructing the population of cultural groups throughout North America. Using culture area estimates and early census data, Kroeber (1939) estimated that the population of the New World just prior to 1492 was 8.4 million, with 900,000 people inhabiting North America (see table 1.1).

In contrast, recent researchers have regarded the historical census records as representing populations already diminished by epidemics and social disruption. Dobyns (1966, 1983, 1989), for example, contends that epidemics spread rapidly through New World populations, ahead of direct contact with Europeans. Historical descriptions of specific groups, therefore, do not portray pristine cultures, but societies in a post-epidemic state of cultural and biological ruin. To reconstruct aboriginal populations, Dobyns (1966, 412) calculated a "standard" New World depopulation ratio based on the size of "the known

Table 1.1. Estimates of aboriginal population prior to European contact

	Western Hemisphere	North America	California
Merriam (1905)	—	—	260,000
Mooney (1910)	—	1,153,000	260,000
Kroeber (1939)	8,400,000	900,000	133,000
Borah (1964)	100,000,000	—	—
Dobyns (1966)	90,043,000	9,800,000	—
Cook (1976)	—	—	310,000
Ubelaker (1988)	—	1,894,350	221,000
Denevan (1992)	53,904,000	3,790,000	—

or confidently estimated preconquest population in 1 area and a known or closely estimated nadir population in that same area." Dobyns then compared ratios calculated for various areas to test for "consistency," and suggested a constant depopulation ratio of 20 to 1. The use of such a ratio assumes a mechanistic relationship between European contact and Native American population decline that is unaffected by environment, culture, or time: contact automatically led to the demise of 95 percent of every indigenous population.

The pitfalls of this method can be illustrated using population estimates for California (table 1.1). A depopulation ratio of about 8 to 1 over a period of 140 years is derived from Kroeber's (1939) estimate of the precontact California population of 133,000, divided by a nadir population of 15,850 in 1912 (Dobyns 1966, 413). Using Cook's (1976, 1978) estimate of a precontact population of 310,000 and 1900 nadir of 15,377 (based on U.S. census data), however, yields a depopulation ratio of 20 to 1 over 130 years, a figure more acceptable to Dobyns (1966, 413). Ubelaker's (1988, table 2) estimate of 221,000 for precontact California and 1950 nadir population of 10,542 yields a ratio of about 21 to 1 over a span of 180 years. Controlling for the number of years from contact to nadir, however, yields variable results, with depopulation *rates* from 0.5 to 0.73 percent per annum.

Clearly, no constant depopulation ratio or rate can be derived over different time spans and among disparate populations ranging from the Amazon to the Andes and central Mexico to California. Dobyns (1966, 412–14) makes no attempt to control for the length of time from contact to nadir, ranging from 12 to 140 years for the groups he discusses. Use of a standard depopulation ratio also assumes that mortality rates from different diseases are the same, and neither environmental variables (e.g., climate, altitude) nor cultural factors (e.g., settlement and subsistence patterns, sociopolitical organization) affect them. Furthermore, uniform rates of morbidity and mortality are assumed in subsequent epidemics, despite previous exposure to the pathogen (cf. Thornton et al. 1991). If epidemics occurred every $4\,^1/_6$ years, as suggested by Thornton (1987, 45) for the period from 1520 to 1900, some level of immunity would have resulted from prior exposure to a disease (cf. Joralemon 1982, 122).

An illustration of the vagaries of uniformly applying mortality data to different populations is provided by Shea (1992). Shea (1992, 159–61) describes how use of data derived from the central valley of Mexico is inappropriate for estimating rates of decline for groups inhabiting the central Andes (cf. Dobyns 1966). While villages were located evenly throughout the Valley of Mexico, settlements in the Andes were distributed in a linear manner. Taking into consideration cultural factors linking these settlements together, Shea (1992, 161) uses mathematical reasoning to describe rates of infection in these regions. In Mexico disease would spread from Mexico City in widening concentric circles. In the Andes disease would spread along the river valleys and down from the highlands. As a result of the settlement configuration and linkages between villages, Shea concludes that the infection rate would be more than three times (3.14) higher in Mexico. Concomitantly, the mortality rate in Mexico would be much higher than in the Andes. Thus, application of mortality data derived from Mexico would result in an unrealistic estimate of death and decline in Andean populations.

Extrapolations based upon standard ratios of depopulation have resulted in estimates of precontact New World population as high as 18 million in North America alone (Dobyns 1983). While such high precontact population estimates are extremely controversial (e.g., Denevan 1992; Fawcett and Swedlund 1984; Henige 1986; Johansson 1982, 1985; Storey 1985; Sturtevant 1984), it is generally accepted that the precontact Native American population was higher and denser than proposed by most researchers during the first half of this century. Explanations of the causes for, and processes by which, depopulation occurred are subject to even greater contention than the size of the precontact population.

An Alternative Approach

Adherents of the demographic collapse of Native American populations assume that *all* indigenous groups were fatally susceptible to contagious diseases, *all* were severely affected in the same way, and *all* failed to rebound demographically until recent decades. However, the evidence gleaned from the archaeological and historical records clearly indicates cultural and biological responses to epidemics were highly variable, disease dispersal was circumscribed, and demographic recovery was experienced by many populations; all of which challenge uniformitarian assumptions.

The view presented here is that different questions must be asked to elucidate how Native American groups reacted to European contact. Epidemic disease undoubtedly was a factor in depopulation, but was it the primary cause? How did individual cultures respond to the invasion of foreign bodies (both Europeans and their diseases)? How did they adapt biologically and culturally to these new contacts? What cultural factors, both European and Native American, circumscribed the choices available for adaptation? To what extent were Old and New World pathogens exchanged and modified, and what factors affected the dissemination and maintenance of specific diseases? What is the evidence for dispersal of disease in advance of direct contact and how can it be evaluated archaeologically and biologically? Even more fundamentally, are disease and depopulation directly related, or can they be viewed as independent variables whose relationship must be investigated? Finally, how does the examination of skeletal remains contribute to answering questions about adaptation, epidemiology, and depopulation?

Although this list of questions appears daunting, it provides a point of departure for studying the biological and cultural consequences of European and Native American interaction. Rather than assuming that disease was the prime cause of depopulation, we suggest that it should be considered as one of multiple causes and studied as part of locally complex cultural and biological contexts.

This is not a new or unique idea; others (e.g., Henige 1986, 305) have advocated approaching the problem with questions in mind rather than preconceived answers in hand, but the burgeoning literature that assumes epidemic disease caused demographic collapse (e.g., Ramenofsky 1987; Smith 1987; Thomas 1989, 1990, 1991) precludes a more rigorous evaluation of the problem. For example, in discussing the similarity between Mooney's precontact population estimates and Catlin's counts for 37 populations in the 1830s, Thornton's (1978) bias precludes the consideration that both figures are correct. Instead, since Thornton assumes that indigenous populations declined sharply due to epidemics in the intervening periods—ranging from 50 to 230 years after contact for these groups—he concludes that Mooney's estimates are much too low and must be revised accordingly. A more objective consideration of these population estimates provokes questions regarding the rates of disease dispersal and mortality among Plains Indians.

Extensive evidence confirms that Native Americans did adapt, both culturally and biologically, to European contact. The twentieth-century demographic recovery of Native American populations (figure 1.1) portrays the resilience of indigenous groups (Johansson 1982; Thornton 1987; Thornton et al. 1991; Ubelaker 1988, 293–94). That distinct cultural groups had variable demographic responses to contact has been demonstrated by numerous authors (e.g., Denevan 1992; Griffen 1979; Hann 1988; Larsen and Milner 1994; Meister

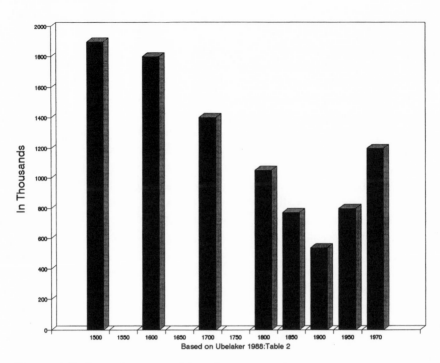

Figure 1.1. Decline and recovery of the indigenous North American population, 1500–1970.

1976; Snow 1995; Verano and Ubelaker 1992). The focus on demographic disaster, however, has encouraged the neglect of more significant cultural calamities and their biological consequences.

incorrect definition

Two phases of depopulation after 1492 can be separated analytically: the period preceding direct contact by Europeans in a region, referred to as the protohistoric period; and the period of direct contact, known as the historic or contact period. Diachronic investigations must evaluate the changes that occurred in both periods due to contact. The evidence for depopulation in these two periods is derived from different sources. For the protohistoric period the majority of evidence is obtained from archaeological and bioarchaeological data. For the contact period these data are supplemented by historical records.

THE FOCUS OF THE VOLUME

The essays collected in this volume reflect the necessity of using a broad range of evidence to assess the issue of Native American response to European contact diachronically. It is not necessary to rely upon estimates of the size of precontact populations to evaluate cultural upheaval after 1492. Demographic collapse may be inferred from both cultural and biological evidence. Discontinuities in settlement pattern, site size, and mortuary practices, as well as diachronic changes in mortality profiles and health status obtained from skeletal remains, can aid in determining biological responses of indigenous groups to European imperialism.

The consequences of Spanish colonization in the area known as the Spanish Borderlands provide the focus of the following essays. Geographically, the eastern Spanish Borderlands were what is now the southeastern United States, from Florida to South Carolina and westward to the Mississippi River valley. The western Spanish Borderlands encompassed what is now the American Southwest, including Texas, New Mexico, Arizona, and California. It is in these areas that the Spanish presence was established through military and civil settlements and missions.

The volume is divided into three parts, each consisting of three chapters. The contributors use a variety of theoretical or methodological approaches in examining their data sets. As a result, their conclusions do not always coincide. These differences highlight not only how complex and multifaceted the biocultural processes of contact were, but also how multidimensional our inquiries need to be.

Part 1, "Bioarchaeological Investigations," begins with Cassandra Hill's study of cultural and biological change during the protohistoric period in west-central Alabama. Hill compares Mississippian and protohistoric mortuary assemblages, including both archaeological evidence (burial practices and settlement patterns) and skeletal data (age and sex composition and stress indicators) to investigate changes in health status. The higher frequency and greater severity of porotic hyperostosis in the later groups suggest an increasing reliance on maize agriculture during the protohistoric period. Hill suggests that protohistoric populations were in decline prior to direct contact, with the disintegration of the Mississippian culture. These groups may, in fact, have experienced nutritional stress for generations, limiting their ability to cope with new diseases.

In contrast to Hill's emphasis on skeletal indicators of stress, Jay Johnson and Geoffrey Lehmann in chapter 3 analyze settlement patterns in northern Mississippi to clarify the subsistence and organizational changes following the Mississippian period. Johnson and Lehmann find that late protohistoric groups exploited more diversified upland habitats, away from the classic Mississippian pattern of intensive floodplain agriculture. Settlement data indicate that a major shift took place *prior* to European contact in Mississippi and, perhaps, throughout an extensive portion of the Southeast. Such shifts in settlement patterns and subsistence may have created chronic nutritional stress, leading eventually to patterns of skeletal stress similar to those found by Hill in adjacent areas.

Chapter 4 is a review by Lisa Kealhofer of archaeological and historical evidence for demographic collapse in the Canalino and Central Valley areas of California. Kealhofer suggests that the Spanish agenda constrained the adaptive choices available to indigenous societies, leading to a reorganization of social roles and values that eventually affected a group's biological response. Her analysis of published demographic and skeletal biological data highlights the diversity of aboriginal cultural and biological responses to contact, and she emphasizes the importance of local cultural and environmental variables for understanding a culture's response to both direct and indirect contact. While epidemic disease is not precluded in the investigations found in part 1, other equally disruptive cultural and biological changes contributing to depopulation are explored.

The chapters in part 2, "Skeletal Biology and Paleoepidemiology," further delineate the diverse trajectories of aboriginal change from the late prehistoric through historic periods. Changes in health status and ways in which aboriginal populations adapted to European contact are addressed through examinations of human skeletal remains.

In chapter 5, Clark Larsen, Christopher Ruff, and Mark Griffin evaluate skeletal morphology for changes in activity patterns among the Guale populations of Florida and Georgia before and after contact. Both osteoarthritis and biomechanical differences are used as indicators of changing behavioral patterns through time. Rather than specifically addressing the impact of epidemics on the Guale, the authors' analysis reveals the biological adaptations of epidemic survivors to changing circumstances. As Larsen and his coworkers have noted previously, Spaniards extracted heavy labor from groups already affected by epidemics (Larsen et al. 1992, 26–28; Hann 1988). Reduction of the labor force during repeated epidemics resulted in increased physical demands on those who survived. The similarities in prevalence and pattern of osteoarthritis, and the decrease in gender differences found in limb morphology in comparison to precontact skeletal assemblages, indicate that physical demands were made on men and women alike.

In chapter 6, Elizabeth Miller investigates variability in health status between prehistoric hunter-gatherers and mission Indians in Texas. She examines several indicators of biological stress in four different skeletal assemblages. Interestingly, Miller finds that both short- and long-term contact had the same effect on the health of missionized groups. Health status among these groups declined most significantly because of subsistence changes (to agricultural products) and resettlement.

In chapter 7, Ann Lucy Stodder looks at multiple indicators of stress to compare the health status of several Pueblo communities of New Mexico during the protohistoric and early contact periods. Her study focuses on contemporaneous skeletal assemblages from San Cristobal and Hawikku. While these communities are culturally quite similar, Stodder finds significant differences in their health, thus illustrating the mosaic of biological responses and adaptations among these societies.

Part 3, "Theoretical Perspectives and Prospects," begins with chapter 8, in which Ann Palkovich confronts the problems encountered when using epidemiological models to address depopulation. In her thought-provoking discussion of the evaluation of health status, she suggests that different underlying cultural and biological factors can result in similar skeletal manifestations of stress. She illustrates her points with examples drawn from the Arroyo Hondo site in New Mexico. Her theoretical and methodological approach challenges skeletal biologists and paleopathologists to examine rigorously the underlying contexts for skeletal manifestations of stress when comparing samples.

In chapter 9, George Milner uses the data presented in earlier chapters to evaluate ongoing research problems and suggest prospects for future investigations of biological, cultural, and demographic change in contact-era populations. He reiterates the importance of studying the nature of accommodations to drastically altered social and biotic milieus as a counterpoint to the focus on cultural and demographic catastrophe.

The volume editors elaborate in chapter 10 on the trends identified by the other contributors and emphasize the importance of using various types of data to explore the disparate reasons for aboriginal change during the contact period.

We seek to demonstrate the astonishing complexity of aboriginal change from late prehistory into historic times. Refinement of regional chronologies indicates that, in many areas, major cultural changes began prior to contact and continued through the contact period. An array of independent cultural, biological, and environmental factors contributed to the often dramatic changes traditionally ascribed to European contact alone. These papers indicate that detailed studies of individual cultures from the late prehistoric through the historic periods paint a rich and variable portrait of ongoing cultural and biological adaptation. It is our hope that these studies will stimulate a reevaluation of the evidence for epidemic disease-driven demographic collapse and, more importantly, promote thorough, localized investigations of aboriginal change from late prehistoric to recent times.

REFERENCES

Ashburn, P. M.
    1947   *The Ranks of Death.* Edited by Frank D. Ashburn. New York: Coward-McCann.

Axtell, James
  1981   *The European and the Indian: Essays in the Ethnohistory of Colonial North America.* New York: Oxford University Press.
  1985   *The Invasion Within: The Contest of Cultures in Colonial North America.* New York: Oxford University Press.
  1992   *Beyond 1492: Encounters in Colonial North America.* New York: Oxford University Press.
Borah, Woodrow
  1964   America as Model: The Demographic Impact of European Expansion upon the Non-European World. *Actas y Memorias del XXXV Congreso Internacional de Americanistas, Mexico, 1962* 3:379–87.
Cook, Sherburne F.
  1943   The Conflict between the California Indian and White Civilization I: The Indian Versus the Spanish Mission. *Ibero-Americana* 21.
  1976   *The Population of the California Indians, 1769–1970.* Berkeley: University of California Press.
  1978   Historical Demography. In *California,* edited by Robert F. Heizer, 91–98. *Handbook of North American Indians,* vol. 8, William C. Sturtevant, general editor. Washington, D.C.: Smithsonian Institution.
Crosby, Alfred W., Jr.
  1972   *The Columbian Exchange: Biological and Cultural Consequences of 1492.* Westport, Conn.: Greenwood.
Denevan, William
  1992   Native American Populations in 1492: Recent Research and a Revised Hemispheric Estimate. In *The Native Population of the Americas in 1492,* 2d edition, edited by William Denevan, xxvii–xxxviii. Madison: University of Wisconsin Press.
Denevan, William, ed.
  1992   *The Native Population of the Americas in 1492.* 2d edition. Madison: University of Wisconsin Press.
Dobyns, Henry F.
  1966   Estimating Aboriginal American Population 1: An Appraisal of Techniques with a New Hemispheric Estimate. *Current Anthropology* 7:395–449.
  1983   *Their Number Become Thinned: Native American Populations Dynamics in Eastern North America.* Knoxville: University of Tennessee Press.
  1989   More Methodological Perspectives on Historical Demography. *Ethnohistory* 36:285–99.
Duffy, John
  1953   *Epidemics in Colonial America.* Baton Rouge: Louisiana State University Press.
Fawcett, William B., Jr., and Alan C. Swedlund
  1984   Thinning Populations and Population Thinners: The Historical Demography of Native Americans. *Reviews in Anthropology* 11:264–69.
Griffen, William B.
  1979   *Indian Assimilation in the Franciscan Area of Nueva Vizcaya.* Anthropological Papers no. 33. Tucson: University of Arizona Press.

Hann, John H.
   1988   *Apalachee: The Land Between the Rivers.* Gainesville: University Press of
           Florida.
Henige, David
   1986   Primary Source by Primary Source? On the Role of Epidemics in New World
           Depopulation. *Ethnohistory* 33:293–312.
Jennings, Francis
   1975   *The Invasion of America: Indians, Colonialism, and the Cant of Conquest.*
           Chapel Hill: University of North Carolina Press.
Johansson, S. Ryan
   1982   The Demographic History of the Native Peoples of North America: A Selec-
           tive Bibliography. *Yearbook of Physical Anthropology* 25:133–52.
   1985   Review of *Their Number Become Thinned* by Henry F. Dobyns. *American
           Journal of Physical Anthropology* 67:291–92.
Joralemon, Donald
   1982   New World Depopulation and the Case of Disease. *Journal of Anthropologi-
           cal Research* 38:108–27.
Kroeber, Alfred L.
   1939   *Cultural and Natural Areas of Native North America.* University of Califor-
           nia Publications in American Archaeology and Ethnology no. 38. Berkeley:
           University of California Press.
Larsen, Clark Spencer, and George R. Milner, eds.
   1994   *In the Wake of Contact: Biologicl Responses to Conquest.* New York: Wiley-
           Liss.
Larsen, Clark Spencer, Christopher B. Ruff, Margaret J. Schoeninger, and Dale L.
           Hutchinson
   1992   Population Decline and Extinction in La Florida. In *Disease and Demography
           in the Americas,* edited by John W. Verano and Douglas H. Ubelaker, 25–39.
           Washington, D.C.: Smithsonian Institution.
Meister, Cary W.
   1976   Demographic Consequences of Euro-American Contact on Selected Ameri-
           can Indian Populations and Their Relationship to the Demographic Transi-
           tion. *Ethnohistory* 23:161–72.
Merriam, C. Hart
   1905   The Indian Population of California. *American Anthropologist* 7:594–606.
Milner, George R.
   1980   Epidemic Disease in the Postcontact Southeast: A Reappraisal. *Mid-Conti-
           nental Journal of Archaeology* 5:39–56.
Mooney, James
   1910   Population. In *Handbook of American Indians North of Mexico,* edited by F.
           W. Hodge, 286–87. Bureau of American Ethnology Bulletin 30, part 2. Wash-
           ington, D.C.: U.S. Government Printing Office.
Ramenofsky, Ann F.
   1985   Review of *Their Number Become Thinned* by Henry F. Dobyns. *American
           Antiquity* 50:198–99.

1987   *Vectors of Death: The Archaeology of European Contact.* Albuquerque: University of New Mexico Press.

Reff, Daniel T.

1987   The Introduction of Smallpox in the Greater Southwest. *American Anthropologist* 89:704–8.

1991   *Disease, Depopulation, and Culture Change in Northwestern New Spain, 1518–1764.* Salt Lake City: University of Utah Press.

Rouse, Irving

1992   *The Tainos: Rise and Decline of the People Who Greeted Columbus.* New Haven, Conn.: Yale University Press.

Sale, Kirkpatrick

1990   *The Conquest of Paradise: Christopher Columbus and the Columbian Legacy.* New York: Penguin.

Salisbury, Neal

1982   *Manitou and Providence: Indians, Europeans, and the Making of New England.* New York: Oxford University Press.

Shea, Daniel E.

1992   A Defense of Small Population Estimates for the Central Andes in 1520. In *The Native Population of the Americas in 1492,* 2d edition, edited by William Denevan, 157–80. Madison: University of Wisconsin Press.

Smith, Marvin T.

1987   *Archaeology of Aboriginal Culture Change in the Interior Southeast: Depopulation during the Early Historic Period.* Ripley P. Bullen Monographs in Anthropology and History no. 6. Gainesville: University Press of Florida.

Snow, Dean R.

1995   Microchronology and Demographic Evidence Relating to the Size of Pre-Columbian North American Indian Populations. *Science* 268:1601–4.

Stannard, David E.

1992   *American Holocaust: Columbus and the Conquest of the New World.* New York: Oxford University Press.

Stearn, E. Wagner, and Allen E. Stearn

1945   *The Effect of Smallpox on the Destiny of the Amerindian.* Boston: Bruce Humphries.

Steele, Ian K.

1994   *Warpaths: Invasions of North America.* New York: Oxford University Press.

Storey, Rebecca

1985   Review of *Their Number Become Thinned* by Henry F. Dobyns. *American Anthropologist* 87:455–56.

Sturtevant, William C.

1984   Review of *Their Number Become Thinned* by Henry F. Dobyns. *American Historical Review* 89:1380–81.

Thomas, David Hurst

1991   Cubist Perspectives on the Spanish Borderlands: Past, Present, and Future. In

Columbian Consequences, vol. 3: *The Spanish Borderlands in Pan-American Perspective,* edited by David Hurst Thomas, xv–xxii. Washington, D.C.: Smithsonian Institution.

Thomas, David Hurst, ed.

1989   *Columbian Consequences,* vol. 1: *Archaeological and Historical Perspectives on the Spanish Borderlands West.* Washington, D.C.: Smithsonian Institution.

1990   *Columbian Consequences,* vol. 2: *Archaeological and Historical Perspectives on the Spanish Borderlands East.* Washington, D.C.: Smithsonian Institution.

1991   *Columbian Consequences,* vol. 3: *The Spanish Borderlands in Pan-American Perspective.* Washington, D.C.: Smithsonian Institution.

Thornton, Russell

1978   Implications of Catlin's American Indian Population Estimates for Revision of Mooney's Estimates. *American Journal of Physical Anthropology* 49:11–14.

1987   *American Indian Holocaust and Survival: A Population History since 1492.* Norman: University of Oklahoma Press.

Thornton, Russell, Tim Miller, and Jonathan Warren

1991   American Indian Population Recovery Following Smallpox Epidemics. *American Anthropologist* 93:28–45.

Trigger, Bruce G.

1985   *Natives and Newcomers: Canada's "Heroic Age."* Montreal: McGill-Queens University Press.

Ubelaker, Douglas H.

1988   North American Indian Population Size, A.D. 1500 to 1985. *American Journal of Physical Anthropology* 77:289–94.

Upham, Steadman

1986   Smallpox and Climate in the American Southwest. *American Anthropologist* 88:115–28.

Verano, John W., and Douglas H. Ubelaker, eds.

1992   *Disease and Demography in the Americas.* Washington, D.C.: Smithsonian Institution.

Viola, H. J., and C. Margolis

1991   *Seeds of Change: A Quincentennial Commemoration.* Washington, D.C.: Smithsonian Institution.

Zubrow, Ezra

1990   The Depopulation of Native America. *Antiquity* 64:754–65.

PART ONE

Bioarchaeological Investigations

In this section the bioarchaeological data from Alabama, Mississippi, and California are discussed. Each chapter presents a different type of data set, as well as a disparate perspective, but all the authors grapple with the issue of how to identify the archaeological traces of the biological and cultural changes from the protohistoric to the historic periods in the Spanish Borderlands.

In a study of sites from three Alabama river valleys, Hill (chapter 2) analyzes four types of data to evaluate how European contact affected the inhabitants during the protohistoric period. Settlement patterns, burial practices, artifact assemblages, and skeletal pathology all changed substantially from the late Mississippian to the protohistoric period. The shift in burial practices and associated mortuary assemblages reflects an abrupt change in cultural and demographic circumstances. Hill has begun the enormous task of detailing the cultural changes related to maize agriculture and shifting economic and political alliances, and the relationship of these to the effects of European contact in this region. She suggests that protohistoric populations experienced periods of nutritional stress, beginning with the disintegration of the Mississippian societies. The diseases introduced by Europeans, therefore, led to major cultural and biological disruption because they attacked an already compromised society.

In the adjacent Black Prairie region of northeastern Mississippi and west-central Alabama, Johnson and Lehmann (chapter 3) study the settlement patterns of the late prehistoric and protohistoric periods. Their data show that the settlement pattern and subsistence system changed prior to European contact in this region, as the population dispersed into small upland sites. Despite this dispersal, economic strategies at the sites reflect late prehistoric specialization rather than decentralization or collapse. This settlement pattern change, just prior to contact, seems to have buffered the immediate effects of early European contact in this area.

The work of Hill and Johnson and Lehmann demonstrates the same pattern of settlement-system devolution in adjacent regions during the late prehistoric period. Intensification of economic reliance on upland resources and nutritional stress may be responses to the same stimuli, with an as yet unknown causal relationship between the two. As these studies illustrate, the late prehistoric period is crucial to our understanding of the biological and cultural impact of contact. Only with increasing chronological resolution can we discern the causal relationships between these variables.

Kealhofer (chapter 4) summarizes the archaeological and bioarchaeological evidence for demographic collapse during the protohistoric and historic periods in California, focusing primarily on the Central Valley and the southern coastal region. Despite the constraints of the data sets, no evidence can be found for demographic collapse prior to direct contact in California. On the contrary, populations were expanding and cultures were at their most complex during the protohistoric period. Major population disruption and loss was initiated during the Spanish Colonial period (1769–1822), as entire coastal populations were relocated at and adjacent to mission settlements. The most dramatic population decline seems to postdate the Colonial period, a ramification of the gold and land rushes in California during the 1840s to 1880s. The historic period evidence from different regions of California suggests that the precolonial period demography, cultural organization, and the extent of European contact led to very different patterns of postcontact demographic decline and cultural response.

These three examples reveal the potential of, and need for, more intensive settlement pattern studies focusing on the late prehistoric and protohistoric periods of the Spanish Borderlands to elucidate the regionally defined arenas in which cultural, demographic, and biological changes occurred during the protohistoric and early historic periods.

Chapter 2

Protohistoric Aborigines in West-Central Alabama

Probable Correlations to Early European Contact

M. CASSANDRA HILL

The examination of cultural transition is never an easy task. In most instances the analyst eventually resorts to comparing former and later cultural modes, and then draws conclusions about what might have taken place in between the two. The protohistoric period in Alabama is nebulously defined. Researchers have disputed its time constraints for years. In fact, earlier researchers were so perplexed by the seemingly instantaneous appearance of the dominant characteristics used to identify this period in stratigraphic contexts that they referred to it as a separate cultural entity: The Burial Urn Culture (Brannon 1938, 1948; Moore 1904). The fact that archaeologists and historians are still somewhat puzzled by this period is reflected in their use of the synonymous interchange of the terms "Protohistoric" and "Mississippian Decline," and simultaneous use of the initial European contact period (A.D. 1500–1700) as the definition of its temporal limits (see Brannon 1935; Curren 1984; Curren et al. 1982; Sheldon 1974). Formerly known by a single phase designation (the Alabama River phase), sites with evidence of protohistoric occupation more recently have been identified with at least three different phases: Summerville IV (Peebles, ed., 1981), Moundville IV (Curren 1984; Curren and Little 1991), and Alabama River phase (Sheldon 1974), according to their location on each of the major waterways in the state (figure 2.1). The general consensus is that "sometime between A.D. 1450 and 1550, a series of unknown events and processes brought an end to the cultural florescence at Moundville" (Sheldon 1974, 9; Sheldon and Jenkins 1986). One dominant theory is that the changes in the Mississippian sociocultural system were brought about by European contact (Curren 1984; Smith 1987). This chapter summarizes much of the archaeological and biological data for the protohistoric period from the state of Alabama and offers some suggestions for the mutually causal relationships of the patterns observed.

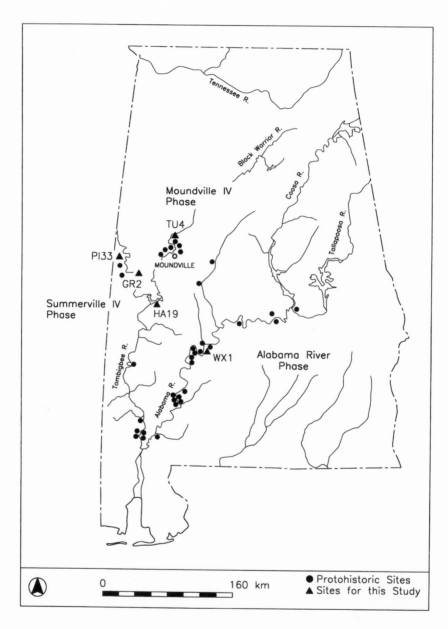

Figure 2.1. Map of Alabama showing protohistoric sites and sites used for this study.

Archaeologists recognize the Mississippian Decline by a loss or decline of numerous cultural traits, the most notable of which were as follows: (1) the change in burial procedure from predominantly primary, extended, flexed, or semi-flexed to predominantly bundles and urn interments; (2) the change from elaborate, highly stylized burial accoutrement inclusions to an almost total lack of inclusions, with simple artifact embellishment; (3) a change from large, fortified villages surrounding mounds, to small, isolated hamlets of 30 individuals or less, or larger villages without mounds; and (4) an abandonment of the construction of large earthworks (DeJarnette 1952; Sheldon 1974; Curren 1984). It is postulated, however, that the subsistence pattern of riverine hoe agriculture heavily supplemented by hunting and gathering established during the Mississippian period continued through historic times (Sheldon 1974; Sheldon and Jenkins 1986). Archaeologists originally felt that the individuals from protohistoric sites surrounding Moundville were probably the direct descendants of the Mississippian population (Sheldon 1974). More recent analysis, however, indicates that direct descent may not have been true in some instances (Sheldon and Jenkins 1986). Sheldon and Jenkins (1986) suggested that some of the protohistoric sites in Alabama possibly were the result of migrations from western Mississippi and Tennessee. It also was assumed that individuals of the protohistoric period were the ones with whom the Spanish had made initial contact. However, it is now felt by some researchers that the Spanish explorers encountered fully developed chiefdoms, and that the protohistoric subsistence and settlement patterns emerged after the first European contact (Curren 1984; Curren and Little 1991). In contrast, Johnson and Lehmann (chapter 3 below) present data for a nearby survey area in Mississippi that reveal changes in subsistence and settlement *prior* to European contact.

Urn Burial in Alabama

Urns containing the remains of deceased individuals are the hallmark of the protohistoric period. The most common type of burial urn (figure 2.2) is wide-mouthed, shell-tempered, globular in shape, and ranges in size from 10 to 20 inches in diameter, although some as large as 28 inches in diameter have been noted (Brannon 1938; DeJarnette 1952; Sheldon 1974). The larger urns are the most common, although some very small ones have been encountered—one even appearing to be a miniature representation (Curren 1984). The mouths of these urns are usually covered, either with an inverted urn, a bowl, or the broken bottom of a bowl. The presence of loops or strap handles around the rims of urns has led to the speculation that they may have been covered with skins (Brannon 1938, 230).

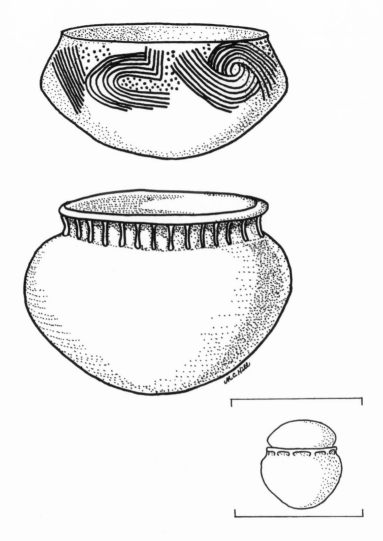

Figure 2.2. A burial urn and cover typical of the protohistoric period in Alabama (based on Holmes 1903). The inset shows the cover in place.

The urns appear to have been deliberately interred, either singly or in groups or clusters.

At Durant's Bend they are found placed in rows; at Pintlala they were apparently arranged in plots; at Taskigi they seem to be scattered about the cemetery among non-urn burials, although there is a suggestion of grouping in rows running east and west.

At Pintlala two unusual groups of urns were discovered. In 1915 nine urns were encountered in a group. Four, serving as containers for bones, were placed close together and each was covered with another urn. The ninth urn rested on the center of the pile formed by the eight others. A covering of burned clay protected the mass, and the entire structure was within a well made vault-like encasement of periwinkle and mussel shells, with which much ash had been mixed. In another part of the same site an orderly group of twelve urns was found in 1930. Eleven of the urns were arranged around a very large one in which there were parts of eight skeletons. Each of the eleven smaller urns contained the parts of one to three skeletons. All of the urns were covered with bowls, except the two smallest which had crudely shaped broken bowl bottoms fitted over them. Near at hand, and just to the north of the urns, was a square pit into which the remaining bones of the skeletons had been thrown in a jumbled mass. (Brannon 1938, 230)

The vessels are usually rather plain, with decoration limited to the rims of the urns and bowls. Some may have been of utilitarian origin, perhaps used for storage of various staples. However, some appear to have been new at the time of interment. Regardless of whether they had been used prior to interment, vessels of this size require larger amounts of time to produce, as well as great skill in manufacturing.

Of the urns found by Brannon (1938, 231) 75 percent contained the remains of children and infants. In these instances the urns were used for primary interment. When the urns contain portions of several adults, they are secondary deposits. Sometimes the urns contain ashes and fragments of burned bones. Brannon (1938, 231) suggested that the cremations were of two types: (1) cremation prior to being placed into the urns; and (2) bones placed in the urns, which were then filled with hot or live coals and ashes at the time of interment. Fire seemed to have played a significant role in the finalization of the interments—as evidenced by the ashes in and around the urns themselves— and by the overall deposits being frequently capped with puddled or moist clay that had subsequently been fired. This fired clay capping also has been observed for single primary interments from the protohistoric period at several sites. For example, Burial 1 at the Baker site (1TU49), excavated in 1975, displayed this fired clay capping, while Burial 6, excavated in 1958, contained the long bones and crania of three individuals and was filled to the rim with burned corn cobs and wood.

The urns themselves are usually the only accompanying accoutrements for the interments, with the rare inclusion of single strands of shell (or, even more rarely, glass) beads, earspools, or other single artifacts such as awls. Because of this cultural impoverishment relative to the preceding Mississippian period, combined with archaeologists' early focus on artifact retrieval, sites from the protohistoric period were, for the most part, overlooked. When excavations were conducted, the urns were removed and their contents emptied and reburied without further analysis. Adding insult to injury, these sites have been periodically looted over the last 150 years by local collectors because it was rumored that the large urns contained "Indian gold." The unfortunate consequence is that literally thousands of individuals representative of this period have been lost forever. For example, 1,500 burials were excavated between 1924 and 1935 from the Taskigi site (1EE1), a very large protohistoric village, but none were saved (Curren 1984). Despite the resulting impoverishment of biological collections, much can still be learned about protohistoric peoples from the extant skeletal remains.

Skeletal Biology of Selected Sites

This author's examination of skeletal material from the period of Mississippian decline has taken the form of primary, secondary, and tertiary levels of analysis, all within the context of a general systems theory model (Hill 1979, 1981a, 1981b, 1985; Hill and Clark 1981, 1984). Demographic data were collected from a series of 182 individuals from five sites in Alabama considered to be representative of the Mississippian-protohistoric transition (figure 2.1). These demographic data include age at death, sex, pathology and anomalies, and cranial and postcranial measurements (see Bass 1971; Krogman 1973, for standard methods of analysis). The sites are located along each of the waterways believed to have been on the route of the de Soto entrada (see Hudson et al. 1990, 109; and Little and Curren 1990, 175, for maps and discussion of the proposed route).

The designation of Mississippian and protohistoric is based on the original field notes from the excavations of the sites (see Bozeman 1963, 1980; Cottier 1968, 1970; Hill 1981b; Hill and Clark 1981; Jenkins 1982; Sheldon 1974; site files, University of Alabama). A total of 82 individuals (51 from site 1GR2 and 31 from site 1PI33) represents the Mature Mississippian period, and 100 individuals (33 from site 1WX1, 46 from site 1TU4, and 21 from site 1HA19) comprise the protohistoric sample. These sites are also in close proximity to Moundville.

Initially, the analysis of the skeletal material from the period of decline focused on the testing of the hypothesis of a continuation of riverine hoe agriculture, heavily supplemented by hunting and gathering (Hill 1979, 1981b). The results were interesting in that the pathology data indicate a steady increase in the percentage of the populations exhibiting nutritional stress, particularly porotic hyperostosis, though the percentage of infection essentially

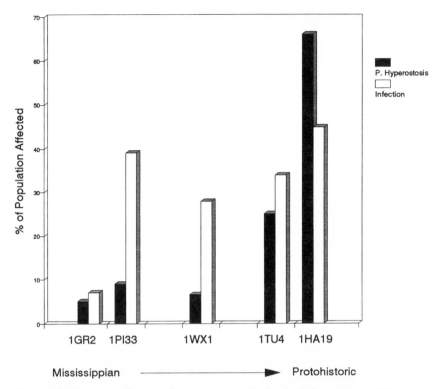

Figure 2.3. Histogram showing the percentage of individuals from Mature Mississippian (1GR2 and 1PI33) and protohistoric (1WX1, 1TU4, and 1HA19) sites exhibiting infection and porotic hyperostosis.

remained the same (figure 2.3). The low percentages of pathological conditions at site 1GR2 are an artifact of burial deposition. The soil composition included a large amount of clay, and most individuals were interred in six mass graves, with five to 18 individuals in each. These conditions resulted in poor and fragmentary preservation, making diagnosis extremely difficult. Additionally, dental pathology associated with a maize-dependent diet, including caries, periodontal disease, and heavy calculus deposits, is present. Evidence of infectious lesions ranged from localized to diffuse.

Also notable among the pathology found at the protohistoric sites are hydrocephalus and bifurcated roots of the incisors and canines. The hydrocephalus and dental anomaly are rare, congenital traits. The hydrocephalic individual (figure 2.4) is an infant (less than 1 year old) from site 1WX1. (It was first diagnosed by the late Dr. Carl Sensenig, chairman of the Department of Anatomy, University of Alabama Medical School, and by Dr. T. Dale Stewart, professor emeritus, Smithsonian Institution, during a visit to the Moundville site [David DeJarnette, personal communication 1974]. The specimen was sub-

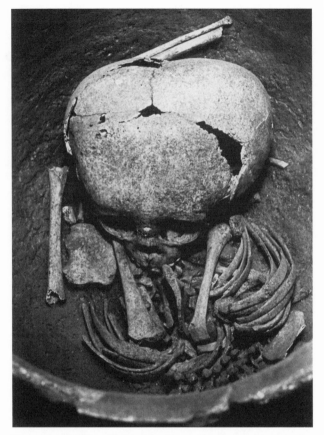

Figure 2.4. Unidentified infant in urn from protohistoric site
1WX1.

sequently examined and diagnosed by Dr. Juan Villa Nova, chairman of the
Department of Pathology, Druid City Hospital, Tuscaloosa, Alabama, 1976.)
Studies of the dental anomaly have correlated it with homogeneous populations (Alexandersen 1963). This anomaly was present in four individuals from
sites 1WX1 and 1HA19, but has not been observed in the Mississippian individuals.

A secondary level of analysis of the porotic hyperostosis itself, along with
other prevalent pathology, was rather surprising. Not only did a dramatic increase in porotic hyperostosis occur during the latter part of the protohistoric
period, but the expression of the pathology shows a marked increase in the
percentage of the population affected (figure 2.3), and also in the severity and
duration of the lesions themselves (Hill 1981b, 1985). The adolescent female
(Burial A, site 1TU4), depicted in figure 2.5, for example, displays pathology

Figure 2.5. Adolescent female from site 1TU4. One of two young female bundle burials interred together. Both exhibited porotic hyperostosis.

comparable in severity to that sometimes seen in Mediterranean individuals with hemolytic anemias (Mahmoud El-Najjar, personal communication 1978). All cohorts of the sample populations were seemingly affected by porotic hyperostosis. Turner's (1985) examination of the pathology also demonstrates the high incidence of porotic hyperostosis in protohistoric samples (table 2.1).

A tertiary analysis of the porotic hyperostosis is still being conducted. This analysis explores the lesions in terms of their size, shape, and location and attempts to correlate them with other stress indicators, including Harris lines and enamel hypoplasias, which have established chronologies. This analysis will allow the determination of episodes of stress of sufficient duration and intensity to leave permanent biological remnants in individuals' skeletal material. Turner (1985) also has examined the correlation between enamel hypoplasias and porotic hyperostosis (table 2.1).

Table 2.1. Prevalence of lesions indicative of general stress within protohistoric and historic skeletal series from Alabama

	Protohistoric	Historic
Porotic Hyperostosis	13/45 = 0.29	0/13 = 0.00
Enamel Hypoplasia	9/30 = 0.30	1/20 = 0.05

Source: Turner 1985.

Table 2.2. Age and sex distribution of skeletal material

Site	1GR2			1PI33			1WX1			1TU4			1HA19		
Gender Cohorts	M	F	U	M	F	U	M	F	U	M	F	U	M	F	U
0-3	0	0	9	0	0	5	0	0	19	0	0	13	0	0	5
4-10	0	0	5	0	0	3	0	0	6	0	0	7	0	0	3
12-16	0	1	1	2	1	2	0	2	0	0	3	0	2	0	2
18-22	2	2	1	1	1	0	0	0	0	1	3	1	0	1	1
25-30	9	7	9	2	2	1	1	1	1	0	1	4	0	3	0
30+	4	1	0	7	4	1	0	3	0	6	6	1	1	3	0
Totals	51			32			33			46			21		

Note: U = undetermined.

There was a noticeable lack of young adult males from all three protohistoric sites (table 2.2), the significance of which will be discussed in the summary remarks.

ADDITIONAL ARCHAEOLOGICAL AND BIOLOGICAL DATA

Burial Practices

The most outstanding change in burial practices is from primary to secondary interment (Brannon 1938; Curren 1982, 1984; DeJarnette 1952; Hill 1979; Peebles 1974; Powell 1981; Sheldon 1974). While more than half of the Mississippian burials at Moundville were single, extended interments (Peebles and Turner cited in Curren 1982; Powell 1981), by far the most common forms of interment for the protohistoric period were secondary bundles (for adults and adolescents) and urns (for children and extremely few adults). Most urns contain multiple primary remains of infants and young children. Many of the urns were literally filled to their rims with cremated remains (Brannon 1938; Moore 1904). Field notes from several of the large protohistoric village sites refer to burials of multiple urns along with several bundles and primary interments (e.g., the Taskigi site, 1EE1). This pattern indicates accumulation of the dead, with primary processing of some of the individuals, before subsequent cumulative interment (Hill 1979; Powell 1981). Urns that contain the remains of adults and adolescents include only selected skeletal elements; some urns hold portions of as many as four individuals (e.g., Burial 1, site 1TU49, 1958 excavations).

Artifact Assemblages

The use of urns is unprecedented in this area. Sociotechnic items suggest the continuation of the subsistence base that was established during the Mississippian period. "Exotic" items identified with the Southern Cult are extremely rare (Curren 1982, 1984; DeJarnette 1952; Sheldon 1974). Urns are the only possible indicator of status, since very few adults were interred in them. Production of these urns would have taken great skill and time expenditure, and most indicate their use as strictly associated with burial. Even if they were secondarily used as repositories for the dead, such use would imply a great amount of time sacrificed for the deceased, as the vessels in their utilitarian role would have to be replaced. Therefore, it could be postulated that the dead interred in these vessels were a precious concern. Except for the size of these vessels, there is little remarkable about them, as they are plainly adorned. Very few, if any, other artifacts were included with the interments.

Settlement Patterns

Mississippian settlement patterns generally are classified as major ceremonial centers, minor ceremonial centers, and farming hamlets (Mistovich 1989; Peebles 1974, 1987; Steponaitis 1983, 1986). Protohistoric settlements tended to be primarily large, sometimes fortified, villages (Curren 1984; Sheldon 1974). Very little horizontal excavation and survey data are available to provide a more complete settlement pattern for the protohistoric period in Alabama. However, in reviewing the data reported by various surveys (site data presented in Curren 1984), almost *all* of the major protohistoric sites are multicomponent. Interestingly, the larger components are Woodland and protohistoric. Moundville has only a small protohistoric component. Sites with preceding Mississippian components show only moderate occupation in comparison to protohistoric components, or no Mississippian component at all. It appears, then, that the dispersed settlement pattern favored during the Woodland period was again favored during the protohistoric. In fact, groups may actually have returned to many of the same sites utilized during the Woodland period, with total or at least partial abandonment of the large Mississippian centers (see Peebles 1987 for more complete discussion).

THE MODEL

A model of positive feedback loops taken from general systems theory, and the statistical concept of multicollinearity, lend themselves well to the explanation of the patterns of pathology, anomalies, and cultural data from these populations. Systems theory has been a popular analytical tool for anthropologists. Both systems theory and multicollinearity were applied to the data from these sites (Hill 1981a, 1981b, 1985; Hill and Clark 1981). Modified from cybernetics (Wiener 1954), systems theory proposes relationships of mutual causality between and among components comprising a particular system (see Maruyama 1963, 1968).

In his discussion of evolutionary developments using systems theory, Bowlby (1969) used the phrase "environment of evolutionary adaptedness," which can be defined as the environment to which a species has become adapted over its phylogenetic history (see Freedman 1974). Bowlby emphasized that evolutionary developments are as much a product of the environment as they are of the organism (see Freedman 1974).

Maruyama (1968, 80) stated that "mutual causality can be applied equally between either a small or large number of elements, and within either a microscopic or a complex social phenomenon, because physical size or degree of complexity is irrelevant." This is an important issue to be considered when studying the etiology of disease expression, either within the individual or among individuals within a population.

Positive feedback serves as a reinforcement for change or amplification within a system, while negative feedback functions to maintain equilibrium. Maruyama (1968, 84) states that "How the system behaves as a whole depends on the strength of each loop [between elements within the system] and their interrelationships, and can only be solved by resort to analytical or numerical analysis for a given system. A system may have states in which it attains an equilibrium, and may have limiting conditions beyond which no amplification takes place." In another article, Maruyama (1963, 164) defines deviation-amplification processes as "all processes of mutual causal relationships that amplify an insignificant or accidental initial kick, build up deviation and diverge from the initial condition."

Multicollinearity refers to relationships that exist among or between elements within an equation or system. These elements are mutually dependent or influential, and cannot be separated for analysis to determine the amount of significance in contribution of each element to the overall equation (see Hanushek and Jackson 1977, 86–96).

Discussion

Numerous authors have discussed the relationship between the pathological expression of porotic hyperostosis and dependence on maize agriculture (Angel 1967; El-Najjar 1976; El-Najjar and Robertson 1976; El-Najjar et al. 1976; Lallo 1973; Mensforth et al. 1978; Steinbock 1976). One might interpret the increase in the percent affected, and the severity of the lesions, as an increasing dependence on maize agriculture (Hill 1979, 1985). Researchers have also noted that the expression of porotic hyperostosis lesions tends to be confined to the younger individuals of populations, primarily because the lesions are subject to the normal process of bone absorption and deposition in the maintenance of skeletal tissues if the diet is stabilized (El-Najjar et al. 1976). However, in the protohistoric Alabama populations, the lesions were severe enough that they are evident even in the elderly individuals. The lesions range in expression from slight to extreme in all age classes from childhood to older adult.

This pattern indicates that nutritional stress was essentially a way of life, at least by the latter part of the protohistoric period. The cranial lesions on the elderly individuals show considerable remodeling but are still evident, suggesting that the original, unremodeled lesions probably looked like those on the cranium of the adolescent seen in figure 2.5. Therefore, nutritional stress was critical, but survivable, if all other factors were held in balance.

Priestly (1928, 215) quoted the Sauz reports (the documentation of the second Spanish expedition into the interior) as saying that the Indians' agricultural lands were "so scant that as soon as an ear of corn is gathered they immediately plant again at the foot of the selfsame stalk. Even with this they have for their principal food bitter acorns, shoots of canes, and roots, wherewith they pass and sustain their lives." If this account is accurate, it is certainly indicative of nutritional stress.

The increased use of urns as the principal means of interment throughout the protohistoric period implies that the groups were on the verge of not being able to replace themselves. Considerable energy was focused on *dead* subadults, suggesting they were precious even after death. The urns frequently contained more than one individual, indicating there were more dead than there was time or energy to bury them individually. In other words, at any given time of the year there were several individuals to be interred. The subadults were not surviving to the age of reproductive maturity.

Institutionalized warfare among neighboring groups in the Southeast is well documented (Dye 1990; Elvas 1973; Gibson 1974; Larson 1972; Varner and Varner 1951). Design motifs of the Southern Cult—showing severed heads, limbs, and scalps—are proof that life during the Mature Mississippian period was not harmonious. This warfare created geographic constraints on subsistence activities. If the agricultural lands of each village were too severely restricted, as the quote from the Sauz reports may indicate, nutrient depletion of the soil would eventually occur as well.

Metal artifacts have been discovered in Alabama that may be evidence of direct contact with the early Spanish expeditions (Curren 1984). Similar metal artifacts have also been found at the King site in Georgia (Hally 1988) and the Margin site in Florida (Ewen 1990, 87). Other evidence for possible direct contact includes a Nueva Cadiz bead found on site 1TU4 by an amateur collector in 1992. Nueva Cadiz beads have also been found at other sites in the Southeast and have been suggested as providing evidence of de Soto's route (Ewen 1990, 86). Documentation of these expeditions noted conflicts with the European intruders as well (Elvas 1973; Gibson 1974; Hudson 1976, 205; Ranjel 1922, 43–150; Steele 1994, 7–20; Swanton 1946; Varner and Varner 1951).

Warfare just prior to and during the initial Spanish contact could have re-sulted in annihilation of large portions of the male population, and may have had long-term consequences for food production (Walthall 1980, 246–77). Potentially half of the workforce may have been eliminated, including almost all those usually associated with hunting activities. The Spanish expedition-ary forces also either traded for or took food surplus from the Indian groups they encountered (Hann 1988; Hudson 1990; Larsen et al. 1992, 26–28; Ranjel 1922; Steele 1994, 14; Varner and Varner 1983). There were over 1,000 men and animals (horses, pigs, and "dogs of war") in the de Soto expedition, which lasted approximately two years (Curren 1984; Steele 1994, 14). Large amounts of food must have been necessary to support a group of this size for such an extended period of time (Hann 1988; Larsen et al. 1992; Larsen et al. chapter 5 below; Ranjel 1922; Steele 1994, 14).

Nutritional stress is usually the result of multiple stimuli. The presence of numerous systemic infections, most commonly attributed to microorganism infection, probably further complicated the nutritional stress in the people from these sites. Microorganism infection is one of the most common conse-quences of a more sedentary subsistence and settlement pattern. The accumu-lation of wastes and garbage, coupled with joint use of cooking vessels—par-ticularly unglazed pottery—resulted in high microorganism infection rates among prehistoric groups (Brothwell 1967, 63). Disposal of the dead would have been a factor in waste management, particularly in the perpetuation of infectious agents, while rigid geographic boundaries between villages would have accentuated environmental pollution within those villages. In addition, foreign explorers may have introduced new pathogens to the indigenous popu-lations they encountered (Dobyns 1983; Ramenofsky 1987; Smith 1987). Many of these pathogens compete with the host for nutrients or so sicken the indi-viduals that they are unable to maintain any semblance of a normal diet. For villages that were already on the brink of decline, foreign-induced pathogens would have been the proverbial final straw.

SUMMARY

Quite frequently in historic records unusual cultural manifestations seem to occur at the time of decadence or decline of highly sophisticated cultures. The practice of urn burial in the Southeast seems to be one such manifestation. Milner (1980; chapter 9 below) notes that the sudden appearance of cultural traits, changes in mortuary customs, mass interments, and high mortality of certain cohorts (such as infants and children) are all possible indicators of foreign-induced crowd infections. Each of these indicators is present in the protohistoric period in Alabama.

The pathology and anomalies can be viewed as physiological expressions of the positive feedback elements within this particular system. The increased incidence of genetically linked pathology and elderly individuals with evidence of childhood pathology indicate that a crumbling foundation had been in place for several generations.

Chiefdoms are inherently unstable (Anderson 1990; Carneiro 1981; Wright 1984). Site spatial analysis suggests that the large Mississippian chiefdoms were no longer in existence in the protohistoric period. The population had returned to outlying areas and established separate factions or polities with rigid geographic and social constraints (Dye 1990; Hudson 1976, 184–257).

Nutritional stress results from the interaction of multiple stimuli. Mensforth and coworkers (1978) observed that the synergistic relationships between constitutional factors, diet, and infectious disease tend to be expressed together in skeletal populations as porotic hyperostosis and periosteal reactions. This pattern characterizes protohistoric populations in Alabama as well. Other components in the feedback system besides maize-dependent diet and infectious disease were small, isolated, sedentary communities (based on archaeological data); exhaustion of certain available food resources in the environment (documented during the Spanish expeditions); inbreeding (the identification of rare, homogeneous, congenital anomalies and pathology); and European contact, which served a multiplicity of roles.

In addition to depleting the population by warfare and nutritional stress, the Spanish expeditions devitalized the indigenous people by introducing strains of infectious diseases to which they had no immunity (Dobyns 1983; Milner 1980; Smith 1987). Turner's (1985) analysis of porotic hyperostosis in protohistoric and historic samples from Alabama revealed a high frequency of pathology in protohistoric samples, which he postulates may be directly related to the introduction of new infectious diseases followed by the development of immunity in subsequent historic groups. Repeated exposure would eventually have led to different cohorts being affected by the pathogens (Turner 1985). When observed separately, each of these factors would perhaps not be of any critical significance. When combined into an interrelated system, however, these variables amplified deviations in health, expressed as the severe porotic hyperostosis lesions in this sample.

In conclusion, the analyses of demographic data from a series of individuals representative of the protohistoric period in Alabama, combined with the archaeological data and historical accounts of initial contact, indicate that this period was no less complex in many ways than its antecedent. The intricate interplay of critical variables such as settlement location, availability of subsistence resources, genetic isolation, and European contact resulted in a series of deviation amplification feedback relationships that had a profound effect on the individuals studied here.

REFERENCES

Alexandersen, V.
   1963   Double-Rooted Human Lower Canine Teeth. In *Dental Anthropology*, edited
           by Don R. Brothwell, 235–44. Elmsford, N.Y.: Pergamon.
Anderson, David G.
   1990   Stability and Change in Chiefdom-Level Societies: An Examination of Mis-
           sissippian Political Evolution on the South Atlantic Slope. In *Lamar Archae-
           ology: Mississippian Chiefdoms in the Deep South*, edited by Mark Williams
           and Gary Shapiro, 187–213. Tuscaloosa: University of Alabama Press.
Angel, J. Lawrence
   1967   Porotic Hyperostosis, Anemias, Malarias, and Marshes in the Prehistoric East-
           ern Mediterranean. *Science* 153:760–63.
Bass, William M.
   1971   *Human Osteology: A Laboratory and Field Manual of the Human Skeleton.*
           Columbia: Missouri Archaeological Society.
Bowlby, John
   1969   *Attachment.* New York: Basic Books.
Bozeman, Tandy K.
   1963   The Camden Site, 1WX1. *Journal of Alabama Archaeology* 9(1):4–12.
   1980   Moundville Phase Sites in the Black Warrior Valley, Alabama: Preliminary
           Results of the UMMA Survey. Paper presented at the 37th Annual South-
           eastern Archaeological Conference, New Orleans.
Brannon, Peter A.
   1935   The Archaeology of Taskigi. *Arrowpoints* 20(5–6).
   1938   Urn-Burial in Central Alabama. *American Antiquity* 3(3):228–35.
   1948   Urn Burial, an Opinion. *Journal of the Alabama Academy of Science* 20:10–
           13.
Brothwell, Don R.
   1967   The Bio-Cultural Background to Disease. In *Diseases in Antiquity*, edited by
           Don R. Brothwell and A. T. Sandison, 56–68. Springfield, Ill.: Charles C. Tho-
           mas.
Carneiro, Robert L.
   1981   The Chiefdom: Precursor of the State. In *The Transition to Statehood in the
           New World*, edited by Grant D. Jones and R. R. Kautz, 37–79. Cambridge:
           Cambridge University Press.
Cottier, John W.
   1968   Archaeological Salvage Investigations in the Miller's Ferry Lock and Dam
           Reservoir. University of Alabama, Office of Archaeological Research. Unpub-
           lished report submitted to the National Park Service, U.S. Department of the
           Interior.
   1970   The Alabama River Phase: A Brief Description of a Late Phase in the Prehis-
           tory of South-Central Alabama. Appendix to Archaeological Salvage Investi-

gations in the Miller's Ferry Lock and Dam Reservoir. University of Alabama, Office of Archaeological Research. Unpublished report submitted to the National Park Service, U.S. Department of the Interior.

Curren, Caleb B.
1982   The Alabama River Phase: A Review. In *Archaeology in Southwestern Alabama, A Collection of Papers,* edited by Caleb B. Curren, 103–14. Camden: Alabama-Tombigbee Regional Commission.
1984   *The Protohistoric Period in Central Alabama.* Camden: Alabama-Tombigbee Regional Commission.

Curren, Caleb B., and Keith J. Little
1991   Moundville IV Phase of the Black Warrior River: A Definition. Paper presented at the meeting of the Alabama Academy of Science, Jacksonville State University.

Curren, Caleb B., Keith J. Little, and George E. Lankford
1982   Archaeological Research Concerning Sixteenth-Century Spanish and Indians in Alabama. Unpublished report submitted to the Alabama-Tombigbee Regional Commission.

DeJarnette, David L.
1952   Alabama Archaeology: A Summary. In *Archaeology of the Eastern United States,* edited by J. B. Griffin, 272–84. Chicago: University of Chicago Press.

Dobyns, Henry F.
1983   *Their Number Become Thinned: Native American Population Dynamics in Eastern North America.* Knoxville: University of Tennessee Press.

Dye, David H.
1990   Warfare in the Sixteenth-Century Southeast: The de Soto Expedition in the Interior. In *Columbian Consequences,* vol. 2: *Archaeologial and Historical Perspectives on the Spanish Borderlands East,* edited by David Hurst Thomas, 211–22. Washington, D.C.: Smithsonian Institution.

El-Najjar, Mahmoud Y.
1976   Maize, Malaria, and the Anemias in the Pre-Columbian New World. *Yearbook of Physical Anthropology* 20:329–488.

El-Najjar, Mahmoud Y., and A. L. Robertson, Jr.
1976   Spongy Bones in Prehistoric America. *Science* 193:141–43.

El-Najjar, Mahmoud Y., Dennis J. Ryan, Christy G. Turner II, and Betsy Lozoff
1976   The Etiology of Porotic Hyperostosis among the Prehistoric and Historic Anasazi Indians of the Southwestern United States. *American Journal of Physical Anthropology* 44:477–88.

Elvas, Gentleman of
1973   Discovery of Florida, the True Relation by a Fidalgo of Elvas. In *Narratives of the Career of Hernando de Soto in the Conquest of Florida,* vol. 1, edited by Edward G. Bourne. 1922. Reprint, New York: AMS.

Ewen, Charles R.
1990   Soldier of Fortune: Hernando de Soto in the Territory of the Apalachee, 1539–

1540. In *Columbian Consequences,* vol. 2: *Archaeological and Historical Perspectives on the Spanish Borderlands East,* edited by David Hurst Thomas, 83–91. Washington, D.C.: Smithsonian Institution.

Freedman, Daniel G.

1974   *Human Infancy: An Evolutionary Perspective.* Hillsdale, N.J.: Lawrence Erlbaum.

Gibson, Jon L.

1974   Aboriginal Warfare in the Protohistoric Southeast: An Alternative Perspective. *American Antiquity* 39(1):130–33.

Hally, David J.

1988   Archaeology and Settlement Plan of the King Site. In *The King Site: Continuity and Contact in Sixteenth-Century Georgia,* edited by Robert L. Blakely, 3–16. Athens: University of Georgia Press.

Hann, John H.

1988   *Apalachee: The Land Between the Rivers.* Gainesville: University Press of Florida.

Hanushek, Eric A., and John E. Jackson

1977   *Statistical Methods for Social Scientists.* New York: Academic Press.

Hill, M. Cassandra

1979   The Alabama Phase: A Biological Synthesis and Interpretation. Master's thesis, Department of Anthropology, University of Tennessee, Knoxville.

1981a   Analysis, Synthesis, and Interpretation of the Skeletal Material Excavated for the Gainesville Section of the Tennessee-Tombigbee Waterway. In *Bio-cultural Studies in the Gainesville Lake Area,* by G. M. Caddell, A. Wookrick, and M. Cassandra Hill, 211–334. Tuscaloosa: Office of Archaeological Research, University of Alabama/University of Alabama Press.

1981b   The Mississippian Decline in Alabama: A Biological Analysis. Paper presented at the 50th Annual Meeting of the American Association of Physical Anthropologists, Detroit.

1985   A Biological Assessment of Protohistoric Populations in Alabama. Paper presented at the 84th Annual Meeting of the American Anthropological Association, Washington, D.C.

Hill, M. Cassandra, and George A. Clark

1981   Skeletal Analysis of Burials from 1TU4 and 1HA19. In *Archaeological Investigations (1933–1980) of the Protohistoric Period of Central Alabama,* edited by Caleb B. Curren and Keith J. Little, 135–84, 200–33, 281–96. Camden: Alabama-Tombigee Regional Commission.

1984   [Site data sections, by site.] In *The Protohistoric Period in Central Alabama,* by Caleb B. Curren. Camden: Alabama-Tombigee Regional Commission.

Holmes, William H.

1903   Aboriginal Pottery of the Eastern United States. *Bureau of American Ethnology, Annual Report, 1898–1899* 20:1–237.

Hudson, Charles M.

1976   *The Southeastern Indians.* Knoxville: University of Tennessee Press.

1990   Conversations with the High Priest of Coosa. In *Lamar Archaeology: Missis-*
        sippian Chiefdoms in the Deep South, edited by Mark Williams and Gary
        Shapiro, 214–30. Tuscaloosa: University of Alabama Press.

Hudson, Charles M., John E. Worth, and Chester B. DePratter
1990   Refinements in Hernando de Soto's Route Through Georgia and South Caro-
        lina. In *Columbian Consequences,* vol. 2: *Archaeological and Historical Per-*
        spectives on the Spanish Borderlands East, edited by David Hurst Thomas,
        107–19. Washington, D.C.: Smithsonian Institution.

Jenkins, Ned J.
1982   *Archaeology of the Gainesville Lake Area: Synthesis.* Office of Archaeologi-
        cal Research, Report of Investigations no. 12. Tuscaloosa: University of Ala-
        bama Press.

Krogman, Wilton M.
1973   *The Human Skeleton in Forensic Medicine.* Springfield, Ill.: Charles C. Tho-
        mas.

Lallo, John W.
1973   The Skeletal Biology of Three Prehistoric American Indian Societies from
        Dickson Mounds. Ph.D. diss., University of Massachusetts, Amherst. Ann
        Arbor, Mich.: University Microfilms.

Larsen, Clark Spencer, Christopher B. Ruff, Margaret J. Schoeninger, and Dale L.
        Hutchinson
1992   Population Decline and Extinction in La Florida. In *Disease and Demography*
        in the Americas, edited by John W. Verano and Douglas H. Ubelaker, 25–39.
        Washington, D.C.: Smithsonian Institution.

Larson, Lewis H., Jr.
1972   Functional Considerations of Warfare in the Southeast during the Mississippi
        Period. *American Antiquity* 37:383–92.

Little, Keith J., and Caleb Curren
1990   Conquest Archaeology of Alabama. In *Columbian Consequences,* vol. 2: *Ar-*
        chaeological and Historical Perspectives on the Spanish Borderlands East, ed-
        ited by David Hurst Thomas, 169–95. Washington, D.C.: Smithsonian Insti-
        tution.

Maruyama, Magorah
1963   The Second Cybernetics: Deviation-Amplifying Mutual Causal Process. *Ameri-*
        can Scientist 51(2):164–79.
1968   Mutual Causality in General Systems. In *Positive Feedback,* edited by J. H.
        Milsum, 80–100. Elmsford, N.Y.: Pergamon.

Mensforth, Robert P., C. Owen Lovejoy, John W. Lallo, and George J. Armelagos
1978   The Role of Constitutional Factors, Diet and Infectious Disease in the Etiol-
        ogy of Porotic Hyperostosis and Periosteal Reactions in Prehistoric Infants
        and Children. *Medical Anthropology* 2(1):1–59.

Milner, George R.
1980   Epidemic Disease in the Postcontact Southeast: A Reappraisal. *Mid-Conti-*
        nental Journal of Archaeology 5(1):39–56.

Mistovich, Timothy
    1989   Toward an Explanation of Variation in Moundville Phase Households in the
            Black Warrior Valley, Alabama. Paper presented at the 54th Annual Meeting
            of the Society for American Archaeology, Atlanta.
Moore, Clarence B.
    1904   Aboriginal Urn-Burial in the United States. *American Anthropologist*
            6(n.s.):660–69.
Peebles, Christopher S.
    1974   Moundville: The Organization of a Prehistoric Community and Culture. Ph.D.
            diss., Department of Anthropology, University of California, Santa Barbara.
    1987   The Rise and Fall of the Mississippian in Western Alabama: The Moundville
            and Summerville Phases, A.D. 1000 to 1600. *Mississippi Archaeology* 22(1):1–
            31.
Peebles, Christopher S., ed.
    1981   Prehistoric Agricultural Communities in West-Central Alabama. University
            of Michigan. Unpublished report submitted to the Heritage Conservation,
            Recreation Service, and the U.S. Army Corps of Engineers.
Powell, Mary L.
    1981   Post-Mississippian Mortuary Variability in the Gainesville Reservoir, West-
            Central Alabama. *Southeastern Archaeological Conference Bulletin* 24:12–13.
Priestly, Herbert I.
    1928   *The Luna Papers.* 2 vols. Freeport, N.Y.: Books for Libraries.
Ramenofsky, Ann F.
    1987   *Vectors of Death: The Archaeology of European Contact.* Albuquerque: Uni-
            versity of New Mexico Press.
Ranjel, Rodrigo, trans.
    1922   *Narratives of the Career of Hernando de Soto in the Conquest of Florida,*
            edited by Edward G. Bourne. New York: Allerton.
Sheldon, Craig T., Jr.
    1974   The Mississippian-Historic Transition in Central Alabama. Ph.D. diss., De-
            partment of Anthropology, University of Oregon, Eugene. Ann Arbor, Mich.:
            University Microfilms.
Sheldon, Craig T., Jr., and Ned J. Jenkins
    1986   Protohistoric Development in Central Alabama. In *The Protohistoric Period
            in the Mid-South: 1500–1700,* edited by David H. Dye and Ronald C. Brister,
            95–102. Proceedings of the 1983 Mid-South Archaeological Conference. Jack-
            son: Mississippi Department of Archives and History.
Smith, Marvin T.
    1987   *Archaeology of Aboriginal Culture Change in the Interior Southeast: De-
            population during the Historic Period.* Ripley P. Bullen Monographs in An-
            thropology and History no. 6. Gainesville: University Press of Florida.
Steele, Ian K.
    1994   *Warpaths: Invasions of North America.* New York: Oxford University Press.

Steinbock, R. Ted
    1976   *Paleopathological Diagnosis and Interpretation.* Springfield, Ill.: Charles C. Thomas.

Steponaitis, Vincas P.
    1983   *Ceramics, Chronology, and Community Patterns: An Archaeological Study at Moundville.* New York: Academic Press.
    1986   Prehistoric Archaeology in the Southeastern United States, 1970–1985. *Annual Review of Anthropology* 15:363–404.

Swanton, John R.
    1946   *The Indians of the Southeastern United States.* Bureau of American Ethnology Bulletin 137. Washington, D.C.: U.S. Government Printing Office.

Turner, Kenneth R.
    1985   Epidemic Disease in the Early Historic Southeast. Paper presented at the Southeastern Archaeological Conference, Birmingham, Alabama.

Varner, John G., and Jeannette J. Varner
    1983   *Dogs of the Conquest.* Norman: University of Oklahoma Press.

Varner, John G., and Jeannette J. Varner, trans.
    1951   *The Florida of the Inca.* Austin: University of Texas Press.

Walthall, John A.
    1980   *Prehistoric Indians of the Southeast: Archaeology of Alabama and the Middle South.* Tuscaloosa: University of Alabama Press.

Wiener, Norbert
    1954   *The Human Use of Human Beings: Cybernetics and Society.* 2d edition. Garden City, N.Y.: Anchor Books.

Wright, Henry T.
    1984   Prestate Political Formations. In *On the Evolution of Complex Societies: Essays in Honor of Harry Hoijer 1982,* edited by Timothy K. Earle, 41–77. Malibu, Calif.: Undena.

Chapter 3

Sociopolitical Devolution in Northeast Mississippi and the Timing of the de Soto Entrada

Jay K. Johnson and Geoffrey R. Lehmann

Amid the hardships and dangers we have described, our Spaniards overcame the problem of crossing the first river in the province of Chicaza; and on finding themselves rid of their enemies, they dismantled the boats, preserving the nails to make other craft when such should be necessary. This work done, they continued their exploration, and after marching four days through level country, which though populated contained only scattered villages of few houses, they came to Chicaza, the principal settlement from which the rest of the province derives its name. This town was situated on a flat hill extending north and south between some ravines which contained little water but numerous groves of walnuts, live oaks and oaks. (Varner and Varner 1951, 397)

Garcilaso de la Vega's dramatic description of de Soto's Tombigbee River crossing and entrance into Chickasaw territory on December 16, 1540, sets the stage for this first contact between Europeans and Indians in northeast Mississippi. This depiction, and other accounts (Elvas 1973, 100–110; Ranjel 1973, 131–37), suggests that Chickasaw settlement at that time was concentrated on the Black Prairie—a long, relatively narrow physiographic zone in northeast Mississippi and west-central Alabama.

There are several clues in the chronicles that suggest the Black Prairie was the setting for Chicasa. In the first place, this zone is underlain by relatively impermeable chalk that is more severely eroded than the sands bounding it to the east and west (Stephenson and Monroe 1940). Consequently, it is the only relatively level country to be encountered in the region.

Studies of the earliest land survey notes of 1834 (Johnson et al. 1984; Stubbs 1983), as well as other reconstructions of the forest cover for the Black Prairie

(Kuchler 1964; Lowe 1911; USDA 1958), show the uplands to have been for-
ested in hickory and scrub oak on the deep soils with cedar glades and grasslands (the savannahs of the chronicles) where the chalk is close to the surface.
The stream bottoms were covered with oaks and hickories. Because the substratum is impermeable, many of the streams in the Black Prairie flow only
during and immediately after rainfall, a point to be considered when contrasting the Tombigbee, which was over its banks at the time of crossing (Ranjel
1973, 131; Varner and Varner 1951, 393), with the low water in the ravines
near Chicasa four days later.

    Important implications for the dynamics of aboriginal culture change in
the sixteenth century follow from this interpretation of the de Soto accounts.
There has been a tendency in the past to view the European impact on native
societies as the prime mover of social change during this period, casting the
Indians of the Southeast as passive victims. If Chicasa and the other Chickasaw
settlements were located on the uplands of the Black Prairie, the major shift in
settlement strategy—and, by implication, social organization that marks the
protohistoric in northeast Mississippi—preceded rather than resulted from this
first contact, and provides evidence of the adaptive capacities of late prehistoric Chickasaw culture. Moreover, if the dispersed upland settlement pattern
was already in place before the entrada, the potential impact of epidemic disease in the region would have been considerably reduced. The outlines of this
shift to upland settlement have been formulated on the basis of recent work in
the central portions of the Black Prairie (Johnson 1991a, 1991b; Johnson et al.
1984, 1991; Johnson and Curry 1984; Johnson and Sparks 1986). Middle Mississippian sites in the region are almost exclusively located on the terraces of
the major streams. They are often quite large and some contain platform
mounds. Protohistoric sites, on the other hand, are typically located on narrow upland ridges extending out into the bottoms of the smaller streams that
drain the prairie. They are generally quite small.

    The Mississippian settlement pattern is easy to interpret, with its charac-
teristic emphasis on the rich flood plain resources and arable soil. Bruce Smith
(1978, 1985) highlights the importance of the "energy subsidy" provided by
flooding in major rivers and argues this is a critical aspect of Mississippian
adaptation.

    In a project conducted jointly by the Mississippi Department of Archives
and History and the University of Mississippi, fieldwork was directed toward
expanding our knowledge of the nature and timing of the move into the prairie uplands. During the months of June, July, and August 1989, a five-person
field crew completed the fieldwork phase of the project. First, a 33 percent
sample of the area along two east-west transects in the region of West Point,
Mississippi, was searched for sites (figure 3.1). A total of 3,305 hectares was

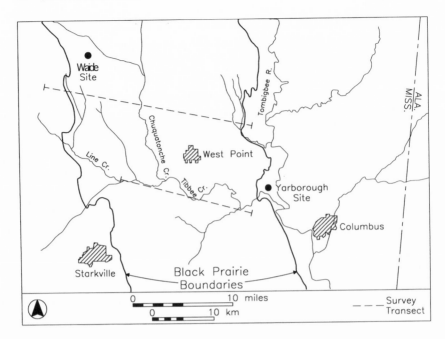

Figure 3.1. Survey area, near West Point, Mississippi.

surveyed using an interval of 30 meters for pedestrian transects. Shovel testing was employed in areas where vegetation covered the ground surface. Once
a site was located, shovel testing and surface collecting were used to secure a
sample of artifacts. We now have collections from 109 sites, 96 of which were
previously unknown. More than half (64) of these sites contain shell-tempered pottery. The vast majority of these sherds are plain. Only four sites can
be assigned to a specific phase: one Middle Mississippian and three protohistoric.

Technically, the protohistoric period in northeast Mississippi dates from de
Soto's initial contact to the beginning of regular historic documentation by
the French—A.D. 1540 to about A.D. 1700. One of the goals of our research
project was to date the beginning of the protohistoric settlement pattern in
the Black Prairie. We now know this pattern originated in the late fifteenth
century and continued through the historic Chickasaw.

For the purposes of the following analysis of protohistoric settlement, all
sites containing protohistoric ceramics or shell-tempered ceramics with no
Middle Mississippian markers were considered potential protohistoric sites.
The locations of these sites were digitized and patterns in their distribution
relative to soils and streams were examined using a PC-based geographic information system (GIS) software known as ERDAS. The three data planes
that will be discussed were recorded at a 30 meter resolution. The basic opera-

tion in a GIS analysis consists of overlaying two or more data planes and examining patterns in the coincidence of features of interest. For example, table 3.1 shows the total protohistoric site area in our survey sample broken down by soil type in the column marked "observed." The "expected" column shows the percentage of the total survey area made up by each of the soil types. If sites were located randomly in relation to soils, this would be the expected proportion of the site area to be made up by that soil. There are obvious and very interesting differences between the observed and expected values in table 3.1 that can be expressed easily in terms of the observed to expected ratio. When this value exceeds 1.0, sites occur in frequencies higher than expected for that particular soil type. All but one (cpo) of the soils for which this condition holds in table 3.1 are upland soils. Moreover, seven of the nine soils for which the O/E ratio exceeds 2.0 are shallow upland prairie soils.

This obvious selection during the protohistoric for shallow, upland soils in the Black Prairie comes as no surprise, confirming as it does a pattern noted in earlier research (Johnson and Sparks 1986). Furthermore, a recent, preliminary analysis of historic Chickasaw settlement in the Tupelo region (Johnson et al. 1989) has demonstrated not only that the shallow soils are likely locations for settlement, but the areas in the vicinity of the shallow soils do show concentrations of settlement. Therefore, a proximity analysis of the Clay County survey data was performed (table 3.2). In GIS this is done by projecting distance contours around each occurrence of the area in question; in this case, shallow prairie soils. The contour interval is fixed at 30 meters since that is the resolution of the data. The O/E ratio for all shallow soils is a relatively high 3.09 with a drop to 1.60 in the area within 30 meters, and 1.09 at 60 meters, beyond which the ratio is equal to or less than 1.0. There is clear patterning here. However, 48.04 percent of the site area falls beyond the 300 meter contour. Consequently, a proximity analysis was conducted for deep, upland soils (table 3.3). The O/E ratio for the combined deep soils is much lower than that for shallow soils and there is much less patterning in the distance contours.

In an effort to refine the pattern, a data plane was created specifying areas that were deep upland soils, or shallow upland soils, or within 60 meters of shallow upland soils. This amounted to 35.38 percent of the survey area and accounted for 73.46 percent of the protohistoric site area, yielding a quite respectable O/E of 2.08.

Still, we know from earlier work (Johnson and Sparks 1986) that another factor, stream order, was critical in the location of protohistoric sites. Accordingly, streams were classified and digitized, and sites were classified as to closest stream order. Stream order was designated by classifying the smallest streams in the drainage as first order. When two first-order streams join, the

Table 3.1. Protohistoric site area broken down by soil type

Soil type	Observed %	Expected %	O/E ratio
cod	8.10	1.81	4.48
sub2	8.38	2.58	3.25
svb2	3.63	1.18	3.08
klb2	2.23	0.73	3.05
bnb	4.47	1.53	2.92
oka	7.26	2.65	2.74
sub2	1.12	0.52	2.15
svc2	5.59	2.66	2.10
sud2	0.84	0.42	2.00
gse	2.23	1.50	1.49
kpb2	3.46	15.80	1.48
okb	7.82	5.36	1.46
vab2	0.84	0.71	1.18
cpo	3.35	3.07	1.09
un	0.84	1.09	0.77
kpc2	2.79	4.14	0.67
bra	0.84	1.51	0.56
suc2	1.12	2.02	0.55
kia	0.28	0.58	0.48
gr	3.63	7.65	0.47
le	7.82	16.56	0.47
kpa	1.68	4.25	0.40
brb	1.12	2.95	0.38
cpl	0.00	0.03	0.00
klc2	0.00	0.03	0.00
loa	0.00	0.07	0.00
ote3	0.00	0.20	0.00
vac2	0.00	0.23	0.00
ord2	0.00	0.37	0.00
svd3	0.00	0.44	0.00
oz	0.00	0.57	0.00
mha	0.00	0.62	0.00
lel	0.00	0.64	0.00
orc2	0.00	0.77	0.00
vaa	0.00	0.84	0.00
sre	0.00	0.90	0.00
be	0.00	1.28	0.00
orb	0.00	3.49	0.00
se	0.00	3.85	0.00
tl	0.00	4.40	0.00

Table 3.2. Protohistoric site area broken down by proximity to shallow prairie soils

Zone	Observed %	Expected %	O/E ratio
Shallow soils	30.17	9.75	3.09
30m	8.94	5.59	1.60
60m	3.63	3.32	1.09
90m	2.51	2.52	1.00
120m	2.51	2.77	0.91
150m	1.40	1.64	0.85
180m	1.12	1.68	0.67
210m	0.56	1.28	0.43
240m	0.28	1.27	0.22
270m	0.56	1.35	0.41
300m	0.28	0.97	0.29
>300m	48.04	67.85	0.71

result is a second-order stream. A second-order stream that is joined by a first-order stream remains a second-order stream. Tibbee Creek, the largest stream in the survey area, was classified as a sixth-order stream.

A cross-tabulation of sites by time and stream order of nearest water (table 3.4) shows that more than half (38) of the sites with protohistoric components are located high in the drainages nearest a first- or second-order stream, and the observed values for these cells exceed the expected. Proximity analyses of first- and second-order stream locations (tables 3.5 and 3.6) show definite patterning. Moving away from the streams, O/E exceeds 1.0 at 60 meters in both

Table 3.3. Protohistoric site area broken down by proximity to deep upland soils

Zone	Observed %	Expected %	O/E ratio
Deep soils	38.55	23.78	1.62
30m	7.54	9.80	0.77
60m	4.19	6.06	0.69
90m	5.87	4.96	1.18
120m	6.70	5.47	1.22
150m	1.96	2.97	0.66
180m	1.96	2.88	0.68
210m	1.40	2.03	0.69
240m	0.56	1.94	0.29
270m	0.56	1.94	0.29
300m	0.84	1.32	0.64
>300m	29.89	36.86	0.81

Table 3.4. Sites cross-tabulated by order of nearest stream and phase assignment

	First	Second	Third	Fourth	Fifth	Sixth
			Stream Order			
Earlier						
	O = 9.0	O = 9.0	O = 0.0	O = 10.0	O = 2.0	O = 17.0
	E = 16.2	E = 7.7	E = 0.9	E = 4.7	E = 1.7	E = 15.8
Protohistoric						
	O = 29.0	O = 9.0	O = 2.0	O = 1.0	O = 0.0	O = 20.0
	E = 21.8	E = 10.3	E = 1.1	E = 6.3	E = 2.3	E = 21.2

cases, confirming the fact that sites are not located in these relatively narrow bottoms but on the bluffs overlooking them. There follows a roughly symmetrical increase and then decrease until the O/E approaches 1.0 at about 210 meters for first-order and 180 meters for second-order streams.

Combining stream and soil data, a final data layer was created that specified all the area that was deep upland soil, or shallow upland soil, or within 120 meters of shallow upland soil, *and* within 60 to 210 meters of a first-order stream or within 60 to 180 meters of a second-order stream. This ability to create synthetic data planes using logical arguments is a powerful aspect of GIS analysis. The resulting zone amounted to 15.07 percent of the survey area and accounted for 39.94 percent of the site area with an O/E ratio of 2.65. This balances quite well the need to maximize both the amount of site area included and the O/E ratio.

The protohistoric settlement pattern, as delineated by our research, is more difficult to understand than the Mississippian pattern. Not only does it occur primarily on the minor first- and second-order streams, rather than the much larger sixth-order streams where Mississippian sites predominate, but the majority of the protohistoric sites in our sample are located on or near thin, upland prairie soils. The relationship between thin prairie soils and protohistoric settlement might be explained in terms of deer habitat. Today these soils characteristically support cedar glades and grasslands. Whether or not cedar glades were a prehistoric feature of the prairie is open to question (Johnson 1990; Peacock and Miller 1990). At any rate, wildlife studies in Arkansas have shown that cedar glades are an important foraging locality for deer during the winter (Segelquist and Green 1968). Forest edge and grasslands are also a critical source of deer browse. Bottomland hardwoods are an important warm-weather food source. The situation of the protohistoric sites on the edge of the stream bottoms at those points where thin soils occur suggests that they were located to maximize opportunities to hunt deer.

Table 3.5. Protohistoric site area broken down by proximity to first-order streams

Zone	Observed %	Expected %	O/E ratio
Stream	0.84	2.72	0.31
30m	4.10	6.97	0.60
60m	4.47	5.19	0.86
90m	6.42	5.10	1.26
120m	10.80	7.41	1.47
150m	7.82	5.18	1.51
180m	8.10	6.06	1.34
210m	5.03	4.93	1.02
240m	4.47	5.28	0.85
270m	3.91	5.70	0.69
300m	4.75	4.08	1.16
>300m	39.11	41.30	0.95

Some of the prairie drainages, however, contain more protohistoric settlement than others. There is good evidence that the stream bottoms with silt loam and silty clay-loam soils were preferred over those with finer-textured soils. The importance of silt loam soils to the Mississippian settlement system is generally recognized (Green and Munson 1978, 317; Larson 1972; Muller 1978, 400; Price 1978, 207; Ward 1965). It is likely that this soil texture class was selected by the protohistoric inhabitants of the Black Prairie for exactly the same reasons advanced to explain the Mississippian preference: it is amenable to aboriginal agricultural practices.

Table 3.6. Protohistoric site area broken down by proximity to second-order streams

Zone	Observed %	Expected %	O/E ratio
Stream	0.00	1.00	0.00
30m	0.28	2.72	0.10
60m	1.12	2.02	0.55
90m	3.07	2.07	1.48
120m	7.26	3.20	2.27
150m	6.70	2.32	2.89
180m	5.03	2.93	1.72
210m	2.23	2.52	0.88
240m	2.51	2.81	0.89
270m	1.96	3.29	0.60
300m	0.84	2.55	0.32
>300m	68.99	72.57	0.95

Summarizing, the typical protohistoric site setting in the study sample appears to be the tops of the low ridges and bluffs of the Black Prairie overlooking the upper reaches of small streams carrying a relatively coarse sediment load. This points to agriculture, but the preference for thin soils and their cedar glade-prairie cover indicates site selection balancing the needs of agriculture with those of hunting.

All of this stands in contrast to the Mississippian emphasis on the broad terraces of the major streams. The only point of resemblance between the two settlement strategies is the preference for silt loam bottom soils. The protohistoric pattern can be interpreted to represent a deemphasis on intensive, large-scale agriculture and a reemphasis on hunting. There is a concurrent decentralization. While most Mississippian sites in the survey area are large enough to suggest several families living together, most protohistoric sites are too small to contain more than two or three houses (recall Garcilaso's description of the settlement pattern on the way to Chicasa). There is little evidence for mound building or other indicators of the religious and political centralization that occurred during the preceding Mississippian period.

The eighteenth-century Chickasaw settlement around present-day Tupelo, Mississippi, fits the protohistoric pattern almost exactly. That is, all of the factors that were important during the protohistoric come together in their optimal expression at this point. The chalk substratum in this region ensures large areas of prairie. Several large streams flow across this prairie originating in the sand deposits of the Pontotoc Ridge to the west, thereby creating large bottoms filled with coarse-textured soils. Major settlement in the area occurs on the bluffs overlooking these stream bottoms (Jennings 1941; Johnson et al. 1989; Stubbs 1982, 1983). If we are correct in arguing continuity in subsistence systems from the sixteenth through the eighteenth centuries, it is easy to see why the Chickasaw competed so successfully in the deerskin trade for the Apalachee market in the seventeenth century and the English market in the eighteenth century. They were, in a sense, preadapted for it.

Data recovered in the excavation phase of the 1989 research suggest it may be possible to distinguish the Mississippian and protohistoric subsistence systems. During the last months of the field season, we conducted test excavations at five sites that appeared to have the potential of yielding additional information about the nature of protohistoric settlement. All but one of these were badly disturbed by agricultural practices. The exception, the Waide site (22CL764), provided a rare glimpse of what seems to be a typical protohistoric hamlet. The site is in pasture, with very little evidence of having been plowed. Excavations revealed a human burial located just outside an arch of post holes that probably marked the outer wall of a house. A large sample of artifacts

Table 3.7. Faunal assemblage composition (% by weight) and diversity indices for the Lubbub Creek, Yarborough, and Waide sites

Site	Large mammal	Small mammal	Bird	Turtle	Snake	Amphibian	Fish	Diversity
Lubbub								
I	84.5	4.6	6.2	3.9	0.1	0.1	0.1	0.60
II/III	83.4	4.1	7.1	0.1	0.1	0.1	0.6	0.47
IV	83.4	4.3	8.4	2.9	0.2	0.1	0.8	0.65
Yarborough	73.7	6.4	4.6	13.3	0.9	0.2	1.0	0.83
Waide	94.4	2.5	3.4	0.8	0.1	0.0	0.1	0.31

Source: Data for Lubbub and Yarborough sites derived from Peebles 1987, tables 2 and 3.

was recovered, particularly from a trash midden situated on a downslope edge of the site. This midden was particularly rich in animal bones.

Slightly more than 1,300 animal bones from the Waide site were identified as to species, body part and, in some cases, age at death by Susan Scott, a zooarchaeologist working in southern Mississippi. These data give an excellent picture of a subsistence system that focused primarily on deer, but also utilized a number of other animals, perhaps even bison (Johnson et al. 1994). These faunal remains document habitation at the site in at least late winter and early summer.

Peebles (1987) utilized data from several sources, including the Lubbub Creek site nearby in Alabama (Scott 1983) and the Yarborough site located not far from our survey area in Clay County (Scott 1982), to demonstrate an increase in diversity in the exploitation of faunal resources during the protohistoric period. We anticipated that the Waide faunal assemblage would fit this pattern. However, using the same measure (Shannon-Weiner), the Waide site assemblage proves to be less diverse even than the Middle Mississippian Summerville II-III assemblage from Lubbub (table 3.7). This diversity measure has been used extensively in biology (Margalef 1968), where it was borrowed from information theory (Shannon 1949). The index is based on the summation of a natural logarithmic transformation of the proportional breakdown of an assemblage. An absolutely homogeneous assemblage (one class containing all specimens) would have a diversity index of 0.00 and an absolutely heterogeneous assemblage (each class containing 0.14 of the total in a seven-class example) would yield a diversity value of 1.95.

A glance at the composition percentage of the Waide site fauna shows its relatively low diversity to be the result of the remarkably large amount of large mammal bones (primarily deer) from that site. This emphasis on deer ties in well with an earlier interpretation of the potential of the prairie (Johnson and Sparks 1986), but Scott (personal communication) has cautioned that the depositional environment at Waide had subjected the bones to considerable mechanical stress as a result of the tendency for prairie soils to expand and contract. This may have biased the collection in favor of the relatively more durable bones of the large mammals.

After the bone was identified, two large (more than 500 grams) samples were sent to Beta Analytic for bone collagen dating. The two samples produced raw dates that differed by only 20 years. After C13/C12 correction, they were identical. The dendro correction shows a 2σ range from A.D. 1442 to 1535 with a central intercept of A.D. 1490. These dates lend strong support to the argument that the historic Chickasaw settlement pattern was prehistoric, and that the shift to upland prairie hamlets occurred prior to the intrusion of Europeans into the area.

Moreover, the ceramics associated with the Waide site dates are stylistically distinctive and homogeneous. The assemblage is distinguished by a high proportion of Alabama River Applique and O'Byam Incised, both of which are common at the nearby Yarborough site (Solis and Walling 1982) where similar prehistoric radiocarbon dates were obtained. Seriation of the decorated ceramics from Yarborough, Waide, and two seventeenth-century Chickasaw assemblages from the Tupelo area supports the early, almost surely prehistoric timing of the shift to upland settlement in northeast Mississippi (Johnson et al. 1994).

Finally, there are the de Soto chronicles themselves. There can be little doubt that the Chickasaw were located up on the prairie at the time of first contact. That being the case, the move to the uplands must have preceded the entrada.

One of the things that makes delineating the Mississippian to protohistoric transition in the Black Prairie so important in understanding the dynamics of culture change in the Southeast is the discontinuity in settlement pattern. The protohistoric Alabama River phase just to the east in Alabama, for example, is viewed as a breakdown and simplification of the Mississippian system, but settlement strategy is essentially the same (Curren 1984; Sheldon 1974). Likewise, data from the Lubbub Creek site, located between the Alabama River phase area and the Black Prairie of northeast Mississippi, shows an in situ development from Mississippian through protohistoric (Peebles 1986, 1987). There is controversy over the timing of the beginning of the Alabama River phase. Peebles (1986, 1987) has argued that Moundville, the Mississippian ceremonial center that controlled much of northwestern Alabama, was abandoned at the time of the de Soto entrada. According to this view, the Alabama River phase grew out of the collapse of the complex, centralized social organization implied by Moundville, and this collapse was due to internal causes.

On the other hand, Sheldon and Jenkins (1986) place the beginning of the Alabama River phase at the middle of the sixteenth century. Curren (1984, 244–47) considers this phase to have been the result of epidemic disease introduced by the de Soto expedition. Marvin Smith (1987) develops a similar thesis in his review of the archaeology and ethnohistory of northwestern Georgia, eastern Tennessee and northeastern Alabama. Although there can be little doubt that the groups de Soto met in this area were full-blown Mississippian chiefdoms that devolved in the centuries to follow, the evidence for disease and depopulation is not so clear (Johnson 1988).

In fact, recent evidence from north Georgia (Kowalewski and Hatch 1991) suggests that there was actually a population increase in the Oconee drainage that began in the sixteenth century and continued into the seventeenth century. What is even more interesting about this increase is that it is characterized by a dispersed settlement and a move into the uplands. The parallels between this area and northeast Mississippi are remarkable. Not only are the settlement patterns similar, the sites themselves are alike in terms of their generally small size.

Kowalewski and Hatch (1991) are able to document a population increase for the protohistoric period in their research area on the basis of a fine-tuned ceramic chronology and a relatively large number of large-scale survey and excavation projects in the region. As a result, they can plot changes in site density through time.

Although a great deal of archaeological surveying was done in preparation for the construction of the Tennessee-Tombigbee waterway in northeast Mississippi, it is impossible to compute site density using many of the Tenn-Tom reports since survey coverage was not specified. Futato (1989) compiled the available data to study changes in settlement patterns through time in the Tenn-Tom corridor. In bringing together these data he developed a data base that, at our request, he used to examine Mississippian and protohistoric site densities.

For the Black Prairie and Pontotoc Ridge physiographic zones in Mississippi covered by Futato's sample, 3,436 hectares were classified as bottoms or terraces and 2,420 hectares were uplands. Because it was not always clear in the reports that he was using, Futato was not able to tell whether a site yielding shell-tempered pottery in this region was Mississippian or protohistoric. However, it has become evident on the basis of our work in the Black Prairie that sites with shell-tempered pottery located in the uplands are protohistoric, while those found in the stream bottoms and on the terraces are primarily Mississippian. Site density for shell-tempered assemblages in the uplands is

3.3 sites/km^2, slightly lower than the 3.8 sites/km^2 density recorded for the terraces and bottoms. This compares to a site density of 2.2 sites/km^2 for the 2,064 hectares of upland prairie surveyed during the course of our project. Although the data are inconclusive, it can at least be said that there was not a dramatic change in settlement density that coincided with the move to the uplands. Moreover, Futato's data for the historic Chickasaw show an upland site density of 5.0 sites/km^2, higher than either of the previous periods.

There are, however, two points of difference between the Georgia and Mississippi protohistoric data. First there is the timing of the shift to upland settlement. Kowalewski and Hatch (1991) attribute the major shift to upland settlement to the Dyar phase, from 1520 to 1580. The timing of this phase creates an ambiguity in evaluating the relationship between the reorientation in settlement and the de Soto entrada. Kowalewski and Hatch (1991) argue that the dramatic increase in upland settlement is the result of a reduction in interregional conflict with the collapse of neighboring chiefdoms, as they felt the disruption of European contact. In Mississippi, however, it is reasonably clear that the shift occurred before contact. Not only are there a growing number of radiocarbon dates, but there is a complete lack of European material in any of the upland settlements in the central part of the prairie in Mississippi.

The second contrast between the two regions is in settlement hierarchy. Kowalewski and Hatch (1991) note the presence of Dyar phase material at mound centers in the Oconee drainage. A two-tiered site hierarchy continued into the sixteenth century in the region, albeit much reduced from the preceding Mississippian occupation. There is little evidence for mound-centered ceremonialism in the northeast Mississippi protohistoric period. However, the small mound center at Lubbub Creek in nearby western Alabama was occupied during the early protohistoric. The point to be made here is that different things appear to have been happening at different times in different places on this late time level. Archaeologists sometimes lose track of this possibility in their effort to construct phases and search for common causes and effects.

Given that the shift away from the classic Mississippian pattern is prehistoric in northeast Mississippi, what are the implications for assessing the impact of European contact on indigenous groups? Two questions require immediate attention. First, what caused the shift? Now that we have eliminated the easy answer (that de Soto did it), we are left with the much more difficult and interesting problem of searching for indigenous causes. This search has just begun.

The second problem involves placing the sixteenth-century protohistoric period along the sociopolitical continuum from the complex chiefdoms of the eleventh century to the less centralized tribes of the historic Chickasaw. Dispersed settlement, in itself, is not an adequate measure of political decentralization since it appears as a riverine phenomenon during the height of the Mississippian period in the region surrounding Moundville in western Alabama (Peebles 1987; Steponaitis 1991). In fact, Steponaitis relates dispersed settlement to a domestic security, resulting from an increase in centralized control. Certainly, the meager evidence for mound-centered ceremonialism suggests that the devolution of social complexity had begun in northeast Mississippi prior to the first contact with Europeans. Here also we have a great deal of work to do (Johnson 1996).

Regardless, the prehistoric timing of the shift to a dispersed, upland settlement in northeast Mississippi has important implications for assessing the impact of de Soto on the Chickasaw. It would be considerably more difficult for epidemic disease to spread among the small and isolated hamlets we recorded in Clay County than it would be in a more centralized settlement system. It seems likely that there never was a demographic collapse among the Chickasaw and this, in part, may account for their prominence during the early historic period. Galloway (1994) has developed a parallel argument to account for similar data from the Choctaw region of southeastern Mississippi.

Acknowledgments

This paper has benefited from conversations with a number of people. Chief among them are Pat Galloway, Eugene Futato, James Hatch, and George Milner. We also need to acknowledge the tremendous hospitality of the people of Clay County, among whom Rufus Ward stands out. This was a joint University of Mississippi–Mississippi Department of Archives and History project with funding provided by the National Geographic Society and the National Endowment for the Humanities, an independent government agency.

References

Curren, Caleb B.
   1984   *The Protohistoric Period in Central Alabama.* Camden: Alabama-Tombigbee Regional Commission.
Elvas, Gentleman of
   1973   Discovery of Florida, the True Relation by a Fidalgo of Elvas. In *Narratives of the Career of Hernando de Soto in the Conquest of Florida*, vol. 1, edited by Edward G. Bourne. 1922. Reprint, New York: AMS.
Futato, Eugene M.
   1989   *An Archaeological Overview of the Tombigbee River Basin, Alabama and Mississippi.* University of Alabama, State Museum of Natural History, Division of Archaeology, Report of Investigations 59.

Galloway, Patricia K.

1994   Confederacy as a Solution to Chiefdom Dissolution: Historical Evidence in the Choctaw Case. In *Spanish Explorers and Indian Chiefdoms,* edited by Charles M. Hudson and Carmen McClendon, 393–420. Athens: University of Georgia Press.

Green, Thomas J., and Cheryl A. Munson

1978   Mississippian Settlement Pattern in Southwestern Indiana. In *Mississippian Settlement Patterns,* edited by Bruce D. Smith, 293–330. New York: Academic Press.

Jennings, Jesse D.

1941   Chickasaw and Earlier Indian Cultures of Northeast Mississippi. *Journal of Mississippi History* 3:155–226.

Johnson, Jay K.

1988   Review of *Archaeology of Aboriginal Culture Change in the Interior Southeast* by Marvin T. Smith. *Mississippi Archaeology* 23(1):73–75.

1990   Cedar Glades and Protohistoric Settlement: A Reply to Peacock and Miller. *Mississippi Archaeology* 25(2):58–62.

1991a   Aboriginal Settlement and First Contact in Northeast Mississippi. *National Geographic Research and Exploration* 7(4):492–94.

1991b   Settlement Patterns, GIS, Remote Sensing and the Late Prehistory of the Black Prairie in East-Central Mississippi. In *Applications of Space-Age Technology in Anthropology,* edited by Cliff Behrens and Tom Sever, 111–19. Bay St. Louis, Miss.: NASA, Science and Technology Laboratory, John C. Stennis Space Center.

1996   Chiefdom to Tribe in Northeast Mississippi: A Culture in Transition. In *Historiography of the Hernando de Soto Expedition,* edited by Patricia K. Galloway. Lincoln: University of Nebraska Press.

Johnson, Jay K., and Hugh K. Curry

1984   Final Report, Cultural Resources Survey in the Chuquatonchee Creek Watershed, Chickasaw, Clay, Monroe, and Pontotoc Counties, Mississippi. Center for Archaeological Research, University of Mississippi. Unpublished report submitted to Soil Conservation Service, Jackson, Mississippi, contract no. 53-4423-3-439.

Johnson, Jay K., Hugh K. Curry, James R. Atkinson, and John T. Sparks

1984   Final Report, Cultural Resources Survey in the Line Creek Watershed, Chickasaw, Clay, and Webster Counties, Mississippi. Center for Archaeological Research, University of Mississippi. Unpublished report submitted to the Soil Conservation Service, Jackson, Mississippi, contract no. 53-4423-2-314.

Johnson, Jay K., Patricia K. Galloway, and Walter Belokon

1989   Historic Chickasaw Settlement Patterns in Lee County, Mississippi: A First Approximation. *Mississippi Archaeology* 24(2):45–52.

Johnson, Jay K., Geoffrey R. Lehmann, James R. Atkinson, Susan L. Scott, and Andrea B. Shea

1991   Protohistoric Chickasaw Settlement Patterns and the de Soto Route in Northeast Mississippi. Unpublished report submitted to the National Endowment for the Humanities and the National Geographic Society.

Johnson, Jay K., Susan L. Scott, James R. Atkinson, and Andrea B. Shea

1994   Late Prehistoric Settlement and Subsistence on the Black Prairie: Buffalo Hunting in Mississippi. *North American Archaeologist* 2:167–80.

Johnson, Jay K., and John T. Sparks

1986   Protohistoric Settlement Patterns in Northeastern Mississippi. In *The Protohistoric Period in the Mid-South: 1500–1700,* edited by David H. Dye and Ronald C. Brister, 64–82. Archaeological Report no. 18. Jackson: Mississippi Department of Archives and History.

Kowalewski, Stephen A., and James W. Hatch

1991   The Sixteenth-Century Expansion of Settlement in the Upper Oconee Watershed, Georgia. *Southeastern Archaeology* 10(1):1–17.

Kuchler, August W.

1964   *Potential Natural Vegetation of the Coterminous United States.* Special Publications no. 36. New York: American Geological Society.

Larson, Lewis H., Jr.

1972   Functional Considerations of Warfare in the Southeast during the Mississippian Period. *American Antiquity* 37(3):383–92.

Lowe, Edwin N.

1911   *Soils of Mississippi.* Bulletin 8. Jackson: Mississippi State Geological Survey.

Margalef, Ramón

1968   *Perspectives in Ecological Theory.* Chicago: University of Chicago Press.

Muller, Jon

1978   The Kincaid System: Mississippian Settlement in the Environs of a Large Site. In *Mississippian Settlement Patterns,* edited by Bruce D. Smith, 269–92. New York: Academic Press.

Peacock, Evan, and W. Frank Miller

1990   Protohistoric Settlement Patterns in Northeast Mississippi and the Cedar Glade Hypothesis. *Mississippi Archaeology* 25(2):45–57.

Peebles, Christopher S.

1986   Paradise Lost, Strayed and Stolen: Prehistoric Social Devolution in the Southeast. In *The Burden of Being Civilized. An Anthropological Perspective on the Discontents of Civilization,* edited by Miles B. Richardson and Malcolm C. Webb, 24–40. Southern Anthropological Society Proceedings 18. Athens: University of Georgia Press.

1987   The Rise and Fall of the Mississippian in Western Alabama: The Moundville and Summerville Phases, A.D. 1000 to 1600. *Mississippi Archaeology* 22(1):1–31.

Price, James E.

1978   The Settlement Pattern of the Powers Phase. In *Mississippian Settlement Patterns,* edited by Bruce D. Smith, 201–32. New York: Academic Press.

Ranjel, Rodrigo

1973   A Narrative of de Soto's Expedition Based on the Diary of Rodrigo Ranjel, His

Private Secretary. In *Narratives of the Career of Hernando de Soto in the Conquest of Florida*, vol. 2, edited by Edward G. Bourne, 41–191. 1922. Reprint, New York: AMS.

Scott, Susan L.

1982   Yarborough Site Faunal Remains. *In Archaeological Investigations at the Yarborough Site (22CL814), Clay County, Mississippi*, by Carlos Solis and Richard Walling, 140–52. Report of Investigations no. 30. Tuscaloosa: University of Alabama, Office of Archaeological Research.

1983   Analysis, Synthesis, and Interpretation of Faunal Remains from the Lubbub Creek Archaeological Locality. In Studies of Material Remains from the Lubbub Creek Archaeological Locality, edited by Christopher S. Peebles, 272–379. Prehistoric Agricultural Communities in West-Central Alabama, vol. 2. University of Michigan Museum of Anthropology. Submitted to National Park Service, Interagency Archaeological Services, Atlanta.

Segelquist, Charles A., and Walter E. Green

1968   Deer Food Yields in Four Ozark Forest Types. *Journal of Wildlife Management* 32(2):330–37.

Shannon, Claude E.

1949   The Mathematical Theory of Communication. In *The Mathematical Theory of Communication*, edited by Claude E. Shannon and Warren Weaver, 29–125. Urbana: University of Illinois Press.

Sheldon, Craig T., Jr.

1974   The Mississippian-Historic Transition in Central Alabama. Ph.D. diss., University of Oregon. Ann Arbor, Mich.: University Microfilms.

Sheldon, Craig T., Jr., and Ned J. Jenkins

1986   Protohistoric Development in Central Alabama. In *The Protohistoric Period in the Mid-South: 1500–1700*, edited by David H. Dye and Ronald C. Brister, 95–102. Archaeological Report no. 18. Jackson: Mississippi Department of Archives and History.

Smith, Bruce D.

1978   Variation in Mississippi Settlement Patterns. In *Mississippian Settlement Patterns*, edited by Bruce D. Smith, 479–503. New York: Academic Press.

1985   Mississippian Patterns of Subsistence and Settlement. In *Alabama and the Borderlands: From Prehistory to Statehood*, edited by R. Reid Badger and Lawrence A. Clayton, 64–80. Tuscaloosa: University of Alabama Press.

Smith, Marvin T.

1987   *Archaeology of Aboriginal Culture Change in the Interior Southeast: Depopulation During the Early Historic Period.* Ripley P. Bullen Monographs in Anthropology and History no. 6. Gainesville: University Press of Florida.

Solis, Carlos, and Richard Walling

1982   *Archaeological Investigations at the Yarborough Site (22CL814), Clay County, Mississippi.* Report of Investigations no. 30. Tuscaloosa: University of Alabama Office of Archaeological Research.

Sparks, John T.
  1987   *Prehistoric Settlement Patterns in Clay County, Mississippi.* Archaeological
           Report no. 20. Jackson: Mississippi Department of Archives and History.
Stephenson, Lloyd W., and Watson H. Monroe
  1940   *The Upper Cretaceous Deposits.* Bulletin 40. Jackson: Mississippi State Geo-
           logical Survey.
Steponaitis, Vincas P.
  1991   Contrasting Patterns of Mississippian Development. In *Chiefdoms: Power,
           Economy and Ideology,* edited by Timothy K. Earle, 193–228. Cambridge:
           Cambridge University Press.
Stubbs, John D., Jr.
  1982   A Preliminary Classification of Chickasaw Pottery. *Mississippi Archaeology*
           17(2):50–56.
  1983   Archaeological Survey in Lee County, Mississippi. Paper presented at the 4th
           Mid-South Archaeological Conference, Memphis, Tennessee.
USDA (United States Department of Agriculture)
  1958   *Mississippi Forest.* U.S. Forest Service, Southern Forest Experiment Station,
           Forest Survey Release 81, New Orleans, Louisiana.
Varner, John G., and Jeannette J. Varner, trans.
  1951   *The Florida of the Inca.* Austin: University of Texas Press.
Ward, H. Trawick
  1965   Correlation of Mississippian Sites and Soil Types. *Southeastern Archaeologi-
           cal Conference Bulletin* 3:42–48.

Chapter 4

The Evidence for Demographic
Collapse in California

Lisa Kealhofer

Major health and demographic changes occurred during the protohistoric (1492–1769) and historic (1769–present) periods in California. The timing and causes of these changes, however, are poorly understood. Historical, archaeological, and skeletal evidence from two areas during these periods are used to address the prevalent theory of indigenous demographic collapse.

The thesis that early, deadly epidemics caused demographic collapse throughout the New World (e.g., Dobyns 1983, 1989) neglects the highly variable cultural and biological response of indigenous populations, and the significance of several hundred years of regional demographic fluctuation, decline, and recovery. If New World regional and local demographic trends are compared, the extreme variability in response to infectious diseases, from demographic collapse to recovery, demonstrates the importance of the cultural and environmental context of disease (Borah 1964; Cook and Borah 1979; Jackson 1985; Ramenofsky 1987).

Arguments for demographic collapse driven by epidemics of European diseases are inherently difficult to counter using only historical data for several reasons: (1) population decline among indigenous groups in North America during nineteenth-century epidemics makes early demographic disaster plausible; (2) documents often refer to local devastating disease episodes, but rarely discuss the recovery cycle or the distribution of the disease; and (3) selective interpretations of historical documents cumulatively seem to support demographic collapse (cf. Dobyns 1983; Henige 1986; Johansson 1985). One goal of this chapter is to decouple the argument for demographic collapse from the agent of epidemic disease.

The historically documented decline in populations during the eighteenth and nineteenth centuries leaves no doubt that depopulation was ubiquitous among Native American groups, a trend reversed only in the last few decades (Cook 1978; Ubelaker 1988). While examples of major demographic changes due to epidemics exist for the Americas, the evidence for the rapid, uniform demolition of native populations across both American continents is ambiguous (cf. Harvey 1967; Keen 1971; Zubrow 1990). The high mortality rates associated with epidemics, however, make them stand out beyond their true importance (Duffy 1953, 237; Keen 1971, 353). Recent work reveals that the causes for and responses to depopulation are complex, and often environment and culture dependent (Costello 1992; Jackson 1985; Johnson and Lehmann chapter 3 above; Stannard 1991; Walker and Johnson 1992). These studies confirm that indigenous response to contact was highly variable.

The evidence from two regions of California, despite its unevenness, is reviewed here to suggest a need for more detailed regional archaeological surveys, as well as culture-specific evaluations of the biological and cultural interaction and response of Native Americans and Europeans to epidemic diseases (cf. Milner 1988). Rather than assuming epidemic diseases had a uniform biological and cultural impact on Native Americans, the diversity of both cultural and biological responses needs further study.

California: An Illustration

Evidence for demographic collapse in California has to be assessed through diachronic changes in both cultural and biological patterns. Specifically, archaeological characteristics such as settlement pattern, site size, and mortuary practices of indigenous groups between the late prehistoric, protohistoric, and historic periods are appropriate for evaluating the possibility of cultural discontinuity due to demographic collapse.

To study demographic change and its biocultural ramifications in California during the contact period, the demography and cultural patterning prior to contact must be understood. Reconstructions of late prehistoric California cultures and their populations date to the turn of the century, when Merriam (1905) and later Kroeber (1925) derived population estimates for individual aboriginal cultures using a variety of techniques (described in Dobyns 1966). While Merriam (1905, 598) postulated a precontact population of 260,000, Kroeber (1925, 882–84) revised this downward to 133,000–150,000. Cook (1964, 1976) used mission records to arrive at a precontact population of 310,000 for California, a figure still in use, although controversial.

Three questions are discussed here: (1) What evidence is there in California for epidemic-based demographic collapse in the protohistoric period? (2) What evidence is there for epidemic-based demographic collapse in the historic period? And (3) what other factors contributed to the depopulation documented in the nineteenth century? Archaeological (including mortuary and settlement pattern evidence), skeletal, and historical data are used to address these questions, although the types and quality of data available for each period vary considerably.

Each of these three sources of data has intrinsic problems. Much of the skeletal material from California was collected in the late nineteenth and early twentieth centuries with little contextual documentation or systematic osteo-logical analysis, and poor chronological resolution (Moratto 1984, 121–23; Nelson 1936, 199). For example, Chumash cemeteries were rifled by relic hunt-ers beginning in the late 1800s (Moratto 1984, 121). The methods used in early excavations did not recover "populations" or "samples," precluding de-mographic analyses of these collections today. Skeletal material is rarely exca-vated now, due to current stringent California laws, and most recently exca-vated material cannot be analyzed. However, there are large unanalyzed assemblages in storage that still need to be studied.

While archaeological evidence continues to accumulate, many of the late prehistoric (A.D. 500–1500) and protohistoric (A.D. 1500–1769) cultures for which there is skeletal or historical material have little corresponding settle-ment pattern data (e.g., Gabrielino, see below). Historical documentation of California began in A.D. 1542, but was sporadic and infrequent until coloniza-tion in A.D. 1769. Historical records are critical for understanding the colonial era, but must be critically evaluated as their use can introduce an array of problems, as noted in a substantial body of literature (see, for example, the exchange between Dobyns 1989; Reff 1987, 1989; Upham 1986, 1987; also Henige 1986). Careful comparisons of archaeological and historical interpre-tations reveal ambiguities, identifying valuable avenues for subsequent re-search.

Protohistoric Demographic Collapse?

The bulk of the evidence for addressing the question of protohistoric demo-graphic collapse consists of archaeological, mortuary, and osteological data, although a few explorers documented their trips along the coast of California (e.g, Cabrillo 1542). Three archaeological variables (settlement pattern, site size, and mortuary practices), as well as disease patterns and ethnohistoric data are used to evaluate the argument for demographic collapse during the protohistoric period. The discussion focuses on the Canalino area, including the protohistoric Chumash and Gabrielino cultures, and the Central Valley area, including a variety of cultures but particularly the protohistoric Yokuts (figure 4.1). These areas were chosen for being the most intensively studied by archaeologists, ethnohistorians, and physical anthropologists.

Archaeology in these two areas of California began, as elsewhere, with relic hunters and amateur archaeologists in the late nineteenth and early twentieth centuries (e.g., Alliot 1916; Bryan 1927). Systematic excavation began in the early 1920s, leading to the definition of tripartite cultural sequences in the

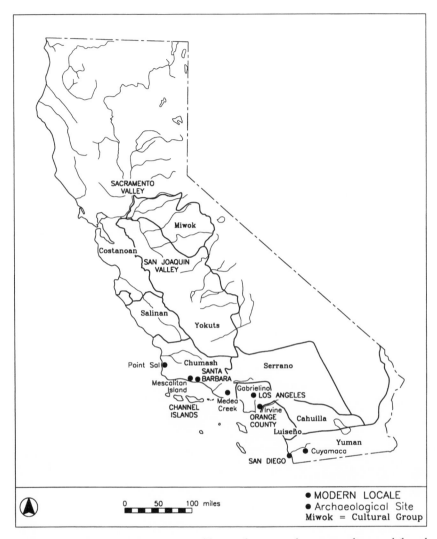

Figure 4.1. California sites, regions, and late prehistoric culture areas discussed (based on Beck and Haase 1974).

1930s (e.g., Gifford and Schenk 1926; Olsen 1930; Orr 1943; Rogers 1929; Schenk and Dawson 1929).

Major construction projects, particularly dams, precipitated an increasing number of salvage projects beginning in the 1950s, specifically in the Central Valley and the coastal regions of southern California. Most cemeteries were excavated before radiocarbon dating was common, and are therefore broadly dated (e.g., Early Horizon 2500–500 B.C.). While some of this material was integrated into published studies, much of it was never published. Many of the collections have not been studied in detail. With the impending repatriation of some of these collections, important analyses are underway. Without more refined chronologies and knowledge of late prehistoric cultures, however, these data will continue to be of limited value for investigating issues of demographic collapse (e.g., Newman 1957).

Mortuary Evidence

Late prehistoric populations in California were most dense in the Santa Barbara Channel region, the Central Valley, and along the coast of northwestern California. The mortuary patterning in these regions reveals the cultural complexity often attendant on greater population density. In much of California burial practices were seemingly in continuous flux during late prehistory. Cremation, secondary bundle burials, and primary cemetery and household burials seem to have co-occurred in many culture areas (e.g., Beardsley 1948; Pritchard 1970; Reinman and Townsend 1960). This complicated patterning makes constructing local population profiles difficult during late prehistory. Most commonly, population reconstructions are based on house and settlement data, given the nature of the mortuary data (e.g., Brown 1967; Slaymaker 1982).

In southern California, near San Diego, mortuary ritual included the use of burial urns for cremations, grave goods with miniature mortuary vessels, and grave markers within the context of spatially defined cemeteries (True 1970). Farther north, near Santa Barbara, cemeteries were also well-defined, with both primary and secondary interments, but cremation was not practiced (Olson 1930, 207; Reinman and Townsend 1960, 29; Rogers 1929, 384). In the intermediate area the Gabrielino (Los Angeles County) seem to have practiced both primary interments (mostly tightly flexed inhumations) and cremation (King et al. 1968, 25–29; Wallace 1955).

What is most interesting is that, while mortuary practices were in flux in all of these areas during late prehistory, no evidence for dramatic changes during the protohistoric period is seen in burial practices, burial goods, or the relationship between settlements and cemeteries. Such changes would be expected if demographic collapse had occurred after A.D. 1521 (see, for example, Hill, chapter 2 above; King 1969; Orr 1943). The pattern of change seen—the slow incorporation of cremation and its divergent ritual elaboration in many areas—reflects the gradual development of cultural complexes, rather than a short-term response to devastating disease episodes (cf. Milner 1980). The elaboration of mortuary ritual until the eighteenth century, with the addition of (interment) preparatory acts, as well as more elaborate (often Euro-American) grave goods in greater quantity, in fact, argues against major demographic disruption until the historic period (e.g., King et al. 1968; True 1966, 1970).

Settlement Pattern and Site Size

The settlement data for particular regions of California are quite good (Greenwood 1972; Leonard 1971; Moratto 1971; O'Connell 1975; Pohorecky 1976; Rozaire 1978; Smith 1961; Smith and Weymouth 1952; Treganza and Heickson 1969; Wallace 1962; Warren et al. 1961), if frequently present only in unpublished contract reports or theses (Goldberg and Arnold 1988; Martz 1984; Moratto 1973; Peak 1976; Theodoratus et al. 1979). Despite the quantity of site information, the lack of resolution in the chronological data makes it difficult to reconstruct changes during the protohistoric (King 1978, 58). While surveys in both the Central Valley and the Chumash area reveal sedentary village sites, often adjacent to junctions of rivers or creeks, survey data alone provide little information about the duration of occupation, size of settlement, or why occupation ceased (e.g., Beardsley 1948; Wallace 1955, 1978).

Survey data do support the increase in site quantity during the protohistoric period (Elsasser 1978, 43). Where sites have been excavated (e.g., King et al. 1968), size and complexity increase through the late prehistoric, and possibly the protohistoric, period (Chartkoff and Chartkoff 1984, 227; King 1978, 66–67).

The patterning at individual sites, such as the Century Ranch sites or Goleta Slough, clearly reflects cultural complexity and population density commensurate with semisedentary and sedentary societies. The development of food storage strategies, the use of ceramics, and the focus on specific resources and territorial definition support this view of the protohistoric (Frederickson 1973; Johnston 1962; Kealhofer 1991).

Those who have attempted to synthesize the data (Chartkoff and Chartkoff 1984; Moratto 1984), note that the largest populations are protohistoric in date. While individual settlement location did change and complex intersite networks developed in many areas, there is no archaeological evidence to indicate settlement pattern disruption or economic disaster. On the contrary, population and cultural complexity increased during the protohistoric, with corresponding shifts in health status related to population concentration.

Demographic disruption at the end of the protohistoric is more difficult to assess, since little material evidence could accumulate in the short interval before contact. However, early explorers' accounts record dense populations in the Central Valley and in coastal southern California (Crespí 1769 in Brown 1965; Trapper 1832 in Cook 1955, 319), with no mention of deserted village sites or disarrayed populations.

The archaeological and mortuary data reflect accelerating change in the late prehistoric and protohistoric periods. Some portion of this change can be attributed to increased contacts, both between indigenous groups and between explorers and indigenous groups. None of the evidence found thus far, however, supports a disruption in the demographic increase seen in late prehistory, except perhaps in the Channel Islands (see below). Large settlements and cemeteries are known up to colonization in 1769 (Chartkoff and Chartkoff 1984, 203, 205).

If demographic collapse occurred in the sixteenth century, as Dobyns (1983) suggests, it is archaeologically invisible to date. While collapse is possible, it seems unlikely that it would be completely unobserved in mortuary and settlement patterning. Renewed attention to protohistoric chronology and more demographically oriented research is needed to convincingly address population changes in these areas.

Disease Patterns

A broad range of infectious diseases was present among precontact central California groups, including treponematosis, tuberculosis, osteomyelitis, various malaria-type fevers, as well as several parasites (Newman 1975, 669; Roney 1966; Stodder 1986, 21). Bone lesions indicate streptococcal and/or staphylococcal infections were also present among some groups (Roney 1966; Suchey et al. 1972). Walker (1986) suggests that gastrointestinal infections were particularly common in the Channel Islands, possibly affecting infant mortality (Walker et al. 1989, 356). Evidence of violence is also seen in Channel Islands assemblages (Walker et al. 1989).

Walker (1986) and coworkers (1989) have completed several analyses of Canalino skeletal material, evaluating prehistoric trends in health across the subregions of the Santa Barbara area. The patterns of pathology, linear enamel hypoplasia, and cribra orbitalia show local variability, with some increases over time, suggestive of a slow rise in disease loads where populations were growing (Walker et al. 1989). No evidence is presented that supports a sharp increase in infectious disease during the protohistoric period.

Dickel and coworkers (1984, 453) suggest that Late Horizon populations in central California had elevated levels of parasitism and infectious diseases due to increasing sedentism and population density, as in the Santa Barbara region. A trend of declining health and/or increasing chronic stress in the protohistoric among southern California and Central Valley cultures may be present, but the lack of skeletal "populations" and poor chronological control makes conclusive interpretations problematic (Dickel et al. 1984; cf. Milner 1980, 49).

The diseases and stress indicators seen in the skeletal remains of these groups suggest that while general health declined in the protohistoric period, this decline was a result of cultural choices and endemic diseases rather than widespread, rampant epidemics. The increasingly compromised health suggests these groups were more susceptible to the cultural disruption and diseases introduced by the Spanish in the Colonial period.

Ethnohistoric Evidence

Spanish explorers discovered Baja California in 1532, and sailed north up the Pacific coast 10 years later (Cleland 1954, 4–9). Between 1532 and 1769, when Alta California was colonized, sailors sporadically stopped along the coast (Castillo 1978, 100). Several of these explorers recorded their brief contacts (e.g., Cabrillo 1542, Unamuno 1587, and Vizcaíno 1602), but many encounters probably went undocumented.

Comparisons of Vizcaíno's 1602 account of the coastal Santa Barbara area with the 1769 explorers' diaries (e.g., Crespí in Brown 1965, 175) indicate a strong continuity in the number and size of settlements. Brown (1967, 77–79) notes that warfare often led to settlement relocation but not to major demographic loss in Chumash groups, and he estimated the Chumash population at about 20,000 in 1769. Castillo (1978, 66) reports that island and mainland Chumash settlement patterns differed: mainland coastal village sites consolidated and grew during the protohistoric, while island site populations dispersed both to other island sites and to mainland villages. One oral tradition mentions that a pestilence afflicted the Chumash just prior to colonization, but its description and distribution are vague (Hudson et al. 1977, 11).

Reconstructions of the prehistoric population for the coastal area were based on mission documents, using an estimated ratio of the number of gentile baptisms to calculate a total population (Cook 1976, 25). While these estimates are useful, there is no way to know what the relationship was between the population immediately prior to 1769 and the population prior to the presence of Europeans in the New World (e.g., Grant 1978, 505). Without this relationship, historical data can reveal little about depopulation in the protohistoric period. Based on a reevaluation of Cook's (1976) estimates and oral history data, Chartkoff and Chartkoff (1984, 234–35) suggest a population maxima in 1700 of 350,000 for all of California, declining to Cook's estimate of 310,000 in 1769.

If early protohistoric demographic collapse did occur, then the explorers' accounts of 1769 suggest recovery had ensued by this time. These overland explorers saw populous, functional, coastal villages, particularly in the Santa Barbara region (Grant 1978, 505). None of the records from 1542, 1602, or 1769 suggest a disarticulated Chumash culture. They do not mention regions with deserted villages, disease, or other evidence of epidemics in Alta California (Brandes 1970). Whether or not these populations were reduced by prior disease episodes, they were fully viable in 1769 (cf. Brown's 1967 estimation of a population of 20,000 for Santa Barbara region coastal villages in 1769).

Epidemics in Baja California in the early eighteenth century, particularly the 1709 smallpox epidemic (Stearn and Stearn 1945, 132), may have spread north to Alta California. The isolation and low population density of Baja California suggest this dispersal was unlikely, but the possibility should be considered. Jackson (1992, 366–67) notes that the pattern of overall mortality seen in mission documents during epidemics indicates that "virgin soil" conditions existed in California, with little evidence for the spread of European infectious diseases during the protohistoric period.

Summary

Setting aside the difficulties of demographic reconstruction, abrupt, society-wide demographic upheaval has not been identified among the protohistoric Chumash or Yokuts (Castillo 1978, 65–66; King 1981). Despite a large number of skeletal assemblages, dated skeletal series are too rare to address demographic shifts within this period.

Mortuary patterns display continuity in the patterning of change from the late prehistoric period, with increasingly complex and elaborate burial rituals. Archaeological site and settlement pattern data support the presence of demographically successful, culturally articulated groups during the protohistoric. These settlement data are as yet not sufficiently detailed to evaluate the possibility of a rapid demographic change in the years just prior to contact. The ethnohistoric evidence leaves the question of early disease disruption open to discussion.

In sum, our current evidence does not support demographic collapse during the protohistoric period in California. Only further archaeological and settlement pattern research, given the constraints on mortuary site excavations, offer the possibility of a more detailed resolution of this problem.

Historic Demographic Collapse?

During the Colonial period, several observers noted the high frequency of neophyte deaths in the missions (Cook 1943a, 17–19). The mortality rate, however, varied considerably in both the coastal mission and the adjacent interior valley populations (Walker and Johnson 1992). Few epidemics were recorded in the missions during the Colonial period—possibly only three, and at most five. During the Mexican period, in the 1830s, at least two epidemics swept through California, with thousands of deaths reported (Cook 1955). These large-scale epidemics did not occur until 60 years after colonization, raising important questions about pandemics, epidemics, and their relationship to cultural interaction.

Historical Evidence

"Contact" is difficult to pinpoint in California, given its disparate definitions. Using Dobyns' (1983) definition of contact as the indigenous acquisition of European pathogens, the timing is tied to disease events. If disease spread like wildfire through the Americas after Cortés conquered Mexico, then "contact" dates to A.D. 1520–25. If, on the other hand, contact dates to the arrival of the first Europeans on the west coast of North America, then explorations around Baja California in the 1530s, as well as Cabrillo's 1542 and Drake's 1579 voyages along the California coast, are more relevant encounters (Kelsey 1985). Most conservatively, contact could be considered to begin with colonization in 1769. The unevenness of the archaeological and historic data after 1500 in California has led to disparate definitions of the contact period (cf. Moratto 1984; Schuyler 1978).

Baja California was successfully colonized only in 1697 (Kelsey 1985, 502), and Alta California in 1769. Soldiers, missionaries, and settlers founded a total of four forts, 21 missions, and three towns in Alta California by 1823, two years after Mexico became independent from Spain (figure 4.2; Cleland 1954).

Mission registers, which include annual counts of baptisms, confirmations, deaths, marriages, runaways, and crop harvests, as well as economic transactions, are the primary source for demographic reconstruction during the Mission period (1769–1834; Archibald 1978; Bancroft 1884, 1886; Engelhardt 1927, 1930; Walker and Johnson 1992). Sporadic head counts from other settlements augment this data set, but provide little information on Native American demography (cf. Cook and Borah 1979). Travelers' reports provide impressionistic accounts of mission events (e.g., Costello 1992).

Cook (1943a, 1943b, 1976), and later Cook and Borah (1979) made detailed studies of California's mission registers in order to understand the broad patterns of demographic change and their causes. Most recently, Walker and Johnson (1992) studied the missions in the Chumash area. Several of the patterns identified are pertinent to this discussion.

Using mission data, Walker and Johnson (1992, 129) reconstructed a population pyramid for the 1782 nonmissionized Chumash population, which they suggest shows evidence of disease impact between 1769 and 1782 based on the underrepresentation of 0–14-year-olds. However, the 0–9-year-old group makes up 25 percent of the mission population (Walker and Johnson 1992, 130, table 1). Cook (1976, 92) estimated, based on a study of children in the missions during the first years of missionization, that 0–9-year-olds made up about 26 percent of the aboriginal population. If Cook's estimates are correct, Walker and Johnson's population pyramid shows little evidence for disease impact in 1782.

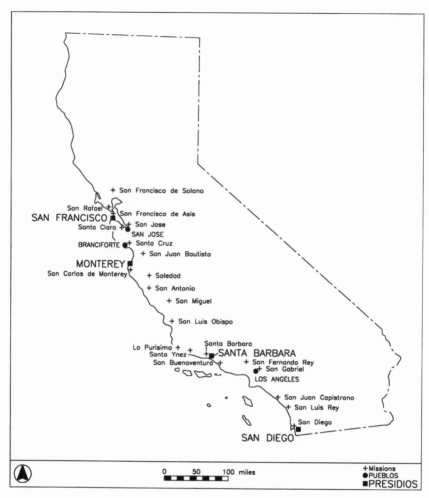

Figure 4.2. Spanish Colonial period settlements in Alta California (based on Beck and Haase 1974, map 19).

Walker and Johnson (1992, 129) note that the number of Chumash bap-tized, beginning in 1782, corresponded to only half the population estimated by Portolá during the first land exploration of California in 1769. They con-clude that this is due to very high mortality between 1769 and 1782 (Walker and Johnson 1992, 129). Undoubtedly, disease and warfare significantly af-fected Chumash population. A loss of half the population—7,000–10,000 people—however, during the early Colonial period seems high, especially if the population pyramid shows little evidence of this loss in the pertinent age categories.

What could have happened to the rest of the population? It is possible that estimates of Chumash population are high (cf. Cook 1976). Or, given the later known patterns of immigration, a demographic shift inland may have occurred (Walker and Johnson 1992, 136). Some communities may have isolated themselves in the mountains and inland valleys, avoiding mission recruitment. The imbalanced sex ratios both at the beginning and the end of the Colonial period, whatever their cause, must have negatively affected fertility rates in both aboriginal and mission populations. Epidemics claimed many Chumash during missionization, but the relative rarity of epidemics in the Colonial period suggests some of the population survived outside the reach of the padres, and were subject to other cultural and environmental stresses. Further evidence is needed to evaluate the nature of Chumash demographic decline after 1769.

Comparisons between missions show that life expectancy after baptism varied strikingly. Life expectancy after conversion was 8.6 years at Santa Cruz, for example, but 17.4 years at San Luis Obispo (Cook and Borah 1979, 211–20). Whether this variability was due to mission management, the environment, or other factors is unclear, but the disparity between relatively closely spaced missions suggests individual padres' behavior contributed to the disparate patterns.

Disparity between missions is clear when the percentage of children (0–9 years) is compared from a group of five southern to 16 central and northern missions. In the southern missions the percentage of children increased throughout the Colonial period, but declined steadily in the northern missions (Cook 1976, 83).

Mission children experienced high mortality rates. While infant mortality was relatively comparable to other parts of the world, child (0–5 years) mortality was over 50 percent in the missions (Cook and Borah 1979, 232, 240–42). The synergism of nutritional deficiencies in weaning diets, sanitation-related diseases, congenitally transmitted diseases, epidemics, and cultural disruption was undoubtedly critical in this pattern. While epidemics accounted for a significant measure of this mortality, they preyed on an already compromised subpopulation.

Although it is difficult to know precontact death rates, these rates apparently soared in the missions. At several missions, however, death rates began to decline by the end of the Mission period (Cook 1943a, 14; 1976, 107).

Birth rates and fertility rates provide other measures of demographic change. Crude birth rates (smoothed) also diverged among the missions, although a pattern of dramatic increase followed by decline seemed widespread (Cook and Borah 1979, 256–59). In southern California there was some evidence of an increase in crude birth rates toward the end of the Mission period (Cook

1976, 107; Cook and Borah 1979, 260), suggesting perhaps the beginning of a demographic recovery.

Crude fertility rates (number of births/number of adult females), again, were highly variable between mission populations (Cook and Borah 1979, 254–55). As Cook and Borah (1979, 249) note, neither of these crude measures of birth rate and fertility would be desirable indices if better census data were available (Cook and Borah 1979, 249).

This variability suggests that the combination of stress and disease loads were not uniform across the colony; both cultural and environmental factors affected demographic response to missionization and disease. The variability may reflect a real difference between mission environments and behavior, based on multiple factors, including the living conditions at the missions, diet, domestic and labor policies of the missionaries, and disease patterns and prevalence.

Disease loads, in general, were high in the missions. Benités, the surgeon who served in California in the early nineteenth century, reported the widespread presence of syphilis, a respiratory ailment (possibly pneumonia), tuberculosis, and debilitating dysentery (cited in Stodder 1986, 39). However, in the adjacent region of Baja California, the Jesuit Father Baegert in 1752 attributed most neophyte deaths to poor diet, inadequate medical care, mercy killing, and abortion rather than epidemic diseases (cited in Kelsey 1985, 504).

Only six epidemics are well documented for both the Colonial and Mexican periods, mostly attributed to measles and smallpox (Cook 1943a, 18–20; Stodder 1986, 39). Estimated deaths based on contemporary reports range from 200–300 to about 1600 (Cook 1943a, 18–20). The distribution of epidemics was also varied. Often only a few missions seem to have been affected. Epidemic duration was also erratic, from weeks to months (Jackson 1983). It is unclear whether the period recorded reflects idiosyncratic record-keeping or actual disease patterns. Our knowledge of historic epidemics is somewhat haphazard, dependent on the survival of informal accounts of the number of missions affected and the deaths reported (cf. Jackson 1983, 36). Cook (1943a, 17–18) noted that, in terms of mortality, only the 1833 and 1834 epidemics were intense. The documentary evidence, thus, records remarkably few true epidemics in Alta California.

Nonmission records mention bouts of sickness in civilian settlements in 1787, 1794, and 1796. In 1797, typhoid and pneumonia may have struck Santa Barbara and San Francisco presidios (Cook 1943a, 21). Only in the 1790s does widespread documentary evidence exist for venereal syphilis (Cook 1943a, 26). Several observers suggest it reached epidemic proportions. As Stodder (1986, 52) noted, syphilis undoubtedly had an impact on fertility as well as mortality. The secondary effects of syphilis on overall health and mortality were also undoubtedly significant, and could explain in part the high childhood mortality (Jackson 1983, 40). In the early 1800s, foreign visitors and missionaries most frequently mentioned syphilis and dysentery as being responsible for neophyte death and ill health, with tuberculosis nearly as serious (Argüello 1807 and Señan 1811, cited in Cook 1943a, 22).

Nutrition was critical to the mortality pattern in Alta California. Mission diets are thought to have provided insufficient protein and calories (e.g., Stodder 1986, 53). Inadequate nutrition can create three types of problems: nutritional deficiency diseases, starvation, and increased susceptibility to infectious diseases (Cook 1943a, 34; Stodder 1986, 3–6). Stodder notes that mission diets were less diverse and higher in carbohydrates than the prehistoric diet. Comparative analysis of prehistoric and mission diets revealed that subclinical nutritional deficiencies significantly contributed to neophyte mortality (Stodder 1986, 39, 53).

Explanations for high mission death rates are diverse. Cook (1943a, 7–8, 30–34) proposed the primary contributing factors were the biological and cultural environment of the missions. Population aggregation in missions enhanced the spread of infectious disease, as did increased interaction between and within societies. The poor sanitation and living conditions within the mission complex, including sewage and water pollution problems, poor diet, crowding, and lack of medical care, together fostered the introduction of new pathogens and synergistically aided others (Jackson 1985).

Violence and fugitivism, in response to mission constraints, increased interaction with interior populations who provided refuge to runaways, thus encouraging the spread of infectious disease into nonmission areas (Cook 1943a, 1943b, 1978). While the missionaries have been accused of using the Indians as virtual slave labor (cf. Cook 1943a, 95–96; Castillo 1989, 378), they seldom extracted excessive labor from the neophytes. However, mission labor requirements and discipline were very different from prehistoric subsistence patterns, and undoubtedly created stress among the neophytes (Cook 1943a, 94–95; Hoover 1989, 401; cf. Larsen et al. chapter 5 below).

The contribution of physical and psychological stress to high mortality rates was emphasized and discussed in detail by Cook (1943a, 30–33, 135; 1978, 92). Not only the living conditions but also the authoritarian regime of the missions (regulating household composition, religious practices, meals, work, childbearing, and marriage) were stressful to neophyte health. The suggestion that stress contributed to mortality patterns is bolstered by comparison with the early European colonists on the eastern seaboard: biological and psychological stress created by the poor sanitation, nutrition, crowding, and fear aboard ship in the early Colonial period led to a mortality rate of nearly 80 percent (Duffy 1953, 13–14). High mission mortality was plausibly enhanced by stress due to poor nutrition, crowding, poor sanitation, and psychological factors.

Skeletal and Mortuary Evidence

Analyzed skeletal material from the historic period is rare (cf. Costello and Walker 1987; Stodder 1986). While excavations at the Santa Barbara and San Diego presidios have encountered burials, problems with preservation, sample size, or control of the skeletal material have often precluded analyses of pathology or demography (e.g., Carrico 1973; Costello and Walker 1987; Reck and Moriarty 1972). The only mission cemetery excavated and reported so far is La Purísima (Humphrey 1965), and this material recently has been subjected to further analysis by Walker and coauthors (1989).

This small assemblage of analyzed mission skeletal material challenges Cook and Borah's (1979) interpretations. They contended that child mortality (0–4 years) was higher in the missions than in other eighteenth- and nineteenth-century societies in Europe and Mexico (greater than 50 percent; Cook and Borah 1979, 242). While life tables are not directly comparable to archaeological mortuary samples, where subadults are often underrepresented, a comparison of the ratio of subadults between archaeological contexts and between documented societies is of interest.

Walker and others (1989, 352) compared subadult mortality from La Purísima mission cemetery samples with an adjacent Middle period Chumash site, Calleguas Creek (VEN-110), and noted that mortality was similar for both groups. At La Purísima 35 percent of the burials were under age 20, while at Calleguas Creek subadults accounted for 31 percent of the skeletal material, although no sample sizes were provided (Walker et al. 1989, 352). Both the (subadult) representativeness of the collections and the variable definition of subadult age range may affect this interpretation.

In the Central Valley, in skeletal material dating to the Late Horizon, 28 percent of the burials were subadults (under 20 years old; Early, Middle and Late Horizon total sample = 1254; Doran 1980; Walker et al. 1989, 352). The pattern of child mortality in both Late Horizon Central Valley and Mission period sites was similar: higher mortality from 0–2 years, significantly dropping off after age 4 (Dickel et al. 1984, 453; Doran 1980). This pattern may relate to similar shifts toward higher carbohydrate diets, as well as increases in settlement size and the contingent health effects during the Late Horizon.

Carbon and nitrogen isotope studies reveal mission neophytes were eating terrestrial (C3 pathway) diets—without a significant marine or maize component (Walker et al. 1989, 354). Given the heavy marine-based diet indicated by isotope studies of late prehistoric remains (Walker et al. 1989, 354), the shift in diet supports mission contribution to, and regulation of, neophyte diet. Comparisons of femoral midshaft dimensions show that La Purísima individuals were smaller than their nonmission counterparts (Walker et al. 1989, 355). Although Walker and coworkers use these dimensions as a measure of overall health, femoral midshaft diameters may represent biomechanical differences between mission and nonmission groups, although long bone length and the ratio of the two were not evaluated (Kealhofer and Baker 1990; cf. Larsen et al. chapter 5 below). The increase in midshaft circularity in the Mission period (Walker et al. 1989, 356, figure 21.2) parallels the increase in circularity seen by Larsen and coworkers (chapter 5 below) in their mission assemblage. Ruff (1987) suggests this increasing roundness in the femur cross section represents a decrease in mechanical loading and an increase in sedentary behavior. The difference between prehistoric and mission subsistence and labor practices supports the hypothesis that biomechanical forces may be responsible for size and shape disparities.

The lack of comparable historic period mortuary populations makes it impossible to evaluate the character of demographic decline from the skeletal evidence. Based on the evidence they studied, Walker, Lambert and DeNiro (1989, 360) concluded that demographic decline was possible during the proto-historic period, steep during the Mission period, but most dramatic during the subsequent gold rush period when violence and land competition claimed the indigenous refuge areas of California. The skeletal and mortuary data do provide insights into how groups physically adapted to changing cultural, nutritional, and economic conditions during the late prehistoric and early historic periods.

Archaeology and Ethnohistory

Historical archaeology in California provides us with the contexts in which colonists and indigenous groups interacted. Where the mission documents show us evidence of demographic decline, presidio, pueblo, and rancho sites demonstrate the active, if selective, participation of Native Americans in the colonial economic and social web. These data cannot *quantitatively* address the issue of demographic collapse in the early historic period, but they do provide a *qualitative* picture of the complex ways individuals and groups of colonists and Native Americans adapted.

In the last 15 years construction projects have necessitated salvage excavations in two pueblo (town) sites in Alta California: urban San Jose and Los Angeles. Smaller projects were undertaken in the third pueblo, Branciforte (Santa Cruz). The urban surroundings of these colonial pueblo sites preclude collecting settlement pattern or demographic data, but these sites provide a unique view of the civilian component of colonial society. The artifacts have been used to assess cultural interaction in the pueblo, and their patterning demonstrates strong indigenous contributions to the society of both pueblos (Fredrickson and Bente 1985; Kealhofer 1990, 1991).

Analysis of the Plaza Church site, in downtown Los Angeles, identified the loci of interaction between the settlers and the local Gabrielino (Kealhofer 1991). The abundance of locally made brownware ceramics in the pueblo suggests trade with local potters continued throughout the Colonial period, and may indicate that indigenous women worked in pueblo households, based on the distribution and types of domestic debris. The faunal material comprised only domesticated species, revealing little interaction between *pobladores* (colonists) and Gabrielino related to native foods, and suggesting few indigenous species were used in the pueblo. Comparisons between this site and data recovered from San Jose demonstrate differences in the interaction patterns between indigenous groups and settlers in northern and southern California (Kealhofer 1991, 577). Both historical and archaeological data from the pueblo sites allow us to reconstruct the variety of ways indigenous groups adapted to colonialism (Mason 1975).

Recent work at postcolonial rancho sites in the Los Angeles area furnishes a growing corpus of data supporting a strong Native American presence until late in the nineteenth century. Chace (1966), Evans (1969), Frierman (1982), Greenwood (1989), and Greenwood and Foster (1986) each described archaeological evidence that ranchos attracted many disenfranchised Native Americans as laborers and provided an alternative context for cultural adaptation and transformation. Rancho sites commonly demonstrate a stronger tie with indigenous groups than is seen in the pueblos. Lithic tools, faunal evidence of wild species, as well as other artifacts, are much more common on rancho sites (Evans 1969; Frierman 1982; Greenwood and Foster 1986; Gust 1982). Pueblos and ranchos, and even the uncolonized desert and mountain areas east of Los Angeles, provided a variety of contexts for indigenous transformation after contact.

Archaeological research at mission sites has increased over the last 15 years. Excavations at Missions Soledad (Farnsworth 1986), San Antonio de Padua (Hoover and Costello 1985), San Buenaventura (Greenwood 1976), and Santa Ynez (Costello 1989a) have greatly expanded our knowledge of acculturation and mission activities. Comparisons of these mission data sets are somewhat hampered by the fact that the areas excavated at each mission are often different, varying from neophyte quarters to the central compound, the padre's quarters, and special activity areas.

Where comparisons can be made, the results confirm the variability between missions in factors such as agricultural yields, craft specialization, cattle and sheep, and in neophyte conversion suggested in the historical records (Archibald 1978; Costello 1989b, 1992; Farnsworth 1987, 506–7). Paralleling the diverse biological responses of neophytes at the missions, the rates of change, types of interaction, and range of economic activities vary in the mission assemblages analyzed (Farnsworth 1987; Kealhofer 1991; Simons and Gust 1985). As both Stodder (1986, 32) and Costello (1992) point out, however, the economic success of a mission did not guarantee the health or success of its neophyte population.

At Soledad, Farnsworth (1987, 577–78) postulated that by the 1810s the missionaries became more interested in economic success than in the spiritual and cultural conversion of the neophytes. Paralleling the missionaries' increasingly economic focus was a decline in the rate of acculturative change in material culture (Farnsworth 1987, 619). This change perhaps reflects the failure of Soledad's missionaries to create a viable community, either biologically or culturally. Costello (1992, 79) suggests the shift to economic pursuits correlates with the beginning of the war for independence (1810), and the increasing divergence between missions continued during the subsequent Mexican period. This shift boded ill for the neophytes.

The southern missions were economically more successful than the northern missions (Archibald 1978), where the geography, environment, cultures, and demography made traditional Spanish agriculture more difficult (Stodder 1986, 22). While there is less archaeological information from the southern missions, it is apparent that the demographic and acculturative patterns are also quite distinct and locally variable (Greenwood 1976; Magalousis and Martin 1981; Beth Padon, personal communication 1989).

The archaeological and ethnohistorical data, therefore, confirm the historical record of variability between missions in the indigenous response to colonization. Despite this variability, missions inherently afforded fewer options for indigenous groups to adapt and more opportunities for stress and disease. Pueblo and rancho sites document the continuing presence of Native Americans, yielding evidence of alternative contexts for indigenous adaptation (Chartkoff and Chartkoff 1984, 269; Evans 1969; Greenwood 1989).

Summary

Even though the statistics Cook (1943a, 1976, 1978) and Cook and Borah (1979) calculated for mortality in the Mission and Mexican periods are high, in absolute terms population decline prior to the American period did not approach the 75 percent figure suggested by Dobyns (1983). From 1770 to 1830, the indigenous population of California decreased from 310,000 to 245,000, based on Cook's (1978, 92) estimation. This represents a more conservative 21 percent demographic decline (Kealhofer and Baker 1990).

Catastrophic decline is not evident in the Mission period, nor is there strong evidence that depopulation was primarily due to epidemics of European diseases. The monthly and annual death counts in mission records fall into only a few groups attributable to epidemic mortality (Jackson 1983, 43; Walker and Johnson 1992, 133). Death rates, while fluctuating annually and between missions, were continuously high (see Jackson 1983, tables 13 and 14, 1992). More detailed analyses of mission per capita death rates would be informative. Most importantly, the mission records demonstrate that each mission was unique in the way its indigenous population responded to missionization. This variable patterning argues against epidemics being the primary cause of depopulation in colonial Alta California.

Cook and Borah's (1979, 254–57, 260) graphs show a measure of demographic recovery had begun in some areas by the end of the Colonial period (see also Cook 1978, 92). This is not to underplay the dramatic demographic loss that occurred, particularly in the American period, up to 1900, when the indigenous population reached a nadir at 10 percent of its estimated precontact size (Cook 1978, 92–94). The high death rates, and the multiplicity of causes associated with these rates, mask the nonepidemic nature of depopulation among California's indigenous groups (Duffy 1953; Keen 1971). As noted above, it is easier to assign causality to a single phenomenon, such as epidemics, than to distinguish the multivariate basis of depopulation. Responses to epidemics are diverse, and mortality rates can vary from 10 percent to 75 percent depending on the form of the disease, the underlying health of the population, and the care available (Stearn and Stearn 1945, 15).

Archaeological and historical data from the two colonial pueblos and the ranchos show that cultural transformation and migration played a role in demographic change. Acculturation and assimilation, including switching ethnic-racial identities, may play a larger part than currently recognized (Jackson 1985, 467). Many indigenous family groups merged into the working class in town and on the ranch. However, the causes of depopulation are multiple and complex. Focus on the cultural contexts in which these changes occurred will provide a broader understanding of how indigenous cultures responded to contact.

Approaches to Depopulation

As discussed above, the terms used to understand Native American depopulation raise several issues. They affect the logic of the questions asked and the ways data are marshaled. For example, demographic collapse is only one form of depopulation, and probably not the most common. How do we define the analytical time frame of demographic collapse? How are demographic changes related to cultural changes? Demographic disaster, in the long term, is relatively rare (Thornton 1987) when compared with such cultural transformations as culture creation, assimilation, acculturation, and pluralism. The numerous examples (e.g., Griffen 1969, 1979; Spicer 1962) of depopulation resulting from disruptive cultural interaction suggest that, rather than beginning with the assumption that epidemics caused depopulation, we should ask what the role of epidemic disease, if any, was in a particular case. Cultural continuity was severely disrupted beginning in 1492, and indigenous trajectories of cultural change were permanently altered. Characterizing this transformation as uniformly abrupt and disastrous, however, is not only misleading, it prevents the evaluation of how cultural and biological variables affected adaptation and change.

Two complementary approaches are advocated for understanding the biological and cultural responses of indigenous societies to interaction with Europeans. One approach, as seen in Creamer (1990), is to focus on collecting detailed reconstructions of late prehistoric and historic cultural chronologies at a regional level. The explicit goal is demographic reconstruction, and involves careful site-by-site demographic assessments, a difficult archaeological goal. However, demographic assessments are less important than the long-term changes in location, concentration, and size of populations (sites). Fine-grained regional sequences of cultural and demographic change allow the role of epidemics and the presence of demographic collapse or depopulation to be evaluated.

The second approach focuses on the synchronic patterns in the historical and cultural context of a given contact situation. Researchers often report in detail on pathology in a "population" and only cursorily link the pathology identified to a general subsistence pattern: "hunter-gatherers" or "agriculturalists." The complexity of indigenous adaptations, even in subsistence terms, cannot be so reduced, nor can a uniform response in a specific subsistence system over time be assumed (Cohen and Armelagos 1984).

One alternative is to look at the broader scope of cultural interaction, where epidemiological models for the spread of disease become part of a wider set of variables that shape and constrain a culture's response to both biological and cultural intrusion (or either individually). That this kind of model is appropriate is apparent from the California evidence.

For example, Shipek's (1987) work on the diachronic changes in historic period Indian land tenure in southern California furnishes an explicit interpretation that could be tested with detailed archaeological survey focused on protohistoric demographic reconstruction. Shipek shows how early colonial patterns constrained the development of the spatial, economic, and cultural structure on the extant reservations. The main Spanish strategy for controlling indigenous groups, and shaping them into producers for the colonial economy, was resettlement into mission communities. In the missions south of Los Angeles, however, Franciscan missionaries often did not resettle local populations into mission communities, since agricultural production was not stable in the early years and could not support a mission pueblo. The regions surrounding the missions thus contained communities of both converted and unconverted Indians. This policy has resulted in the presence of extant, albeit transformed, indigenous communities on circumscribed portions of their former territory. In northern missions, missionary strategies included keeping the neophytes at the missions for several weeks, then letting them return home for a few weeks (Kelsey 1985, 505). Thus, the cultural and environmental variability in California was significant in shaping local colonial policy and had a direct impact on the choices and responses, both cultural and biological, of local indigenous groups (see Cook 1976 on northern and southern missions, cited above).

In another example of contextual historical analysis with strong archaeological implications, Harvey (1967) presents data on the Cahuilla of the southern California deserts. Cahuilla demographic decline presents a picture of a culturally rather than biologically disrupted society. Spanish contact with the Cahuilla was sporadic, and they were only peripherally affected by mission recruitment. Ethnohistoric and census information show the Cahuilla's pattern of depopulation reflected out-migration of the marriage-age cohort (Harvey 1967, 194–95). Over time, this out-migration forced marriage rules, previously based on moiety relationships, to break down. Kin groups were not large, and Cahuilla remnant groups eventually combined with other local groups to reestablish viable social units (Harvey 1967, 197). This cultural recombination created a regional pan-Indian society on local reservations. There is no evidence that epidemics caused Cahuilla depopulation (Harvey 1967, 197).

Harvey (1967, 197–98) emphasized that this depopulation pattern was not unique to the Cahuilla, even though recent authors downplay the role of migration in depopulation (e.g., Thornton 1987, 43). Similar cultural responses were described by Nicks (1980 cited in Johansson 1982, 141) for the Northwest, Hann (1986, 392) for the Apalachee of the Southeast, Ewers (1973, 112–13) for Texas, as well as others. Krech (1978, 724–26; 1983) suggests that residence and marriage patterns among the northern Athapaskans shifted from matrilineal/matrilocal to bilateral/bilocal in response to depopulation. Denevan (1992, 7) and Johansson (1982, 141–43) both underscored the role of out-migration and assimilation, by disrupting social organization and depleting the marriage-age cohort, in the demographic decline of small-scale societies. An annual 1 to 2 percent population decline can lead to significant demographic decline in 50–100 years (Johansson 1982, 140).

The pictures of social disintegration and reconstruction that Harvey and others paint from the ethnohistoric data could easily be tested archaeologically. Detailed comparisons of late prehistoric to historic settlement and material cultural changes among the various Cahuilla groups could not only evaluate the validity of Harvey's thesis, but could demonstrate how and when Cahuilla cultural transformations occurred, and what European contact contributed to these changes.

The recent escalation of research on the dynamics of cultural interaction in eighteenth- and nineteenth-century California shows a growing concern for understanding the historical processes connecting extant Native Americans with their predecessors (Castillo 1989; Costo and Costo 1988; Field et al. 1992; Hurtado 1988; Patterson 1992; Rawls 1988, 1992; Shipek 1987; Vane 1992). This attention has encouraged a reevaluation of the discontinuity inherent in "demographic collapse," as well as a growing dissatisfaction with monocausal explanations for protohistoric and historic indigenous change. No single-cause model can account for the diversity of indigenous cultures and their responses (Johansson 1982, 149).

CONCLUSION

Although epidemics sporadically contributed to high mortality rates, historical, archaeological, and skeletal evidence suggests that the disruption of indigenous social organization and reproduction may have at times been more significant factors in depopulation in California. The breakdown in the rules governing marriage and child raising, both from individual opportunism and Spanish-induced relocation, led to cultural and biological disruption. Many other cultural factors, such as the administrative policies of the Franciscans, methods of agricultural production, the decline of Spanish power, and disruption of Spanish trade, as well as the rules inherent in colonial government, were key variables in restructuring roles and values among indigenous groups.

The transformation of the environment caused by the introduction of domesticated animals, crops, and weeds removed indigenous subsistence choices in many areas, while providing new options, such as raiding. Although most California populations were not resettled into mission communities, the loss of eligible mates through secular recruitment, out-migration, raiding, and warfare affected reproductive potential even among nonmission groups.

Human skeletal remains and demographic data must be approached within a larger biocultural framework to understand the complex nature of European and Native American interaction, depopulation, and cultural and biological responses. Given the limitations of working solely with skeletal data excavated many years ago, as in California, it is important to pursue detailed ethnohistorical and settlement pattern studies of cultural change during the late prehistoric, protohistoric, and historic periods to understand cultural interaction and depopulation at contact.

REFERENCES

Aikens, C. M.
  1978   The Far West. In *Ancient Native Americans*, edited by Jesse D. Jennings, 131–81. San Francisco: Freeman.
Alliot, Hector
  1916   Burial Methods of the Southern California Islanders. *Bulletin of the Southern California Academy of Sciences* 15(1):11–15.
Archibald, Robert
  1978   *The Economic Aspects of the California Missions.* Washington, D.C.: Academy of American Franciscan History.
Baker, Brenda J., and George J. Armelagos
  1988   The Origin and Antiquity of Syphilis. *Current Anthropology* 29:703–37.
Bancroft, Hubert H.
  1884   *History of California,* vol. 1. In *The Works of Hubert H. Bancroft,* vol. 18. San Francisco: History Co.
  1886   *History of California,* vol. 3. In *The Works of Hubert H. Bancroft,* vol. 15. San Francisco: History Co.
Bean, Lowell L.
  1978   Social Organization. In *California,* edited by Robert F. Heizer, 673–82. *Handbook of North American Indians,* vol. 8, William C. Sturtevant, general editor. Washington, D.C.: Smithsonian Institution.
Beardsley, Richard K.
  1948   Cultural Sequences in Central California Archaeology. *American Antiquity* 14:1–28.
Borah, Woodrow
  1964   America as Model: The Demographic Impact of European Expansion upon the Non-European World. *Actas y Memorias del XXXV Congreso Internacional de Americanistas, Mexico, 1962* 3:379–87.
Brandes, Raymond, trans.
  1970   *The Costansó Narrative of the Portolá Expedition.* Newhall, Calif.: Hogarth.
Brown, Alan
  1965   The Various Journals of Juan Crespí. *The Americas* 21(4):175–98.
  1967   *The Aboriginal Population of the Santa Barbara Channel.* Archaeological Survey Report no. 69. Berkeley: University of California Archaeological Research Facility.
Bryan, Bruce
  1927   Collecting Indian Relics on a Desert Island. *Museum Graphic* 1(4):145–50.
  1970   *Archaeological Explorations on San Nicolas Island.* Southwest Museum Papers no. 22. Los Angeles: Southwest Museum.

Carrico, Richard L.

1973   The Identification of Two Burials at the San Diego Presidio. *Journal of San Diego History* 19(4):51–55.

Carter, G. F.

1941   Archaeological Notes on a Midden at Point Sal. *American Antiquity* 6(3):214–26.

Castillo, Edward D.

1978   The Impact of Euro-American Exploration and Settlement. In *California*, edited by Robert F. Heizer, 99–127. *Handbook of North American Indians*, vol. 8, William C. Sturtevant, general editor. Washington, D.C.: Smithsonian Institution.

1989   The Native Response to the Colonization of Alta California. In *Columbian Consequences*, vol. 1: *Archaeological Perspectives on the Spanish Borderlands West*, edited by David Hurst Thomas, 377–94. Washington, D.C.: Smithsonian Institution.

Chace, Paul G.

1966   A Summary Report of PCAS Reconnaissance, the Costa Mesa Estancia, 1965. *Pacific Coast Archaeological Society Quarterly* 2(3):30–37.

Chartkoff, Joseph L., and Kerry Kona Chartkoff

1984   *The Archaeology of California*. Stanford: Stanford University Press.

Cleland, Robert Glass

1954   *From Wilderness to Empire*. New York: Knopf.

Cohen, Mark Nathan, and George J. Armelagos, eds.

1984   *Paleopathology at the Origins of Agriculture*. Orlando, Fla.: Academic Press.

Cook, Sherburne F.

1943a   The Conflict Between the California Indian and White Civilization I: The Indian Versus the Spanish Mission. *Ibero-Americana* 21:1–194.

1943b   The Conflict Between the California Indian and White Civilization II: The Physical and Demographic Reaction of the Nonmission Indians in Colonial and Provincial California. *Ibero-Americana* 22:1–55.

1955   The Epidemic of 1830–1833 in California and Oregon. University of California Publications in American Archaeology and Ethnology no. 43(3). Berkeley: University of California Press.

1964   The Aboriginal Population of Upper California. *Actas y Memorias del XXXV Congreso Internacional de Americanistas, Mexico, 1962* 3:397–403.

1976   *The Population of the California Indians, 1769–1970*. Berkeley: University of California Press.

1978   Historical Demography. In *California*, edited by Robert F. Heizer, 91–98. *Handbook of North American Indians*, vol. 8, William C. Sturtevant, general editor. Washington, D.C.: Smithsonian Institution.

Cook, Sherburne F., and Woodrow Borah

1979   Mission Registers as Sources of Vital Statistics: Eight Missions of Northern California. In *Essays in Population History: Mexico and California*, vol. 3, by Sherburne F. Cook and Woodrow Borah, 171–311. Berkeley: University of California Press.

Cook, Sherburne F., and Robert F. Heizer

1950   *The Archaeology of Central California: A Comparative Analysis of Human Bone from Nine Sites.* Anthropological Records vol. 12, no. 2. Berkeley: University of California Press.

1965   *The Quantitative Approach to the Relation Between Population and Settlement Size.* Archaeological Survey Report no. 64. Berkeley: University of California Archaeological Research Facility.

Costello, Julia

1989a   *Santa Ynez Mission Excavations: 1986–1988.* California Historical Archaeology Series no. 1. Salinas, Calif.: Coyote.

1989b   Variability among the Alta California Missions. In *Columbian Consequences,* vol. 1: *Archaeological and Historical Perspectives on the Spanish Borderlands West,* edited by David Hurst Thomas, 435–49. Washington, D.C.: Smithsonian Institution.

1992   Not Peas in a Pod: Documenting Diversity among the California Missions. In *Text-Aided Archaeology,* edited by B. J. Little, 67–81. Boca Raton, Fla.: CRC.

Costello, Julia, and Phillip L. Walker

1987   Burials from the Santa Barbara Presidio Chapel. *Historical Archaeology* 21(1):3–17.

Costo, Rupert, and Jeanette Henry Costo, eds.

1988   *The Missions of California: A Legacy of Genocide.* San Francisco: Indian Historian Press.

Creamer, Winifred

1990   The Study of Prehistoric Demography in the Northern Rio Grande Valley, A.D. 1450–1680. Paper presented at the 59th Annual Meeting of the American Association of Physical Anthropologists, Miami.

Denevan, William M.

1992   Part I: Estimating the Unknown, Introduction. In *The Native Population of the Americas in 1492,* 2d edition, edited by William M. Denevan, 1–12. Madison: University of Wisconsin Press.

Dickel, David N., Peter D. Schulz, and Henry M. McHenry

1984   Central California: Prehistoric Subsistence Changes and Health. In *Paleopathology at the Origins of Agriculture,* edited by Mark Nathan Cohen and George J. Armelagos, 439–61. Orlando, Fla.: Academic Press.

Dobyns, Henry F.

1966   Estimating Aboriginal American Population 1: An Appraisal of Techniques with a New Hemispheric Estimate. *Current Anthropology* 7:395–449.

1983   *Their Number Become Thinned: Native American Population Dynamics in Eastern North America.* Knoxville: University of Tennessee Press.

1989   Native Historic Epidemiology in the Greater Southwest. *American Anthropologist* 91:171–74.

Doran, G.

1980   Paleodemography of the Plains Miwok Ethnolinguistic Area, Central California. Ph.D. diss., Department of Anthropology, University of California, Davis.

Drover, Christopher
    1975   Early Ceramics from Coastal Southern California. *Journal of California Anthropology* 2(1):101–7.
Duffy, John
    1953   *Epidemics in Colonial America.* Baton Rouge: Louisiana State University Press.
Elsasser, Albert B.
    1978   Development of Regional Prehistoric Cultures. In *California,* edited by Robert F. Heizer, 37–57. *Handbook of North American Indians,* vol. 8, William C. Sturtevant, general editor. Washington, D.C.: Smithsonian Institution.
Engelhardt, Zephyrin
    1927   *San Gabriel Mission and the Beginnings of Los Angeles.* Los Angeles: James H. Barry.
    1930   *The Missions and Missionaries of California.* Vol. 2: *Upper California.* Santa Barbara: Mission Santa Barbara.
Evans, William S.
    1969   California Indian Pottery: A Native Contribution to the Ranchos. *Pacific Coast Archaeological Society Quarterly* 5(3):71–81.
Ewers, John C.
    1973   The Influence of Epidemics on the Indian Populations and Cultures of Texas. *Plains Anthropologist* 18(59):104–15.
Farnsworth, Paul
    1986   Spanish California: The Final Frontier. *Journal of New World Archaeology* 6(4):35–46.
    1987   The Economics of Acculturation in the California Missions: A Historical and Archaeological Study of Mission Nuestra Señora de la Soledad. Ph.D. diss., Department of Archaeology, University of California, Los Angeles.
Field, Les, Alan Leventhal, Dolores Sanchez, and Rosemary Cambra
    1992   A Contemporary Ohlone Tribal Revitalization Movement: A Perspective from the Muwekma Costanoan/Ohlone Indians of the San Francisco Bay Area. *California History* 71(3):412–32.
Finnerty, W. Patrick, Dean A. Decker, N. Nelson Leonard, III, Thomas F. King, Chester D. King, and Linda B. King
    1970   *Community Structure and Trade at Isthmus Cove: A Salvage Excavation on Catalina Island.* Occasional Paper no. 1. Costa Mesa, Calif.: Pacific Coast Archaeological Society.
Fredrickson, David
    1973   Early Cultures of the North Coast Ranges. Ph.D. diss., Department of Anthropology, University of California, Davis.
Fredrickson, David, and Vance Bente
    1985   Report of Phase III Research for Block 1, San Antonio Plaza, San Jose. Theodoratus Cultural Research, Inc. Unpublished report submitted to the Redevelopment Agency, City of San Jose.
Frierman, Jay D., ed.
    1982   The Ontiveros Adobe: Early Rancho Life in Alta California. Greenwood and

Associates. Unpublished report submitted to Redevelopment Agency, City of Santa Fe Springs.

Galdikas-Brindamour, B.
1970   Trade and Subsistence at Mulholland: A Site Report on LAn-246. *University of California, Los Angeles, Archaeological Survey Annual Reports* 12:120–62.

Gifford, E. W., and W. E. Schenk
1926   Archaeology of the Southern San Joaquin Valley. University of California Publications in American Archaeology and Ethnology 23(1). Berkeley: University of California Press.

Glassow, Michael A.
1965   The Conejo Rockshelter: An Inland Chumash Site in Ventura County. *University of California, Los Angeles, Archaeological Survey Annual Reports* 7:19–80.
1979   An Evaluation of Models of Iñezeño Chumash Subsistence and Economics. *Journal of California and Great Basin Anthropology* 1:155–61.
1980   Recent Developments in the Archaeology of the Channel Islands. In *The California Islands: Proceedings of a Multidisciplinary Symposium,* edited by D. M. Power, 79–102. Santa Barbara, Calif.: Santa Barbara Museum of Natural History.

Goldberg, S. K., and J. E. Arnold
1988   Prehistoric Sites in the Prado Basin, California: Regional Context and Significance Evaluation. Unpublished report submitted to the U.S. Army Corps of Engineers, Los Angeles District.

Goodman, Alan H., Debra L. Martin, George J. Armelagos, and George Clark
1984   Indications of Stress from Bone and Teeth. In *Paleopathology at the Origins of Agriculture,* edited by Mark Nathan Cohen and George J. Armelagos, 13–49. Orlando, Fla.: Academic Press.

Gould, Richard A.
1963   *Aboriginal California Burial and Cremation Practices.* Archaeological Survey Report no. 60, 149–68. Berkeley: University of California Archaeological Survey.

Grant, Campbell
1965   *The Rock Paintings of the Chumash.* Berkeley: University of California Press.
1978   Eastern Coastal Chumash. In *California,* edited by Robert F. Heizer, 509–19. *Handbook of North American Indians,* vol. 8, William C. Sturtevant, general editor. Washington, D.C.: Smithsonian Institution.

Greenwood, Roberta S.
1972   *9000 Years of Prehistory at Diablo Canyon, San Luis Obispo County, California.* Occasional Paper no. 7. San Luis Obispo: San Luis Obispo County Archaeological Society.
1976   The Changing Faces of Main Street. Greenwood and Associates. Unpublished report submitted to the Redevelopment Agency, City of San Buenaventura.

1989   The California Ranchero: Fact and Fancy. In *Columbian Consequences,* vol. 1: *Archaeological Perspectives on the Spanish Borderlands West,* edited by David Hurst Thomas, 451–65. Washington, D.C.: Smithsonian Institution.

Greenwood, Roberta S., and Robert O. Browne

1963   Preliminary Survey of the Rancho Canada Larga, Ventura County, California. *University of California, Los Angeles, Archaeological Survey Annual Reports* 5:463–506.

Greenwood, Roberta S., and John Foster

1986   Historic Structure Report, Part II: Archaeological Investigation of the Small Adobe, Olivas Adobe Historical Park. Greenwood and Associates. Unpublished report submitted to Department of Parks and Recreation, City of San Buenaventura.

Griffen, William B.

1969   *Culture Change and Shifting Populations in Central Northern Mexico.* Anthropological Papers no. 13. Tucson: University of Arizona Press.

1979   *Indian Assimilation in the Franciscan Area of Nueva Viscaya.* Anthropological Papers no. 33. Tucson: University of Arizona Press.

Gust, Sherri

1982   Faunal Analysis and Butchering. In The Ontiveros Adobe: Early Rancho Life in Alta California, edited by Jay D. Frierman, 101–44. Greenwood and Associates. Unpublished report submitted to the Redevelopment Agency, City of Santa Fe Springs, California.

Hann, John H.

1986   Demographic Patterns and Changes in Mid Seventeenth Century Timucua and Apalachee. *Florida Historical Quarterly* 64(4):371–92.

Harvey, Herbert R.

1967   Population of the Cahuilla Indians: Decline and Its Causes. *Eugenics Quarterly* 14:185–98.

Heizer, Robert F.

1949   The Archaeology of Central California, I: The Early Horizon. *University of California Anthropological Records* 12(1):1–84.

1955   California Indian Linguistic Records: The Mission Indian Vocabularies of H. W. Henshaw. *University of California Anthropological Records* 15(2):85–202.

Heizer, Robert F., and Franklin Fenenga

1939   Archaeological Horizons in Central California. *American Anthropologist* 41(3):378–99.

Henige, David

1986   Primary Source by Primary Source? On the Role of Epidemics in New World Depopulation. *Ethnohistory* 33(3):293–312.

Hoover, Robert

1973   *Chumash Fishing Equipment.* Ethnic Technology Notes no. 9. San Diego: San Diego Museum of Man.

1989   Spanish-Native Interaction and Acculturation in the Alta California Missions.

In *Columbian Consequences,* vol. 1: *Archaeological Perspectives on the Spanish Borderlands West,* edited by David Hurst Thomas, 395–406. Washington, D.C.: Smithsonian Institution.

Hoover, Robert, and Julia Costello, eds.

1985   *Excavations at Mission San Antonio, 1976–1978.* Monograph 26. Los Angeles: UCLA Institute of Archaeology.

Hornbeck, David

1983   *California Patterns: A Geographical and Historical Atlas.* Palo Alto, Calif.: Mayfield.

Hudson, Dee Travis

1969   The Archaeological Investigations during 1935 and 1937 at ORA-237, ORA-238, and ORA-239, Santiago Canyon, Orange County, California. *Pacific Coast Archaeological Society Quarterly* 5(1):1–68.

Hudson, Dee Travis, Thomas C. Blackburn, Rosario Curletti, and Janice Timbrook

1977   *The Eye of the Flute: Chumash Traditional History and Ritual as Told by Fernando Librado Kitsepawit to John P. Harrington.* Santa Barbara, Calif.: Santa Barbara Museum of Natural History.

Hudson, Dee Travis, and E. Underhay

1978   *Crystals in the Sky: An Intellectual Odyssey Involving Chumash Astronomy, Cosmology, and Rock Art.* Anthropological Papers no. 10. Socorro, N.M.: Ballena.

Humphrey, Richard

1965   The La Purísima Mission Cemetery. *University of California, Los Angeles, Archaeological Survey Annual Reports* 7:179–92.

Hurtado, Albert

1988   *Indian Survival on the California Frontier.* New Haven, Conn.: Yale University Press.

Jackson, Robert

1983   Disease and Demographic Patterns at Santa Cruz Mission, Alta California. *Journal of California and Great Basin Anthropology* 5:33–57.

1985   Demographic Change in Northwestern New Spain. *The Americas* 41(4):462–79.

1992   Patterns of Demographic Change in the Alta California Missions: The Case of Santa Inés. *California History* 71(3):362–69.

Johansson, S. Ryan

1982   The Demographic History of the Native Peoples of North America: A Selective Bibliography. *Yearbook of Physical Anthropology* 25:133–52.

1985   Review of *Their Number Become Thinned* by Henry F. Dobyns. *American Journal of Physical Anthropology* 67:291–92.

Johnson, Jerald T.

1967   *The Archeology of Camanche Reservoir Locality, California.* Paper no. 6. Sacramento: Sacramento Anthropological Society.

Johnston, Bernice E.

1962   *California's Gabrielino Indians.* Los Angeles: Southwest Museum.

Jurmain, Robert

    1990   Paleoepidemiology of a Central California Prehistoric Population from CA-
            Ala-329: Dental Disease. *American Journal of Physical Anthropology* 81:333–
            42.

Kealhofer, Lisa

    1990   Acculturation and Institutional Diversity on the Spanish Colonial Frontier:
            Archaeology in El Pueblo de Los Angeles. Paper presented at the 55th Annual
            Meeting of the Society for American Archaeology, Las Vegas.

    1991   Archaeology and Cultural Interaction in Spanish Colonial California: The Plaza
            Church Site (LAn-1112H). Ph.D. diss., University of Pennsylvania. Ann Ar-
            bor, Mich.: University Microfilms.

Kealhofer, Lisa, and Brenda J. Baker

    1990   Demographic Collapse or Adaptation? A Perspective from California. Paper
            presented at the 59th Annual Meeting of the American Association of Physi-
            cal Anthropologists, Miami.

Keen, Benjamin

    1971   *The Aztec Image in Western Thought.* New Brunswick, N.J.: Rutgers Univer-
            sity Press.

Kelsey, Harry

    1985   European Impact on the California Indians, 1530–1830. *The Americas*
            41(4):494–511.

King, Chester D.

    1974   The Explanation of Differences and Similarities among Beads Used in Prehis-
            toric and Early Historic California. In *?Antap: California Indian Political and
            Economic Organization,* edited by Lowell J. Bean and Thomas F. King, 75–92.
            Anthropological Papers no. 2. Socorro, N.M.: Ballena.

    1978   Prehistoric and Historic Archaeology. In *California,* edited by Robert F. Heizer,
            58–68. *Handbook of North American Indians,* vol. 8, William C. Sturtevant,
            general editor. Washington, D.C.: Smithsonian Institution.

    1981   Chumash Social Organization: An Ethnohistoric Perspective. Ph.D. diss., De-
            partment of Anthropology, University of California, Santa Barbara.

King, Chester D., Thomas Blackburn, and Ernest Chandonet

    1968   The Archaeological Investigation of Three Sites on the Century Ranch, West-
            ern Los Angeles County, California. *University of California, Los Angeles,
            Archaeological Survey Annual Reports* 10:12–107.

King, Linda B.

    1969   The Medea Creek Cemetery [LAn-243]: An Investigation of Social Organiza-
            tion from Mortuary Practices. *University of California, Los Angeles, Archaeo-
            logical Survey Annual Reports* 11:23–68.

Kowta, M., and J. C. Hurst

    1960   Site VEN-15: The Triunfo Rockshelter. *University of California, Los Angeles,
            Archaeological Survey Annual Reports* 2:201–30.

Krech, Shepard

    1978   Disease, Starvation, and Northern Athapaskan Social Organization. *American Eth-
            nologist* 5(4):710–32.

1983   The Influence of Disease and the Fur Trade on Arctic Drainage Lowlands Dene, 1800–1850. *Journal of Anthropological Research* 39(1):123–46.

Kroeber, Alfred L.

1925   *Handbook of the Indians of California.* Bureau of American Ethnology Bulletin 78. Washington, D.C.: U.S. Government Printing Office.

Leonard, N. Nelson III

1966   Ven-70 and Its Place in the Late Period of the Western Santa Monica Mountains. *University of California, Los Angeles, Archaeological Survey Annual Reports* 8:215–42.

1971   Natural and Social Environments of the Santa Monica Mountains (6000 B.C. to A.D. 1800. *University of California, Los Angeles, Archaeological Survey Annual Reports* 13:97–135.

Lillard, Jeremiah B., Robert F. Heizer, and Franklin Fenenga

1939   *An Introduction to the Archaeology of Central California.* Department of Anthropology Bulletin 2. Sacramento: Sacramento Junior College.

Magalousis, Nicholas M., and Paul M. Martin

1981   Mission San Juan Capistrano: Preservation and Excavation of a Spanish Colonial Landmark. *Archaeology* 34(3):60–63.

Martz, Patricia C.

1984   Social Dimensions of Chumash Mortuary Populations in the Santa Monica Mountain Region. Ph.D. diss., Department of Anthropology, University of California, Los Angeles. Ann Arbor: University Microfilms.

Mason, William

1975   Fages' Code of Conduct toward Indians, 1787. *Journal of California Anthropology* 2:90–100.

Meighan, Clement W.

1954   A Late Complex in Southern California Prehistory. *Southwestern Journal of Anthropology* 10(2):215–27.

1955   *Archaeology of the North Coast Ranges, California.* Archaeological Survey Reports no. 30. Berkeley: University of California Archaeological Research Facility.

Merriam, C. Hart

1905   The Indian Population of California. *American Anthropologist* 7:594–606.

Milner, George R.

1980   Epidemic Disease in the Postcontact Southeast: A Reappraisal. *Mid-Continental Journal of Archaeology* 5:39–56.

1988   The American Depopulation: Review of *Vectors of Death. Science* 240:1084–85.

Moratto, Michael J.

1971   *A Study of Prehistory in the Tuolumne River Valley, California.* San Francisco State College, Treganza Anthropology Museum Papers 9:1–177.

1973   *A Survey of Cultural Resources in and Near Redwood National Park.* San Francisco: Frederick Burk Foundation for Education, San Francisco State University.

1984   *California Archaeology.* Orlando, Fla.: Academic Press.

Moriarty, James R., III

1966   Cultural Phase Divisions Suggested by Typological Change Coordinated with Stratigraphically Controlled Radiocarbon Dating in San Diego. *Anthropological Journal of Canada* 4(4):20–30.

Nelson, Nels C.

1936   Notes on the Santa Barbara Culture. In *Essays in Honor of Alfred Louis Kroeber,* edited by Robert H. Lowie, 199–209. Berkeley: University of California Press.

Newman, Marshall T.

1975   Aboriginal New World Epidemiology and Medical Care, and the Impact of Old World Disease Imports. *American Journal of Physical Anthropology* 45:667–72.

Newman, Russell W.

1957   *A Comparative Analysis of Prehistoric Skeletal Remains from the Lower Sacramento Valley.* Archaeological Survey Reports no. 39. Berkeley: University of California Archaeological Research Facility.

O'Connell, James F.

1975   *The Prehistory of Surprise Valley.* Anthropological Papers no. 4. Ramona, Calif.: Ballena.

Olsen, William H., and Louis A. Payen

1968   *Archaeology of the Little Panoche Reservoir, Fresno County, California.* Archaeological Resources Section Report no. 11. Sacramento: California Department of Parks and Recreation.

1969   *Archaeology of the Grayson Site, Merced County, California.* Archaeological Resources Section Report no. 12. Sacramento: California Department of Parks and Recreation.

Olson, C.

1930   Chumash Prehistory. University of California Publications in American Archaeology and Ethnology no. 28. Berkeley: University of California Press.

Orr, Phil C.

1943   *Archaeology of Mescalitan Island, and Customs of the Canaliño.* Occasional Papers no. 5. Santa Barbara, Calif.: Santa Barbara Museum of Natural History.

1951   Ancient Population Centers of Santa Rosa Island. *American Antiquity* 16(3):221–25.

1952   Review of Santa Barbara Channel Archaeology. *Southwestern Journal of Anthropology* 8:211–26.

1956   Radiocarbon Dates from Santa Rosa Island, I. *Santa Barbara Museum of Natural History, Department of Anthropology Bulletin* 2:1–9.

1960   Radiocarbon Dates from Santa Rosa Island, II. *Santa Barbara Museum of Natural History, Department of Anthropology Bulletin* 3.

1968   *Prehistory of Santa Rosa Island, Santa Barbara, California.* Santa Barbara, Calif.: Santa Barbara Museum of Natural History.

Patterson, Victoria D.

1992   Indian Life in the City: A Glimpse of the Urban Experience of Pomo Women in the 1930s. *California History* 71(3):402–11.

Peak, A. S.

1976   Buchanan Reservoir Salvage Project, Madera County, California: Archaeological Excavation. Unpublished report submitted to the U.S. Army Corps of Engineers, Sacramento District, Sacramento.

Pohorecky, Zenon S.

1976   *Archaeology of the South Coast Ranges of California.* Archaeological Research Facility Contribution no. 34. Berkeley: University of California Press.

Pritchard, William E.

1970   *Archeology of the Menjoulet Site, Merced County, California.* Archaeological Report no. 13. Sacramento: California Department of Parks and Recreation.

Ragir, Sonia R.

1972   *The Early Horizon in Central California Prehistory.* Contributions of the University of California Archaeological Research Facility no. 15. Berkeley: University of California Archaeological Research Facility.

Ramenofsky, Ann F.

1987   *Vectors of Death: The Archaeology of European Contact.* Albuquerque: University of New Mexico Press.

Rawls, James J.

1988   *Indians of California: The Changing Image.* Norman: University of Oklahoma Press.

1992   The California Mission as Symbol and Myth. *California History* 71(3):342–61.

Reck, D. Glen, and James R. Moriarty, III

1972   Primary Report on the Discovery of a U.S. Cemetery at the Mission San Diego de Alcalá. *Anthropological Journal of Canada* 10(2):2–12.

Reff, Daniel T.

1987   The Introduction of Smallpox in the Greater Southwest. *American Anthropologist* 89:704–8.

1989   Disease Episodes and the Historical Record: A Reply to Dobyns. *American Anthropologist* 91(1):174–75.

Reinman, Fred M., and Sam-Joe Townsend

1960   Six Burial Sites on San Nicolas Island. *University of California, Los Angeles, Archaeological Survey Annual Reports* 2:1–115.

Riddell, Francis A.

1951   *The Archaeology of Site Ker-74.* Archaeological Survey Reports no. 10. Berkeley: University of California Archaeological Research Facility.

Rogers, David B.

1929   *Prehistoric Man of the Santa Barbara Coast.* Special Publications no. 1. Santa Barbara, Calif.: Santa Barbara Museum of Natural History.

Rogers, Malcolm J.
1936   *Yuman Pottery Making.* San Diego Museum Papers no. 2. San Diego, Calif.:
        San Diego Museum.

Roney, James G.
1966   Paleoepidemiology: An Example from California. In *Human Paleopathology,*
        edited by Saul Jarcho, 99–107. New Haven, Conn.: Yale University Press.

Ross, Lester
1969   The Irvine Complex: A Late Prehistoric Horizon Archaeological Complex for
        the Newport Bay Area, California. Master's thesis, Department of Anthropol-
        ogy, Washington State University, Pullman.
1970   ORA-190: A Descriptive Report of a Late Prehistoric Horizon Site in Orange
        County, California. *Pacific Coast Archaeological Society Quarterly* 6(2–3):1–
        135.

Rozaire, Charles E.
1959   Archaeological Investigations at Two Sites on San Nicolas Island, California.
        Masterkey 33(4):129–52.
1965   *Archaeological Investigations on San Miguel Island.* San Francisco: National
        Park Service.
1967   Archaeological Considerations Regarding the Southern California Islands. In
        Proceedings of the Symposium on the Biology of the Channel Islands, edited
        by R. N. Philbrick, 327–36. Santa Barbara, Calif.: Santa Barbara Botanic Gar-
        den.
1978   *Archaeological Investigations on San Miguel Island, California.* Los Angeles:
        Los Angeles County Museum of Natural History.

Ruff, Christopher B.
1987   Sexual Dimorphism in Human Lower Limb Bone Structure: Relationship to
        Subsistence Strategy and Sexual Division of Labor. *Journal of Human Evolu-
        tion* 16:391–416.

Schenk, W. Egbert, and Elmer J. Dawson
1929   Archaeology of the Northern San Joaquin Valley. University of California
        Publications in American Archaeology and Ethnology no. 25(4). Berkeley:
        University of California Press.

Schuyler, Robert
1978   Indian-Euro-American Interaction: Archeological Evidence from Non-Indian
        Sites. In *California,* edited by Robert F. Heizer, 69–79. *Handbook of North
        American Indians,* vol. 8, William C. Sturtevant, general editor. Washington,
        D.C.: Smithsonian Institution.

Shipek, Florence
1987   *Pushed into the Rocks.* Lincoln: University of Nebraska Press.

Simons, Dwight, and Sherri Gust
1985   Appendix D, Fauna. In Report of Phase III Research for Block 1, San Antonio
        Plaza, San Jose, by David Fredrickson and Vance Bente, D1-D43. Theodoratus
        Cultural Research, Inc. Unpublished report submitted to Redevelopment Agency,
        City of San Jose, California.

Slaymaker, Charles M.
   1982   A Model for the Study of Coast Miwok Ethnogeography. Ph.D. diss., Department of Anthropology, University of California, Davis.
Smith, Clarence E., and W. D. Weymouth
   1952   *Archaeology of the Shasta Dam Area, California.* Archaeological Survey Reports no. 18. Berkeley: University of California Archaeological Research Facility.
Smith, Jack E.
   1961   An Archaeological Survey of Vaquero Reservoir, Santa Maria, California. *University of California, Los Angeles, Archaeological Survey Annual Reports* 3:161–74.
Spicer, Edward H.
   1962   *Cycles of Conquest: The Impact of Spain, Mexico, and the United States on the Indians of the Southwest, 1533–1960.* Tucson: University of Arizona Press.
Stannard, David E.
   1991   The Consequences of Contact: Toward an Interdisciplinary Theory of Native Responses to Biological and Cultural Invasion. In *Columbian Consequences,* vol. 3: *The Spanish Borderlands in Pan-American Perspective,* edited by David Hurst Thomas, 519–39. Washington, D.C.: Smithsonian Institution.
Stearn, E. Wagner, and Allen E. Stearn
   1945   *The Effect of Smallpox on the Destiny of the Amerindian.* Boston: Bruce Humphries.
Stodder, Ann Lucy Wiener
   1986   *Mechanisms and Trends in the Decline of the Costanoan Indian Population of Central California.* Salinas, Calif.: Coyote.
Suchey, J. M., W. J. Wood, and S. Shermis
   1972   Analysis of Human Skeletal Material from Malibu, California (LAn-264). *University of California, Los Angeles, Archaeological Survey Report.*
Tac, Pablo
   1930   Conversión de los San Luiseños de Alta California. *Proceedings of the 23rd International Congress of Americanists, New York, 1968,* 635–48.
Tainter, Joseph A.
   1972   Simulation Modeling of Inland Chumash Economic Interaction. University of California, Los Angeles, *Archaeological Survey Annual Report* 14:79–106.
Theodoratus, Dorothea, Joseph L. Chartkoff, and Kerry K. Chartkoff, eds.
   1979   Cultural Resources of the Gasquet-Orleans (G-O) Road, Six Rivers National Forest, California. Unpublished manuscript on file, Six Rivers National Forest, Eureka, California.
Thornton, Russell
   1987   *American Indian Holocaust and Survival: A Population History since 1492.* Norman: University of Oklahoma Press.
Treganza, Adan E.
   1953   *The Archaeological Resources of Seven Reservoir Areas in Central and Northern California.* San Francisco: National Park Service.

1954   *Salvage Archaeology in the Nimbus and Redbank Reservoir Areas, Central California.* Archaeological Survey Reports no. 26. Berkeley: University of California Archaeological Research Facility.

Treganza, Adan E., and Martin H. Heickson
1969   *Salvage Archaeology in the Black Butte Reservoir Region.* Occasional Papers in Anthropology no. 22, 1–59. San Francisco: San Francisco State College.

True, Delbert L.
1966   Archaeological Differentiation of Shoshonean and Yuman Speaking Groups in Southern California. Ph.D. diss., Department of Anthropology, University of California, Los Angeles.

1970   *Investigation of a Late Prehistoric Complex in Cuyamaca Rancho State Park, San Diego County, California.* Archaeological Survey Monograph no. 1. Los Angeles: Department of Anthropology, University of California, Los Angeles.

Tyson, Rose A.
1977   Human Skeletal Material from the Cape Region of Baja California, Mexico: The American Collections. *Actes du XLIIe Congrès International des Americanistes, Paris, 1976,* 1067–81.

Ubelaker, Douglas H.
1988   North American Indian Population Size, A.D. 1500 to 1985. *American Journal of Physical Anthropology* 77:289–94.

Upham, Steadman
1986   Smallpox and Climate in the American Southwest. *American Anthropologist* 88:115–28.

1987   Understanding the Disease History of the Southwest: A Reply to Reff. *American Anthropologist* 89:708–10.

Van Camp, Gena R.
1979   *Kumeyaay Pottery: Paddle and Anvil Techniques of Southern California.* Socorro, N.M.: Ballena.

Vane, Sylvia Brakke
1992   California Indians, Historians, and Ethnographers. *California History* 71(3):324–41.

Walker, Edwin F.
1947   *Excavation of a Yokuts Indian Cemetery.* Bakersfield, Calif.: Kern County Historical Society.

Walker, Phillip L.
1978   A Quantitative Analysis of Dental Attrition Rates in the Santa Barbara Channel Area. *American Journal of Physical Anthropology* 48:101–6.

1986   Porotic Hyperostosis in a Marine-Dependent California Indian Population. *American Journal of Physical Anthropology* 69:345–54.

1989   Cranial Injuries as Evidence of Violence in Prehistoric Southern California. *American Journal of Physical Anthropology* 80:313–23.

Walker, Phillip L., and Michael J. DeNiro
1986   Stable Nitrogen and Carbon Isotope Ratios in Bone Collagen as Indices of

Prehistoric Dietary Dependence on Marine and Terrestrial Resources in Southern California. *American Journal of Physical Anthropology* 71:51–61.

Walker, Phillip L., and John R. Johnson

1992   Effects of Contact on the Chumash Indians. In *Disease and Demography in the Americas*, edited by John W. Verano and Douglas H. Ubelaker, 127–39. Washington, D.C.: Smithsonian Institution.

Walker, Phillip L., Patricia Lambert, and Michael J. DeNiro

1989   The Effects of European Contact on the Health of Alta California Indians. In *Columbian Consequences*, vol. 1: *Archaeological Perspectives on the Spanish Borderlands West*, edited by David Hurst Thomas, 349–64. Washington, D.C.: Smithsonian Institution.

Wallace, William J.

1955   A Suggested Chronology for Southern California Coastal Archaeology. *Southwestern Journal of Anthropology* 11:214–30.

1962   Prehistoric Cultural Development in the Southern California Deserts. *American Antiquity* 28:172–80.

1978   Post-Pleistocene Archeology, 9000 to 2000 B.C. In *California*, edited by Robert F. Heizer, 25–36. *Handbook of North American Indians*, vol. 8, William C. Sturtevant, general editor. Washington, D.C.: Smithsonian Institution.

Warren, Claude

1968   Cultural Tradition and Ecological Adaptation on the Southern California Coast. In *Archaic Prehistory in the Western United States*, edited by Cynthia Irwin-Williams, 1–14. Contributions in Anthropology no. 1, part 3. Portales: Eastern New Mexico University.

Warren, Claude, Delbert L. True, and Ardith A. Eudey

1961   Early Gathering Complexes of Western San Diego County: Results and Interpretations of an Archaeological Survey. *University of California, Los Angeles, Archaeological Survey Annual Report* 3:1–106.

Wedel, Waldo R.

1941   *Archaeological Investigations at Buena Vista Lake, Kern County, California.* Bureau of American Ethnology Bulletin 130. Washington, D.C.: U.S. Government Printing Office.

Zubrow, Ezra

1990   The Depopulation of Native America. *Antiquity* 64:754–65.

PART TWO

Skeletal Biology and Paleoepidemiology

Diachronic investigations of health and nutritional status in human skeletal assemblages provide direct evidence of biological responses to a variety of stressors. In the following three chapters, skeletal samples from different regions of the Spanish Borderlands are used to appraise the influence of European contact on biological well-being.

Larsen and colleagues (chapter 5) focus on biological adaptations to novel circumstances among the Guale of La Florida. The skeletal series used span four successive temporal periods, from preagricultural through the contact period. These assemblages were obtained through carefully controlled excavations aimed at investigating changes in subsistence and lifestyle through time. As a result, Larsen and his colleagues are in a unique position to evaluate the effects of contact and establishment of missions among the Guale. Rather than specifically addressing the impact of introduced diseases, they emphasize the biological adaptations to physical demands made on the *survivors* of epidemics. These demands included increased workloads, as seen in changes in the shaft morphology of limb bones and patterns of osteoarthritis.

Inferences drawn from skeletal remains are not without difficulties, particularly concerning the representativeness of specific samples and sample comparability (see Palkovich chapter 8 below). Miller (chapter 6) and Stodder (chapter 7) address such problems in their analyses. Miller's examination of skeletal indicators of stress in prehistoric and historic remains from Texas illustrates the need for careful contextualization before individual assemblages can be compared. Her study reveals significant differences between the two mission samples, which she correlates with the duration of contact with Europeans— short term versus long term. Despite these differences, Miller's analysis indicates that both short-term and long-term contact were detrimental to the health of indigenous groups in Texas.

In chapter 7, Stodder examines changes in health status evident in skeletal assemblages from two protohistoric Pueblo sites in New Mexico. In this area, epidemics are thought to have preceded direct contact with Europeans and caused continuing depopulation through the eighteenth century. The timing and extent of this depopulation, however, are debated. Comparison of paleo-epidemiological data from the protohistoric Pueblos with prehistoric skeletal assemblages suggests changes in health status through time. Rates and age-specific patterns of some stress indicators significantly differed between the two protohistoric skeletal assemblages. These differences underscore the variability in the responses to European contact even among closely related groups.

Both Miller and Stodder evaluate health status diachronically by investigating multiple indicators of biological stress. In contrast, Larsen and coworkers focus on specific aspects of biological adaptation seen in the skeleton. Ideally, analyses within and between skeletal assemblages should be integrated to discern the complex repercussions of contact. Each of these chapters demonstrates the contribution of direct examination of skeletal remains to our understanding of change in health status and lifestyle resulting from European contact. Additionally, these data underline the variability in cultural and biological responses to contact.

Chapter 5

Implications of Changing Biomechanical and Nutritional Environments for Activity and Lifeway in the Eastern Spanish Borderlands

CLARK SPENCER LARSEN, CHRISTOPHER B. RUFF,
AND MARK C. GRIFFIN

There can be little doubt that the introduction of new and novel stressors—such as Old World infectious diseases—to native New World populations led to markedly reduced quality of health and catastrophic reductions in population size. Although the topic of demographic catastrophe is important, its emphasis in the popular as well as technical literature has tended to overshadow what we believe to be a highly significant aspect of contact-period human biology: namely, what is known about the *surviving* populations that were in contact with Europeans, sometimes over a period of generations? In what ways did these survivors adapt to wholly new circumstances affecting their lifeways?

This is not to say that epidemic disease in the region discussed in this chapter did not have a horrific effect on native population. Indeed, by the late seventeenth century the region had experienced dramatic population reduction, in no small part due to European-introduced infectious diseases. In all likelihood, the population losses resulted in increased demands on the survivors in a variety of ways. This chapter examines how native populations responded, in part, to these challenges.

In this chapter we address these questions through the study of a sequence of precontact- and contact-era human remains from Guale, a region and a tribal group extending from the mouth of the Savannah River to the area immediately to the south of the mouth of the St. Marys River in coastal northern Florida (figure 5.1). This area of the Atlantic coast is especially important for the study of contact-era biological change because the native populations inhabiting it were among some of the earliest to be encountered by Europeans north of Mexico (Jones 1978; Larsen 1990). Given the well-documented temporal, environmental, and dietary variables for this region, we are provided with an excellent opportunity to look in some detail at responses made by native populations before, during, and after initial contact with Europeans.

Our primary objective in this study is to seek a more comprehensive understanding of biobehavioral changes reflecting population response to the enormous challenges facing them during the period of time preceding their extinction. The present investigation approaches this objective by utilizing a diachronic analysis of two aspects of human variability that are behaviorally significant: (1) skeletal morphology of limb bone diaphyses; and (2) articular joint pathology. Study of skeletal morphology includes the application of beam theory developed by mechanical and civil engineers for structural analysis (Lanyon and Rubin 1985; Nordin and Frankel 1980). In the terminology used by engineers, the long bones of upper and lower limbs can be modeled as hollow beams, and the strength of these beams can be measured. Thus, just as engineers can measure the strength of beams, biological anthropologists can measure the strength of skeletal structures. The application of beam analysis facilitates an understanding of function and behavior by summarizing complex shapes viewed in cross section into a series of readily interpretable properties (Bridges 1989a; Hayes and Gerhart 1985; Ruff 1989).

These properties—called cross-sectional geometric properties—are used to estimate strength or resistance of a bone to two primary forces: bending and torsion (twisting). Limb bones, which are tubular in shape, represent strength under either or both of these forces, depending on the bone (for example, the upper limb versus lower limb) and the location along the shaft. Thus, it is possible to estimate in numerical form the resistance of bone to bending ("bending strength") and torsion ("torsional strength"). The application of this biomechanical approach in the analysis of archaeological skeletal remains has represented an important breakthrough in bioarchaeological study, especially in the elucidation of specific levels and types of activities in now-extinct human groups (e.g., Bridges 1989a, 1989b; Brock and Ruff 1988; Lovejoy et al. 1976; Robbins et al. 1989; Ruff and Hayes 1982, 1983; Ruff et al. 1984; see review in Ruff 1992).

Bone strength reflects distribution of skeletal tissue primarily in response to mechanical forces throughout the years of growth and development as well as adulthood. Thus, bone strength is not a measure of health status. As we will show in this chapter, it is possible for a population to undergo increase in bone strength yet at the same time decline in health status.

Pathology affecting articular joints pertains in this study to a disorder known as osteoarthritis (also called degenerative joint disease). Like structural analysis, study of osteoarthritis by anthropologists has been instrumental in providing insight into activity patterning, lifestyle, and mechanical stresses in many diverse settings worldwide (e.g., Angel et al. 1987; Bennike 1985; Bridges 1990; Hrdlička 1914; Jurmain 1977, 1990; Kelley and Angel 1987; Merbs 1983; Miles 1989; Parrington and Roberts 1990; Stewart 1947, 1966; Walker and

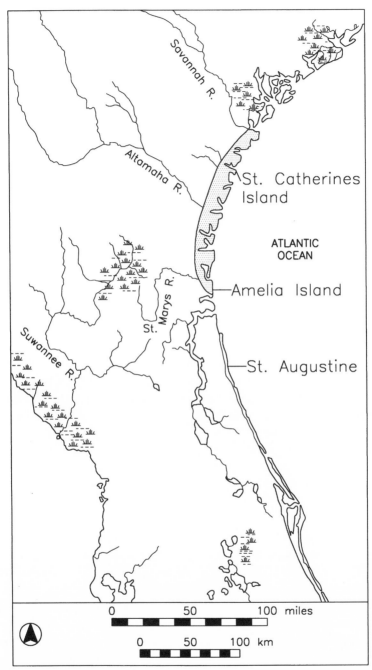

Figure 5.1. Map of northern peninsular Florida and coastal Georgia showing the location of Guale (shaded area) and geographical localities mentioned in the text.

Hollimon 1989; Webb 1989; Wells 1982; Wood Jones 1910; and many others; see reviews in Bourke 1967; Kennedy 1989; Larsen 1987; Ortner and Putschar 1985; Rogers et al. 1987). Osteoarthritis, therefore, offers a source of information complementary to structural analysis for reconstructing and understanding mechanical and behavioral aspects of earlier human populations.

BIOCULTURAL CONTEXT

Human skeletal remains representative of a succession of populations on the southeastern U.S. Atlantic coast have been the focus of a long-term investigation of prehistoric- and historic-era human ecology (Hutchinson and Larsen 1988; Larsen 1982, 1990; Larsen et al. 1990, 1992). These remains are grouped into four successive temporal periods that for purposes of comparison we have called Precontact Preagricultural (before A.D. 1150), Precontact Agricultural (A.D. 1150–1550), Early Contact (A.D. 1607–80), and Late Contact (A.D. 1686–1702). The Precontact Preagricultural–period populations followed an exclusively hunting-gathering-fishing subsistence strategy. Human remains representative of these prehistoric hunter-gatherers are from various Georgia coastal mortuary localities (Larsen 1982; Larsen and Thomas 1982). The Precontact Agricultural–period populations incorporated maize agriculture as a major component of the subsistence economy, but still included nondomesticated terrestrial and marine dietary resources. Human remains representative of these populations are from various late prehistoric sites, but are chiefly from Irene Mound, the largest Mississippian period site in the region (Caldwell and McCann 1941; Hulse 1941; Larsen 1982).

During much of the following contact period, Mission Santa Catalina de Guale on St. Catherines Island served as the northernmost extension of Spanish control in eastern North America (Thomas 1987). Under pressure from the English in the late seventeenth century, particularly following their founding of Charles Town (Charleston, South Carolina), the focus of this control shifted southward when the inhabitants of St. Catherines Island moved below the St. Marys River. They reestablished the mission on Amelia Island, renamed Mission Santa Catalina or Santa Maria de Guale (Hann 1990), but also referred to as Mission Santa Catalina de Guale de Santa Maria (Larsen 1990; Thomas 1987). Historical documentation indicates that, like their late prehistoric predecessors, these contact-period populations utilized dietary carbohydrates (maize), albeit to a greater degree (see below) than prior to the arrival of Europeans in the region. Human remains from the two missions on St. Catherines and Amelia islands are representative of the Early Contact and Late Contact periods, respectively (see Larsen 1990; Hardin 1986; Larsen and Saunders 1987). Archaeological, bioarchaeological, and historical evidence strongly suggests the human remains from these two populations and the earlier prehistoric periods represent a diachronically continuous biological population (Larsen 1982, 1990). This continuum allows us to evaluate the effects of contact and establishment of missions in a well-controlled setting. It is beyond the scope of this chapter to compare these populations with other mission skeletal series where the temporal and biocultural controls are not so tightly defined.

In previous studies we showed that concomitant with the transition from an exclusively hunting and gathering lifeway to one based partly on maize agriculture prior to contact, upper and lower limb bones (represented by humeri and femora, respectively) became shorter, and bone strength, as revealed by structural analysis, declined. These findings reflect, in part, a decrease in mechanical loadings of both limbs (Fresia et al. 1990; Larsen 1981, 1982; Larsen and Ruff 1991; Ruff and Larsen 1990; Ruff et al. 1984). Larsen (1982), moreover, documented a decrease in the prevalence of osteoarthritis in a comparison of Precontact Preagricultural and later agricultural populations. Although a variety of contributing factors have been identified in the etiology of this disorder, excessive and repetitive mechanical loading of articular joints figures most prominently in explaining osteoarthritic remodeling (see DeRousseau 1988; Duncan 1979; Jurmain 1977; Larsen 1982; Merbs 1983; Moskowitz 1987; Pascale and Grana 1989; Radin 1983; Walker and Hollimon 1989). This interpretation is supported by a number of researchers who have shown links between specific occupations and patterns of osteoarthritis (e.g., Kellgren and Lawrence 1958; Lawrence 1955). Thus, a decline in prevalence of osteoarthritis is consistent with a model of reduction in mechanical demand in this region during late prehistory.

What structural or pathological changes should we expect to see in the later contact-period human populations in this region? The written documentation available from historical sources indicates that the arrival of Spanish colonizers and the establishment of missions in the Eastern Borderlands, an area named *La Florida* by Ponce de León in 1513, occasioned dramatic behavioral and workload changes in native populations (Hann 1988). These changes were likely related in part to Spanish interest in native populations as an inexpensive labor source. Native labor was viewed by the Spanish as a central—if not the most important—element in their economic and political success in this region. Various historical accounts note the use of and dependence upon Indian laborers for cargo-bearing, agricultural production, construction projects, woodcutting, and other physically demanding activities (Hann 1988; Larsen 1990). For example, Governor Canzo, in his report to the Spanish Crown in 1602–3, noted: "with all this and the grain from the maize, the labor that they endure in the many cultivations that are given is great, and, if it were not for the help of the Indians that I make them give, and they come from the province of

Guale, Antonico, and from other caciques, it would not be possible to be able to sow any grain" (translation provided by John H. Hann; cited in Larsen 1990).

These historical accounts, therefore, suggest that the workload likely increased during the contact period in response to labor demands placed upon native populations. In answer to the above question, we should expect to see a reversal of the precontact trends in diaphyseal structure and joint pathology in contact-period populations.

Examination of femora and humeri from early Mission period Georgia coastal populations indeed showed a general reversal of the trend documented for precontact populations—limb bones became longer and stronger (Ruff and Larsen 1990). Comparison of males and females revealed somewhat different temporal changes, however. For example, anterior-posterior to medial-lateral bending strength of the femur increased in some males and decreased in others after contact, while female bending strength as a whole continued to decline (Ruff and Larsen 1990). Based on comparative data collected from other human populations (see Ruff 1987), these results suggested some males may have been more mobile after contact—perhaps reflecting their use as long-distance laborers—while females continued to decrease in mobility, a trend established prior to contact.

METHODS OF ANALYSIS

Skeletal Morphology and Size

Determination of cross-sectional geometric properties follow previously described procedures (Ruff and Hayes 1983; Ruff and Larsen 1990). Femora and humeri were oriented in standard anteroposterior (A-P) and mediolateral (M-L) planes and cut transversely using a fine-toothed saw at two locations on the femoral diaphysis and one location on the humeral diaphysis. Measured from the distal ends, the femoral sections are located at 50 percent (midshaft) and 80 percent (subtrochanteric) of bone length, and the humeral section is located at 35 percent (mid-distal) of bone length (figure 5.2). The endosteal (inner surface of bone) and periosteal (outer surface of bone) boundaries were subsequently traced from photographs of these sections rear-projected onto a digitizer screen. Calculations of properties were performed directly on a microcomputer with a digitizer screen. As an indicator of body size, we have recorded a measurement referred to as length' (or "biomechanical length") for femora and humeri (Ruff and Hayes 1983; Ruff and Larsen 1990). For the femur, length' is the distance from the distal surfaces of the condyles (knee region) to the superior margin of the neck (hip region). For the humerus, length' is the distance from the proximal surface of the head (shoulder region) to the distal edge of the lateral lip of the trochlea (elbow region). For the remainder of this chapter, length' will be referred to simply as "length."

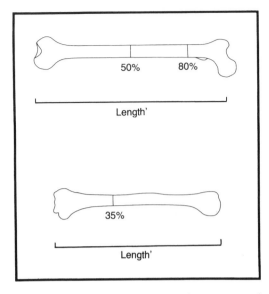

Figure 5.2. Locations of sections on femur (top) and humerus (bottom).

Two types of cross-sectional geometric properties reflecting bone strength—called "areas" and "second moments of area"—were calculated by a modified version of the computer program SLICE from boundary point coordinates (Nagurka and Hayes 1980). Explanation of formulas used to calculate these properties are provided in Ruff (1991). Area properties reflect the *amount* of bone in a cross section. They include cortical area (CA), medullary area (MA), and total subperiosteal area (TA). Second moments of area properties reflect the *distribution* of bone in a cross section relative to particular axes running through the section. The second moments of area properties include maximum and minimum second moments of area (I_{max}, I_{min}), second moments of area about mediolateral (I_x) and anteroposterior (I_y) axes, and the polar second moment of area (J). The "I" and "J" values represent measurements of bending and torsional strength respectively, the two primary loading modes that limb bones are subject to during life. In order to standardize for body size differences between periods and sexes, we have divided areas by bone length^2 and second moments of area by bone length^4 in the analysis (Ruff 1984). Only the length-standardized properties are reported here. We emphasize that these long bone cross-sectional geometric properties do not necessarily represent measures of health status. Rather, they reflect estimated resistance of bones to mechanical loading (their mechanical strength).

Pathology

Osteoarthritis is a complex disorder, but it appears to result from physiological imbalance between mechanical stress of articular joints—comprised of cartilage, bone, and other tissues—and the ability of those tissues to withstand
that stress (Maquet 1983; Radin 1983). As such, it is not a disease per se, but a
group of conditions whereby the common manifestation is joint deterioration
by mechanical means (Radin 1982). Because we are dealing with skeletal remains only, we are only able to view the bone modifications, thus representing but one part of the articular damage seen in living subjects.

We follow DeRousseau's (1988, 7) definition of osteoarthritis in its application to the study of dry bones as including all degenerative articular joint
changes. Articular surfaces and margins of bones representing the major
weight-bearing and nonweight-bearing joints were examined, including intervertebral (cervical, thoracic, lumbar/sacral), shoulder, elbow, wrist, hand,
hip, knee, ankle, and foot (table 5.1). We identified and recorded osteoarthritis
as either present or absent for these articular joints. Presence of osteoarthritic
remodeling was recorded if there was evidence of any one or a combination of
the following hard tissue modifications: (1) proliferation of bone on joint mar-

Table 5.1. Articular surfaces and margins of major adult articular joints observed
for presence or absence of osteoarthritis

Articular joint	Skeletal component observation
Cervical	Intervertebral body; superior and inferior articular processes
Thoracic	Intervertebral body; superior and inferior articular processes
Lumbar/sacrum	Intervertebral body; superior and inferior articular processes
Shoulder	Proximal humerus (head); scapula (glenoid)
Elbow	Distal humerus (trochlea, capitulum); proximal radius (head); proximal ulna (semilunar notch)
Wrist	Distal ulna (head, styloid process); distal radius (lunate-scaphoid articular surfaces); carpals; metacarpals (proximal)
Hand	Metacarpals (heads); proximal, intermediate, and terminal phalanges
Hip	Femur (head); innominate (acetabulum)
Knee	Femur (lateral and medial condyles); patella (condylar surfaces); tibia (lateral and medial condyles)
Ankle	Tibia (talar articular surfaces); tarsals; metatarsals (proximal)
Foot	Metatarsals (heads); proximal, intermediate, and terminal phalanges

Source: Adapted from Larsen 1982.

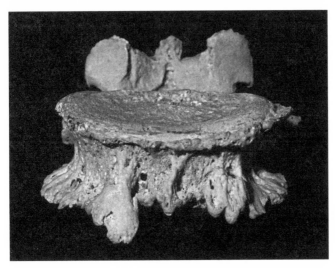

Figure 5.3. Bone proliferation on joint margins of lumbar vertebra (osteoarthritis).

gins (also called marginal or osteophytic lipping); (2) loss of bone on joint surfaces due to resorptive activity; or (3) loss of bone due to mechanical attrition or polishing resulting from direct bone-on-bone articulation following degeneration of cartilage (eburnation). By far, the most frequent manifestation of osteoarthritis in these remains is marginal lipping (figure 5.3).

In the course of data collection we noted that occasionally only one component skeletal element of an osteoarthritic joint was affected by the disorder. For example, in the shoulder the scapular glenoid fossa margin was more commonly affected than the humeral head for most individuals (cf. Wells 1982). However, from a functional perspective, we present summary data in reference to joints, rather than the individual component bones.

For the analysis of osteoarthritis, we do not include the Early Contact period. Data on osteoarthritis for this time period are as yet unavailable for analysis.

Both structural properties and prevalence of osteoarthritis are highly influenced by age structure in human populations. Therefore, consideration of age structure is presented as part of the data analysis. Diachronic assessment of age structure in the four periods has important implications for demographic change, especially in relation to diet and health status. However, this topic is beyond the scope of this chapter (but see the discussion in Larsen et al. 1990).

RESULTS

Skeletal Morphology and Size

Temporal changes in femoral and humeral lengths and their respective cross-sectional geometric properties are presented in table 5.2. These data show important temporal changes for both males and females across the four periods.

Bone lengths, a general indicator of body size, show relatively more change in females than in males in the sequence. Females markedly reduce in body size in the Precontact Agricultural period, increase in body size in the Early Contact period, and slightly decline again in the Late Contact period. Males show a similar trend, but the increase in body size in the Early Contact period remains essentially unchanged in the Late Contact period.

Examination of temporal changes in femoral and humeral cross-sectional geometry shows a number of trends. In the femur both males and females change very little in CA in comparison to the two precontact-period groups, as we have reported earlier (Ruff et al. 1984). However, the endosteal and periosteal surfaces contract in both sexes, resulting in reductions in TA and MA. In the Early and Late Contact periods there are appreciable increases in TA and MA, indicating a reversal of the trends observed before contact. The effects of alteration in geometry are straightforward. That is, with the exception of two properties for males (subtrochanteric I_{max} and J), second moments of area decrease in the Precontact Agricultural period, but increase in the Early Contact period and again in the Late Contact period. This temporal trend demonstrates a consistent increase in these measures of bone strength during the Contact period, from Early to Late.

The humerus shows generally the same pattern of morphological change in comparing the four periods. In males all areas and second moments of area decrease in the Precontact period, but then increase in the Early Contact period and Late Contact period. However, in females humeral properties continue to decline in the Early Contact period. With the exception of CA, in the Late Contact period, the trend reverses. Therefore, humeri show a trend of mechanical strength change that is similar in males and females prior to contact. After contact, however, females continue to decrease while males increase. Both sexes show increases in mechanical strength in the Late Contact period.

Comparison of ratios of second moments of area reveals temporal trends in cross-sectional "shape" of femora and humeri. In males A-P/M-L bending strength in the midshaft femur (I_x/I_y) first decreases, then increases, and finally decreases again. In the mid-distal humerus there is an increase in A-P/M-L bending strength (I_x/I_y), followed by a slight decline in the last period. However, this index shows the same trend for both femur midshaft and mid-distal humerus in the last three periods. A decrease in circularity (reflecting

Table 5.2. Bone size and cross-sectional geometric property means standardized for bone length: PP = Precontact Preagricultural; PA = Precontact Agricultural; EC = Early Contact; LC = Late Contact

	PP	PA	EC	LC	Significant differences[a]
Males					
Femur	(n = 8)	(n = 11)	(n = 11)	(n = 22)	
Length'	424.9	411.2	421.5	419.4	PP/PA
Midshaft					
CA/ln^2	233.6	234.5	234.0	225.1	—
MA/ln^2	82.2	61.8	88.7	99.0	PP/PA, PA/EC, PA/LC
TA/ln^2	315.8	296.3	306.7	324.2	PA/LC
I_{max}/ln^4	88.6	77.9	87.6	93.5	PA/LC
I_{min}/ln^4	65.5	61.0	62.3	66.6	—
I_x/ln^4	86.8	71.7	80.5	81.7	PP/PA, PA/LC
I_y/ln^4	67.3	67.2	69.4	74.5	—
J/ln^4	154.1	138.9	149.9	160.1	PA/LC
I_x/I_y	1.28	1.08	1.20	1.13	PP/PA, PP/LC
Subtrochanteric					
CA/ln^2	225.0	220.8	232.9	225.7	—
MA/ln^2	123.6	83.6	114.7	123.1	PP/PA, PA/EC, PA/LC
TA/ln^2	348.6	304.3	347.6	348.8	PP/PA, PA/EC
I_{max}/ln^4	124.6	92.6	110.0	107.7	PP/PA, PA/EC
I_{min}/ln^4	59.1	51.5	67.5	67.2	PA/EC, PA/LC
J/ln^4	183.7	144.1	177.5	174.9	PP/PA, PA/EC, PA/LC
I_{max}/I_{min}	2.09	1.82	1.65	1.61	PP/PA, PP/EC, PP/LC, PA/EC, PA/LC
Humerus	(n = 15)	(n = 15)	(n = 13)	(n = 22)	
Length'	318.3	312.5	313.2	314.2	—
Mid-distal					
CA/ln^2	215.0	201.2	204.7	216.7	—
MA/ln^2	83.2	70.9	88.3	97.7	PA/LC
TA/ln^2	298.2	272.1	293.1	314.4	PP/PA, PA/LC
I_{max}/ln^4	73.8	62.8	71.1	77.5	PP/PA, PA/LC
I_{min}/ln^4	61.1	48.8	57.3	64.6	PP/PA, PA/LC
I_x/ln^4	66.4	56.0	66.4	73.0	PP/PA, PA/LC
I_y/ln^4	68.6	55.5	62.0	69.1	PP/PA, PA/LC
J/ln^4	135.0	111.6	128.4	142.1	PP/PA, PA/LC
I_x/I_y	0.98	1.01	1.10	1.07	PP/EC, PP/LC, PA/EC
Females					
Femur	(n = 12)	(n = 9)	(n = 11)	(n = 21)	
Length'	415.2	376.4	401.2	392.5	PP/PA, PP/LC, PA/EC, PA/LC

continued

Table 5.2-*continued*

	PP	PA	EC	LC	Significant differences[a]
Midshaft					
CA/ln^2	190.2	186.4	210.0	204.3	PA/EC
MA/ln^2	93.2	70.5	76.2	101.8	PP/PA, PA/LC, EC/LC
TA/ln^2	283.5	256.9	286.2	306.1	PP/PA, PA/EC, PA/LC
I_{max}/ln^4	63.4	54.8	68.9	75.3	PA/EC, PA/LC
I_{min}/ln^4	51.9	44.9	54.4	66.6	PA/EC
I_x/ln^4	62.0	50.6	61.9	65.2	PP/PA, PA/EC, PA/LC
I_y/ln^4	53.4	49.2	61.4	70.7	PP/PA, PP/LC, PA/EC, PA/LC
J/ln^4	115.4	99.8	123.3	141.9	PA/EC, PA/LC
I_x/I_y	1.16	1.03	1.01	0.93	PP/LC
Subtrochanteric					
CA/ln^2	191.5	190.4	216.4	205.4	PA/EC
MA/ln^2	120.2	88.6	99.2	130.7	PP/PA, PA/LC, EC/LC
TA/ln^2	311.7	279.0	315.6	336.1	PP/PA, PA/EC, PA/LC
I_{max}/ln^4	94.7	81.8	95.0	101.1	PA/LC
I_{min}/ln^4	44.9	39.2	54.7	58.2	PP/EC, PP/LC, PA/EC, PA/LC
J/ln^4	139.6	121.0	149.7	159.4	PP/PA, PA/EC, PA/LC
I_{max}/I_{min}	2.14	2.10	1.75	1.78	PP/EC, PP/LC, PA/EC, PA/LC
Humerus	(n = 12)	(n = 14)	(n = 11)	(n = 21)	
Length'	305.8	290.2	302.2	298.0	PP/PA, PA/EC, PA/LC
Mid-distal					
CA/ln^2	179.4	173.2	166.6	161.7	—
MA/ln^2	72.5	71.7	65.5	96.3	PA/LC, EC/LC
TA/ln^2	251.9	244.9	232.1	258.0	EC/LC
I_{max}/ln^4	53.9	50.8	45.3	53.4	—
I_{min}/ln^4	40.7	38.4	34.2	39.5	—
I_x/ln^4	50.4	45.8	41.8	48.5	—
I_y/ln^4	44.3	43.4	37.5	44.5	—
J/ln^4	94.6	89.2	79.5	92.9	—
I_x/I_y	1.13	1.06	1.11	1.10	—

Note: CA = cortical area; MA = medullary area; TA = total subperiosteal area; I_{max} = maximum second moment of area (bending strength); I_{min} = minimum second moment of area (bending strength); I_x = second moment of area about mediolateral axis (anteroposterior bending strength); I_y = second moment of area about anteroposterior axis (mediolateral bending strength); J = polar second moment of area.

Femur length' (in mm) is the distance measured from the condyles to the superior margin of the neck, and humerus length' is the distance from the head to the lip of the trochlea; midshaft and subtrochanteric an increase in the index) in the Early Contact period is followed by an increase in circularity (reflecting a decrease in the index) in the Late Contact period. Temporal trends in midshaft femoral shape are similar in females, although females show no transitory increase in the index from the Precontact Agricultural to Early Contact periods. Females show relatively little change in this index in the humerus.

Finally, comparison of maximum-minimum bending strength in the subtrochanteric femur (I_{max}/I_{min}) shows a considerable temporal decline—that is, an increase in circularity—over all four periods in both males and females.

Pathology

The temporal change in prevalence of osteoarthritis is presented in table 5.3. This pattern is perhaps best revealed by combining all articular joints into a single comparative sample. This comparison indicates first that, for all three periods studied (exluding EC), males have a higher frequency of arthritic joints than females. Second, regardless of gender, a reduction in frequency of affected joints occurred prior to contact. This is followed, in the Late Contact period, by a sharp reversal, with a near tripling in frequency of articular joints affected by osteoarthritis.

Temporal change for individual joints is generally similar to the pattern observed for the combined joints (table 5.3). For example, in the cervical vertebrae 40 percent of Precontact Preagricultural male articular joints are arthritic. In the Precontact Agricultural period only about 10 percent of joints in males are arthritic. In the Late Contact period the frequency of affected joints increases to levels similar to, if not greater than, the Precontact Preagricultural period. In the elbow the Precontact Preagricultural period shows the highest prevalence of osteoarthritis. The knee shows a similar pattern, with the greatest prevalence of osteoarthritis in the Precontact Preagricultural pe-

---

femur refer to 50 percent and 80 percent, respectively, of length' measured from distal end of bone; mid-distal humerus refers to 35 percent of bone length' measured from distal end; area indices over bone length (CA, MA, TA) are multiplied by 10^5, and second moment of area indices over bone length (I_{max}, I_{min}, I_x, I_y, J) are multiplied by 10^8. Humeral properties are averaged for right and left sides, when both were available, or values adjusted for average bilateral differences (see Ruff and Larsen 1990). Area indices (CA, MA, TA) provide relative measures of amount of cortical bone in a cross section and the relative size of the section and medullary cavity; I (bending strength) and J (torsional strength) reflect the distribution of bone about a neutral axis or point; ratios (I_x/I_y, I_{max}/I_{min}) reflect relative distribution of bone about perpendicular axes, and thus cross-sectional "shape" (see Ruff and Hayes 1983; Ruff and Larsen 1990; Ruff et al. 1984).

Sources: Ruff and Larsen 1990; Ruff et al. 1984; Larsen and Ruff unpublished data.

[a]p<0.05, t-test (two-tailed).

riod. Osteoarthritis in the foot shows the most unusual pattern. In Precontact females and males the foot is only very minimally affected by the disorder. However, in the Late Contact period there is a tremendous increase in frequency, especially in males.

Table 5.3. Osteoarthritis prevalence

Joint	PP %	n	PA %	n	LC %	n	Signficant differences[a]
Males							
Cervical	40.0	20	11.3	53	44.4	27	PA/LC
Thoracic	12.5	16	11.8	51	65.4	26	PA/LC
Lumbar/sacral	34.6	26	16.3	80	52.9	51	PP/PA,PA/LC
Shoulder	10.5	38	1.7	120	11.1	27	PP/PA,PA/LC
Elbow	13.7	51	6.1	114	10.3	29	PP/PA
Wrist	2.6	39	0.9	106	10.0	30	PA/LC
Hand	0.0	28	2.0	100	3.2	31	—
Hip	0.0	51	9.1	110	6.4	31	—
Knee	18.6	59	12.6	111	7.4	27	—
Ankle	4.1	49	9.2	109	10.0	30	—
Foot	0.0	26	1.1	93	41.6	24	PA/LC
Combined	9.0	403	6.9	1,047	30.5	333	PP/PA,PA/LC
Females							
Cervical	17.2	29	1.4	73	42.3	26	PP/PA,PA/LC
Thoracic	6.7	30	1.4	72	57.5	33	PA/LC
Lumbar/sacral	19.5	51	9.9	111	54.5	55	PP/PA,PA/LC
Shoulder	2.4	83	0.7	144	56.0	25	PA/LC
Elbow	9.6	94	0.0	167	2.9	34	PP/PA,PA/LC
Wrist	2.6	77	0.0	140	5.3	38	PA/LC
Hand	0.0	50	0.8	129	5.3	38	—
Hip	4.3	93	0.0	148	0.0	36	PP/PA
Knee	15.0	94	3.4	147	8.6	35	PP/PA
Ankle	4.5	88	0.0	139	15.6	32	PP/PA,PA/LC
Foot	0.0	48	0.0	120	11.1	27	PA/LC
Combined	7.0	737	1.5	1,390	23.7	379	PP/PA,PA/LC

Note: PP = Precontact Preagricultural; PA = Precontact Agricultural; LC = Late Contact. The number of articular joints was observed for the presence or absence of osteoarthritis for three periods only; data are not available for the Early Contact period.

Sources: Larsen 1982; Griffin and Larsen 1989.

[a]p<0.05, chi-square.

Interestingly, in the Late Contact period the sex differences in vertebral osteoarthritis became much less pronounced. Females and males in the Late Contact period had similar prevalence of osteoarthritis, unlike the pattern observed in either of the Precontact groups, Preagricultural or Agricultural.

Discussion

The results of this research can be summarized by four primary temporal trends in cross-sectional geometric properties and osteoarthritis in southeastern U.S. Atlantic coastal native populations. First, following a decrease in body size with the adoption of an agricultural lifeway, body size increases in the Early Contact period, followed by a slight decrease in female body size in the Late Contact period. Second, after an initial decline, a reversal developed in relative bone strength, represented by a general expansion of bone cortex in the Early Contact period, followed by further cortical expansion in the Late Contact period. Third, comparison of cross-sectional shape of the midshaft and subtrochanteric sections of the femur shows a general increase in circularity through time. The mid-distal humerus becomes less circular after contact. Fourth, a general pattern of decrease in prevalence of osteoarthritis prior to contact is followed by an increase in the Late Contact period.

These results likely reflect a complex combination of changing nutritional and mechanical loading patterns affecting the skeletal tissues in these populations. We have previously argued that a decrease in body size in the Precontact agriculturalists relative to the Precontact hunter-gatherers likely reflects a decline in nutrition, with the shift to a diet incorporating maize (Ruff et al. 1984). Thus, increase in body size during the Contact period might reflect a general improvement of nutrition—at least in terms of the *quantity* of food consumed, particularly in female body size. Carbon and nitrogen isotopic data derived from analysis of bone collagen samples (table 5.4; Schoeninger et al. 1990), as well as dental caries prevalence (table 5.5; Larsen et al. 1991), would certainly suggest that nutritional improvement, in terms of *quality* of diet, was not operating in this situation. Both the isotopic and caries analyses indicate an increase in consumption of maize in the Contact period, with a probable decline in reliance on marine resources. Maize is a notoriously poor source of protein as it is deficient in several essential amino acids (FAO 1970). This finding alone indicates a decline in nutritional quality. Moreover, archaeological data indicate an increase in consumption of carbohydrates, likely accompanied by a decline in resource diversity, particularly animal sources of protein (Larsen 1990). Historical documentation reveals that native populations experienced periods of food shortages following epidemics or other events such as burning of crops and the taking of stored foods by the Spanish military (Jones 1978).

Table 5.4. Carbon and nitrogen stable isotope summary statistics

	$\delta^{13}C$			$\delta^{15}N$		
Period	Mean	n	Range	Mean	n	Range
PP	-14.5	20	-18.6, -13.4	12.8	20	10.6, 14.4
PA	-13.0	9	-16.4, -10.0	10.7	9	9.5, 13.3
EC	-11.5	22	-14.3, -9.6	9.4	22	7.4, 10.8
LC	-11.5	21	-12.6, -10.0	10.0	22	8.3, 11.6

Note: PP = Precontact Preagricultural; PA = Precontact Agricultural; EC = Early Contact; LC = Late Contact.

Sources: Larsen et al. 1990; Schoeniger et al. 1990.

These accounts very clearly indicate a decline in nutritional quality that almost certainly continued throughout the entire Contact period.

Females appear to show relatively more change than males in body size, as represented by bone lengths. The reason for these differences are not entirely clear, but may relate to the fact that females—who traditionally are associated more closely with settlements than males—may have been more subject to some changes detected in skeletal remains, such as body size. Until more extensive historical documentation of dietary and behavioral differences between males and females is encountered, it will not be possible to provide additional speculation on this point.

With regard to bone geometry, Ruff (1987) has shown that A-P relative to M-L bending strength of the midshaft femur (as measured by the ratio of I_x/I_y) can be used as an index of relative degree of mobility (e.g., amount of running or long-distance travel) in human populations. That is, relatively greater A-P bending strength—as indicated by greater values of I_x/I_y—generally reflects greater mobility in human populations. For example, comparison of prehistoric hunter-gatherers, prehistoric agriculturalists, and industrial (Western) populations by Ruff (1987) revealed that hunter-gatherers have the greatest A-P bending strength and industrial populations have the least A-P bending strength in the femur midshaft. He notes this is consistent with increase in roundness of the bone shaft in recent humans, most likely as a result of reduced mechanical loading of the lower limb in sedentary, industrial populations.

Examination of cross-sectional properties of individuals in the Early Contact period sample from Santa Catalina de Guale on St. Catherines Island shows that, relative to the Precontact Agricultural period, some males became more mobile (although on average they were less mobile) while females continued to decline in mobility. Moreover, both sexes showed an increase in circularity

Table 5.5. Dental caries prevalence

	PP		PA		EC		LC	
Maxilla	%	n[a]	%	n	%	n	%	n
I1	0.8	113	2.3	177	3.8	104	18.8	85
I2	0.0	95	2.8	178	1.5	126	20.0	85
C	0.0	126	8.3	244	1.1	170	23.9	92
P3	0.0	149	17.3	248	5.4	201	29.7	84
P4	0.0	149	11.6	255	4.9	201	38.6	88
M1	0.5	188	14.8	325	10.2	245	45.3	86
M2	1.0	193	12.5	306	11.1	234	66.1	65
M3	4.9	163	13.6	228	17.7	175	63.9	61
dI1	0.0	12	10.5	19	0.0	9	4.3	23
dI2	0.0	10	11.5	18	0.0	10	4.3	23
dC	0.0	18	0.0	28	0.0	20	13.3	30
dM1	0.0	26	19.1	47	20.0	25	24.3	37
dM2	0.0	20	8.2	49	7.5	53	32.0	25
Mandible								
I1	0.0	64	0.0	164	1.6	118	6.9	86
I2	0.0	84	1.5	197	0.7	128	20.6	97
C	0.0	126	2.6	233	1.5	199	24.2	99
P3	0.0	136	5.1	277	2.8	250	30.8	94
P4	0.0	151	10.9	257	3.4	232	46.3	82
M1	1.7	174	22.9	320	13.8	238	68.0	72
M2	3.5	174	24.5	280	15.7	228	80.7	57
M3	2.9	173	25.0	248	23.4	188	72.7	55
dI1	0.0	7	0.0	9	20.0	5	6.8	29
dI2	0.0	11	0.0	15	0.0	10	5.7	35
dC	0.0	19	0.0	26	0.0	21	2.7	36
dM1	0.0	28	5.4	56	0.0	37	0.0	43
dM2	0.0	29	5.4	56	15.2	46	33.3	33
Total	1.3	2,438	11.4	4,260	8.0	3,273	34.2	1,602

Note: PP = Precontact Preagricultural; PA = Precontact Agricultural; EC = Early Contact; LC = Late Contact.

Sources: Larsen 1982; Larsen et al. 1991.

[a]Number of teeth observed for presence or absence of carious lesions for all four periods.

of the subtrochanteric region (as measured by the ratio I_{max}/I_{min}). The increase in circularity has been previously interpreted as representing a decline in general activity levels in human populations (see Ruff and Larsen 1990).

In sum, we interpret the cross-sectional property changes to reflect a combination of decrease in mobility and general activity levels. Reduced levels of activity, both with regard to mobility and general activity, seem to reflect a more sedentary lifeway as Indians relocated near missions during the contact era.

The increases in specific geometric properties (versus ratios) in the Contact-era skeletal remains are more difficult to explain. It is possible that body weight relative to stature was systematically altered in the Contact-period native populations. Mechanical demand on the lower limb is related to stresses derived from a combination of activity *and* body weight. Mechanical loading, therefore, should be proportional to body weight, multiplied by a factor related to level of activity. In the present study we assume that the proportion of body weight to bone length remained constant through the temporal sequence when we divided cross-sectional properties by second and fourth powers of bone length in order to standardize them for size. By length-standardizing the properties, two variables—activity level and body weight/bone length— may have been established that could affect cross-sectional properties (Ruff and Larsen 1990). Bone length is highly correlated with stature. Therefore, this is equivalent to asking whether body weight and/or stature of these populations was altered in the Early and Late Contact periods.

Due to an increase in sedentism and the overall effects of dietary change and population disruption, it is possible to argue that the proportion of body weight to stature increased. A greater dietary focus on carbohydrates in combination with increase in sedentism and confinement of movement could have led to relative weight gain in the Contact-period mission populations. If so, this would increase the body weight-bone length ratio and, thus, the length-standardized properties in the femur, despite declines in level of activity. Moreover, at least in the lower limb, diaphyseal morphology is sensitive to changes in body weight during adulthood (Ruff et al. 1991).

It is difficult to test this hypothesis (primarily because soft tissue is usually not preserved in the archaeological record). However, we suggest that a weight gain interpretation is consistent with the increases in body weight and dietary change in North American native populations undergoing transitions to more sedentary lifestyles in nineteenth- and twentieth-century contexts. Although these populations are not strictly analogous to mission Indians, comparisons provide insight into common experiences regarding sedentism and weight gain. Hrdlička (1908) and Johnston and Schell (1979) have noted, for example, a tendency for high body weight and obesity in relatively sedentary Native American populations consuming greater amounts of dietary carbohydrates, such as those living on reservations or in urban settings. During the contact period in Spanish Florida, native populations were encouraged by either suggestion or coercion to settle around missions and increase maize production. Thus, Bishop Calderón's remark, made in 1675 in reference to the Indians of La Florida, that "They are fleshy, and rarely is there a small one" (cited in

Hann 1988, 158) may reflect these changing settlement and dietary conditions occurring over a century of missionization.

Unlike the femora (or male humeri), female humeri show a continued reduction in bone strength through the Early Contact period. The humerus is subject to mechanical loading patterns derived solely from activity use, and not from forces related to body weight (such as in lower limb bones). Apparently, relatively lower mechanical loads were placed on the upper limbs of females in the Early Contact period relative to the Precontact periods. We have no way of knowing why bone strength in female arms decreased in the Early Contact period. We can only speculate that women used their arms in different functions requiring reduced physical demand.

In both Early and Late Contact males and Late Contact females, an increase in bone strength in the humerus suggests increased use of their upper limbs. In all likelihood these changes in the Late Contact period reflect an increase in mechanical demand on the upper limb. Although it is exceedingly difficult to pinpoint the causal factors behind these changes, they are likely related to the increase in demands placed on these populations by the Spanish in labor-related projects, including subsistence activities. Although females in Southeastern societies were primarily responsible for subsistence-related tasks, such as care of fields and food preparation (Hudson 1976; Swanton 1946), one historical account indicates that pounding of maize into flour by missionized groups was the responsibility of males (Hann 1986). Hann (1988) has also noted the use of Indian laborers in activities involving heavy carrying and lifting, sometimes over great distances. Although these historical references to activities do not provide conclusive evidence as to sexual division of labor, the fact that structural properties increase during the Late Contact period in both females and males suggests that during this time both sexes may have engaged in similar types of activities, or at least activities involving similar loading modes.

Other factors—especially age composition of the skeletal samples—might also influence specific cross-sectional properties. In this regard, Ruff and Hayes (1982, 1983) have compared second moments of area between age groups in the Pecos Pueblo (New Mexico) skeletal series and found subperiosteal expansion and increase in cross-sectional geometric properties with advancing age. These workers suggested that expansion of long bone diaphyses in cross section represents a compensatory response to general bone loss and cortical thinning. Thus, despite general bone loss with advancing age, particularly during and after the fifth decade of life, increase in second moments of area contributes to the ability of the bone to resist bending and torsional loads (Hayes and Gerhart 1985). Comparison of age at death data from the four periods shows a decline in mean age at death in the Precontact Agricultural period, followed by substantial increases in mean age at death in the respective Early and Late

Table 5.6. Mean age at death

Age group	PP	PA	EC	LC
Adult	31.1	25.8	27.2	39.5
Total	26.1	19.7	21.2	28.8

Note: PP = Precontact Preagricultural; PA = Precontact Agricultural; EC = Early Contact; LC = Late Contact.

Contact periods (table 5.6). Therefore, the changing age composition of the skeletal samples may contribute to the temporal trends in areas and second moments of area observed.

With regard to the comparisons of the Precontact Preagricultural and Precontact Agricultural populations, we selected individuals of approximately equal ages at death in order to avoid problems associated with age bias and cross-sectional geometry (table 5.6; and see discussion in Ruff et al. 1984). Therefore, at least with regard to the Precontact comparisons, it is unlikely that age is an important factor in explaining the reduction in cross-sectional geometric properties in the Precontact Agricultural period. The comparisons between the Precontact Agricultural and Early Contact series and between the Early and Late Contact series are more problematic, however. With respect to the two Contact-period groups, it was not possible to select individuals with ages strictly comparable to the Precontact groups because the Contact-period samples represent generally older adults than the Precontact samples. Data comparisons indicate that, although age composition of the skeletal samples may partially explain the temporal changes in cross-sectional geometric properties, behavioral (and perhaps nutritional) considerations are more important. For example, despite an eight-year *increase* in mean age at death of female individuals represented by humeri in the comparison of the Precontact Agricultural and Early Contact periods (table 5.7), all areas and second moments of area *decrease*. If age was the only explanatory factor in determining areas and second moments of area in female humeri, then we would expect to see commensurate increases in these properties. On the contrary, decreases in these properties suggest behaviorally related factors as the underlying cause for these structural changes. This finding strongly suggests, therefore, a reduction in bone strength in female upper limbs occurs during the Early Contact period, and is a factor not simply related to age of the female cohorts.

Additionally, some Late Contact male femora properties are smaller (or of similar magnitude) to those of the Precontact Preagricultural period, despite a greater mean age at death of individuals represented by femora in that group. Therefore, we believe that although age likely contributes (through continued

Table 5.7. Mean age at death for femora and humeri

Period	Sex	Femora	Humeri
PP	Female	30.3	29.8
PP	Male	25.5	29.6
PA	Female	26.1	29.0
PA	Male	23.8	26.8
EC	Female	35.9	37.0
EC	Male	32.5	31.9
LC	Female	42.1	42.1
LC	Male	38.1	38.1

Note: PP = Precontact Preagricultural; PA = Precontact Agricultural;
EC = Early Contact; LC = Late Contact.

medullary and subperiosteal expansion) to the increases in second moments of area during the Contact period, behavioral factors are equally likely, if not more important, in understanding these changes.

Osteoarthritis, too, is strongly influenced by age. Most older adults in modern human populations are affected by the disorder (Eichner 1989; Hough and Sokoloff 1989). Indeed, in each of the series reported in this investigation, the age-progressive nature is well illustrated (tables 5.8 and 5.9). As expected, older individuals have a higher prevalence of osteoarthritis. If prevalence of osteoarthritis was to be predicted by age structure of the samples alone, that predic-

Table 5.8. Individuals affected by osteoarthritis per 5-year age category

	PP		PA		LC		Significant differences
Age	%	n[a]	%	n	%	n	
16.1-20	0.0	9	6.7	30	33.3	3	—
20.1-25	11.1	18	5.7	35	0.0	3	—
25.1-30	10.0	10	9.1	11	60.0	5	PA/LC[b]
30.1-35	0.0	1	42.9	7	25.0	8	—
35.1-40	66.7	6	20.0	10	78.6	14	PP/PA,[b] PA/LC[c]
40.1-45	25.0	4	33.3	3	81.0	21	—
45.1+	46.7	15	62.5	8	85.7	21	—
Total	23.8	63	15.4	104	69.3	75	PA/LC[d]

Note: PP = Precontact Preagricultural; PA = Precontact Agricultural; EC = Early Contact; LC = Late Contact.

[a]Number of aged adult individuals with at least one articular joint affected by osteoarthritis.

[b]p<0.1, Fisher's Exact Test (two-tailed).

[c]p<0.01, chi-square (with Yates' Correction for Continuity).

[d]p<0.0001, chi-square.

Table 5.9. Individuals affected by osteoarthritis per combined age categories

	PP		PA		LC		Significant differences
Age	%	n[a]	%	n	%	n	
16.1-35	7.9	38	9.6	83	31.6	19	PA/LC[b]
35.1+	48.0	25	38.1	21	82.1	56	PA/LC[c]
Total	23.8	63	15.4	104	69.3	75	PA/LC[d]

Note: PP = Precontact Preagricultural; PA = Precontact Agricultural; EC = Early Contact; LC = Late Contact.

[a]Number of aged adult individuals with at least one articular joint affected by osteoarthritis.

[b]p<0.05, chi-square (with Yates' Correction for Continuity).

[c]p<0.0005, chi-square (with Yates' Correction for Continuity).

[d]p<0.0001, chi-square.

tion would likely fit the pattern we have discussed. The decrease in prevalence of osteoarthritis from the Precontact Preagricultural to Agricultural periods should fit the pattern of decline in mean age at death in these two periods. Similarly, the dramatic increase in prevalence of osteoarthritis in comparing the Precontact Agricultural and Late Contact periods should be predicted by the increase in mean age at death.

In order to test the hypothesis that prevalence of osteoarthritis is dependent on the changing age profiles of the skeletal samples, we have categorized the individuals affected by the disorder into respective 5-year age groups (table 5.8). Predictably, within each of the three periods, the prevalence of osteoarthritis increases with age. However, comparison between the three periods within each of the age categories shows, proportionately, a general reduction in prevalence of osteoarthritis in the Precontact Agricultural group relative to the Precontact Preagricultural group. Specifically, proportionately fewer individuals were affected by osteoarthritis in the Precontact Agricultural period than in Precontact Preagricultural period for the 5-year age categories.

The most striking proportionate change, however, is illustrated by comparing the Precontact Agricultural– and Late Contact–period groups (table 5.8). For each of the 5-year age categories, the proportion of individuals affected by osteoarthritis markedly increases in the Late Contact period. Statistically significant increases are found in the 25.1–30 and 35.1–40 age categories. By collapsing the 5-year categories into two groups, young adults (16.1–35) and old adults (35.1+), the proportionate decline in osteoarthritis between the two Precontact groups is shown more clearly among the older adults (table 5.9). The comparison of Precontact Agricultural and Late Contact groups, however, shows significant increases in the proportion of individuals affected by osteoarthritis for both age categories. We conclude that, although the changing frequencies of articular joints showing osteoarthritic remodeling may be related in part to the changing age profiles for each period, the prevalence of osteoarthritis between periods reflects a real rather than an apparent change.

The reversal in prevalence of osteoarthritis indicates that the Late Contact population engaged in activities that excessively loaded articular joints. Moreover, the similarity in prevalence of osteoarthritis between females and males of specific articular areas, such as the intervertebral joints (table 5.3), suggests that differences in gender-based work roles lessened in the Contact period relative to previous periods. This finding is supported by study of upper limb (humerus) asymmetry patterns in cross-sectional geometry that show the least amount of sexual dimorphism during the Contact period relative to Precontact period (see Fresia et al. 1990). On the other hand, other articular joints indicate substantial sex differences in degree of loading. For example, although both sexes show marked increases in foot osteoarthritis, the increase is much greater for males.

The interpretations presented in this chapter are not meant to imply that mechanical changes are the only factors responsible for structural alterations of the skeleton. However, it is interesting to note that standardized values of bone mass or volume (CA) remain largely unchanged for both males and females across the four periods, regardless of bone type (table 5.2). In contrast, over the same temporal span, properties relating to *distribution* of bone within cross sections show large changes. This kind of change suggests structural adaptations of the skeleton to localized (mechanical) rather than systemic (nutritional) factors (cf. Ruff et al. 1984), although the two are obviously interrelated to some degree (see above).

CONCLUSIONS

These findings underscore the importance of looking at native populations as *adapting* during a very critical period of their evolution. In this study we have shown that the investigation of human skeletal remains allows for an examination of responses to alterations in the biomechanical and nutritional environments of precontact- and contact-era native populations.

During the period of colonization of the Southeast coast, native populations did not undergo a reduction in body size or robusticity. These data show that the arrival of Europeans and the establishment of mission centers resulted in behavioral changes that increased robusticity and prevalence of osteoarthritis, the latter of which may reflect increased work demands, particularly those associated with repetitive and stereotypic activities (e.g., heavy lifting), resulting in frequent overloading of articular joints. An increase in body weight in the more sedentary mission Indians may explain increases in specific cross-sectional geometric properties. Thus, an important finding in this study is that although osteoarthritis and bone geometry reflect physical behavior, they represent responses to different types of activity. On one hand, osteoarthritis reflects impact-loading usually unrelated to running or mobility. Cross-sectional properties, on the other hand, reflect long-term habitual behaviors associated more with body movement (e.g., mobility, long-distance travel). Regarding the former, it appears that only certain types of repetitive impact-loading may cause osteoarthritis (Eichner 1989). Experimental and other evidence indicate that running is not a causal factor of osteoarthritis, but it may aggravate the condition if already present in an individual (Eichner 1989). Therefore, while running (or the degree of mobility in general) affects cross-sectional long bone geometry and the shape of the diaphysis, it does not likely play a major role in determination of prevalence of osteoarthritis (see also discussion in Ruff 1992).

The study of behavioral patterning in human skeletal remains by the investigation of long bone cross-sectional geometric properties and osteoarthritis offers important information about past lifeways. Both before and during sustained contact with Europeans and the establishment of mission centers in Spanish Florida, native populations underwent alterations in settlement patterning, diet, and mechanical behavior that resulted in modification of bone morphology (cross-sectional geometric properties) and joint pathology prevalence (osteoarthritis) reflecting those alterations. The establishment of missions, in particular, occasioned a shift to a more sedentary lifeway in native populations and a decrease in level of activity and mobility. At the same time, behaviors involving repetitive motions and heavy impact-loading of articular joints resulted in an increase in prevalence of osteoarthritis in the late seventeenth century.

Although the mechanical changes observed show the same trends generally for both males and females, it is interesting that Early Contact–period females, unlike males, show a reduction in bone strength. Because the humerus is not involved in ambulatory behavior, the changes observed can only be interpreted in relation to activities involving stresses placed on the arm. This finding suggests males increased the use of their upper arms while females did not, at least in the earlier mission era. Based on these findings, we argue that females and males engaged in very different behaviors during this time. What the differences in behaviors were remains unclear.

Acknowledgments

We thank the Edward John Noble Foundation and St. Catherines Island Foundation for support for fieldwork on St. Catherines Island. Dr. and Mrs. George H. Dorion provided generous financial assistance for the excavation of the human remains from Santa Catalina de Guale de Santa Maria on Amelia Island, Florida. The National Science Foundation provided funding for study of the human remains discussed in this chapter (grant awards BNS-8406773, BNS-8703849, and BNS-8747309). We gratefully acknowledge the assistance of Douglas Ubelaker and Donald Ortner in obtaining femora and humeri housed in the collections under their care at the National Museum of Natural History, Smithsonian Institution. Harvey Marshall and Peter Peregrine provided useful suggestions for statistical analysis. Susan Simmons, Katherine Russell, Inui Choi, Dale Hutchinson, Rebecca Shavit, and Joanna Lambert gave invaluable assistance in fieldwork, laboratory, and analysis stages of the investigation. Figures 5.1 and 5.2 were prepared by Lisa Gosciejew and Prisca Kolkowski, with revisions by Sondra Jarvis. The photograph for figure 5.3 was taken by Barry Stark.

An earlier version of this chapter was presented in Miami at the 1990 annual meeting of the American Association of Physical Anthropologists. Thanks are extended to Brenda Baker and Lisa Kealhofer for their invitation to participate in their symposium, "Disease and Demographic Collapse in the Spanish Borderlands."

References

Angel, J. Lawrence, Jennifer Olsen Kelley, Michael Parrington, and Stephanie Pinter
    1987   Life Stresses of the Free Black Community as Represented by the First African Baptist Church, Philadelphia, 1823–1841. *American Journal of Physical Anthropology* 74:213–29.

Bennike, Pia
    1985   *Palaeopathology of Danish Skeletons: A Comparative Study of Demography, Disease and Injury.* Copenhagen: Akademisk.

Bourke, J. B.
    1967   A Review of Paleopathology of Arthritic Disease. In *Diseases in Antiquity*, edited by Don R. Brothwell and A. T. Sandison, 352–70. Springfield, Ill.: Charles C. Thomas.

Bridges, Patricia S.
    1989a   Changes in Activities with the Shift to Agriculture in the Southeastern United States. *Current Anthropology* 30:385–94.
    1989b   Bone Cortical Area in the Evaluation of Nutrition and Activity Levels. *American Journal of Human Biology* 1:785–92.
    1990   Osteological Correlates of Weapon Use. In *A Life in Science: Papers in Honor of J. Lawrence Angel*, edited by Jane E. Buikstra, 87–98. Scientific Papers no. 6. Evanston, Ill.: Center for American Archeology.

Brock, Sharon L., and Christopher B. Ruff
    1988   Diachronic Patterns of Change in Structural Properties of the Femur in the Prehistoric American Southwest. *American Journal of Physical Anthropology* 75:113–28.

Caldwell, Joseph R., and Catherine McCann
    1941   *Irene Mound Site.* Athens: University of Georgia Press.

DeRousseau, C. Jean

1988   *Osteoarthritis in Rhesus Monkeys and Gibbons: A Locomotor Model of Joint Degeneration.* Contributions to Primatology 25. Basel: Karger.

Duncan, Howard

1979   Osteoarthritis. In *Arthritis: Modern Concepts and Ancient Evidence,* edited by Eve Cockburn, Howard Duncan, and Jeanne M. Riddle, 6–9. Henry Ford Hospital Medical Journal 27. Detroit: Henry Ford Hospital.

Eichner, Edward R.

1989   An Epidemiologic Perspective: Does Running Cause Osteoarthritis? *The Physician and Sportsmedicine* 17:147–54.

FAO (Food and Agricultural Organization)

1970   *Amino-Acid Content of Foods and Biological Data on Proteins.* Rome: FAO.

Fresia, Anne F., Christopher B. Ruff, and Clark Spencer Larsen

1990   Temporal Decline in Bilateral Asymmetry of the Upper Limb on the Georgia Coast. In *The Archaeology of Mission Santa Catalina de Guale: 2. Biocultural Interpretations of a Population in Transition,* edited by Clark Spencer Larsen, 121–32. Anthropological Papers 68. New York: American Museum of Natural History.

Griffin, Mark C., and Clark Spencer Larsen

1989   Patterns in Osteoarthritis: A Case Study from the Prehistoric and Historic Southeastern U.S. Atlantic Coast. *American Journal of Physical Anthropology* 78:232.

Hann, John H.

1986   The Use and Processing of Plants by Indians of Spanish Florida. *Southeastern Archaeology* 5:91–102.

1988   *Apalachee: The Land Between the Rivers.* Gainesville: University Press of Florida.

1990   Summary Guide to Spanish Florida Missions and Visitas, with Churches in the Sixteenth and Seventeenth Centuries. *The Americas* 56(4):417–513.

Hardin, Kenneth W.

1986   The Santa Maria Mission Project. *Florida Anthropologist* 39:75–83.

Hayes, W. C., and T. N. Gerhart

1985   Biomechanics of Bone: Applications for Assessment of Bone Strength. In *Bone and Mineral Research,* vol. 3, edited by William A. Peck, 259–94. New York: Elsevier.

Hough, Aubrey J., Jr., and Leon Sokoloff

1989   The Pathology of Osteoarthritis. In *Arthritis and Allied Conditions,* 11th edition, edited by D. J. McCarty, 1571–94. Philadelphia: Lea and Febiger.

Hrdlička, Ales

1908   *Physiological and Medical Observations among the Indians of the Southwestern United States and Northern Mexico.* Bureau of American Ethnology Bulletin 34. Washington, D.C.: U.S. Government Printing Office.

1914   Special Notes on Some of the Pathological Conditions Shown by the Skeletal Material of the Ancient Peruvians. *Smithsonian Miscellaneous Collections* 61:57–69.

Hudson, Charles
1976   *The Southeastern Indians.* Knoxville: University of Tennessee Press.

Hulse, Frederick S.
1941   The People Who Lived at Irene: Physical Anthropology. In *Irene Mound Site,* by Joseph R. Caldwell and Catherine McCann, 57–68. Athens: University of Georgia Press.

Hutchinson, Dale L., and Clark Spencer Larsen
1988   Determination of Stress Episode Duration from Linear Enamel Hypoplasias: A Case Study from St. Catherines Island, Georgia. *Human Biology* 60:93–110.

Johnston, Francis E., and Lawrence M. Schell
1979   Anthropometric Variation of Native American Children and Adults. In *The First Americans: Origins, Affinities, and Adaptations,* edited by William S. Laughlin and Albert B. Harper, 275–91. New York: Gustav Fischer.

Jones, Grant D.
1978   The Ethnohistory of the Guale Coast through 1684. In *The Anthropology of St. Catherines Island: 1. Natural and Cultural History,* by David Hurst Thomas, Grant D. Jones, Roger S. Durham, and Clark Spencer Larsen, 178–210. Anthropological Papers 55. New York: American Museum of Natural History.

Jurmain, Robert D.
1977   Stress and the Etiology of Osteoarthritis. *American Journal of Physical Anthropology* 53:143–50.
1990   Paleoepidemiology of a Central California Prehistoric Population from CA-ALA-329: II. Degenerative Disease. *American Journal of Physical Anthropology* 83:83–94.

Kelley, Jennifer Olsen, and J. Lawrence Angel
1987   Life Stresses of Slavery. *American Journal of Physical Anthropology* 74:199–211.

Kellgren, J. H., and J. S. Lawrence
1958   Osteoarthritis and Disc Degeneration in an Urban Population. *Annals of Rheumatic Disease* 17:388–97.

Kennedy, Kenneth A. R.
1989   Skeletal Markers of Occupational Stress. In *Reconstruction of Life from the Skeleton,* edited by Mehmet Yaşar İşcan and Kenneth A. R. Kennedy, 129–60. New York: Alan R. Liss.

Lanyon, Lance E., and Clinton T. Rubin
1985   Functional Adaptation in Skeletal Structures. In *Functional Vertebrate Morphology,* edited by Milton Hildebrand, Dennis M. Bramble, Karel F. Liem, and

David B. Wake, 1–25. Cambridge, Mass.: Belknap and Harvard University Press.

Larsen, Clark Spencer

1981   Functional Implications of Postcranial Size Reduction on the Prehistoric Georgia Coast. *Journal of Human Evolution* 10:489–502.

1982   *The Anthropology of St. Catherines Island: 3. Prehistoric Human Biological Adaptation*, 155–270. Anthropological Papers 57. New York: American Museum of Natural History.

1987   Bioarchaeological Interpretations of Subsistence Economy and Behavior from Human Skeletal Remains. In *Advances in Archaeological Method and Theory*, vol. 10, edited by Michael B. Schiffer, 339–445. San Diego: Academic Press.

1990   Biocultural Interpretation and the Context for Contact. In *The Archaeology of Mission Santa Catalina de Guale: 2. Biocultural Interpretations of a Population in Transition*, edited by Clark Spencer Larsen, 11–25. Anthropological Papers 68. New York: American Museum of Natural History.

Larsen, Clark Spencer, and Christopher B. Ruff

1991   Biomechanical Adaptation and Behavior on the Prehistoric Georgia Coast. In *What Mean These Bones? Integrated Studies in Southeastern Bioarchaeology*, edited by Mary Lucas Powell, Patricia S. Bridges, and Ann Marie Wagner Mires, 102–13. Tuscaloosa: University of Alabama Press.

Larsen, Clark Spencer, Christopher B. Ruff, Margaret J. Schoeninger, and Dale L. Hutchinson

1992   Population Decline and Extinction in La Florida. In *Disease and Demography in the Americas*, edited by John W. Verano and Douglas H. Ubelaker, 25–39. Washington, D.C.: Smithsonian Institution.

Larsen, Clark Spencer, and Rebecca Saunders

1987   The Santa Catalina de Guale (Amelia Island) Cemeteries. Paper presented at the Southeastern Archaeological Conference, Charleston, S.C.

Larsen, Clark Spencer, Margaret J. Schoeninger, Dale L. Hutchinson, Katherine F. Russell, and Christopher B. Ruff

1990   Beyond Demographic Collapse: Biological Adaptation and Change in Native Populations of La Florida. In *Columbian Consequences*, vol. 2: *Archaeological and Historical Perspectives on the Spanish Borderlands East*, edited by David Hurst Thomas, 409–28. Washington, D.C.: Smithsonian Institution.

Larsen, Clark Spencer, Rebecca Shavit, and Mark C. Griffin

1991   Dental Caries Evidence for Dietary Change: An Archaeological Context. In *Advances in Dental Anthropology*, edited by Marc A. Kelley and Clark Spencer Larsen, 179–202. New York: Wiley-Liss.

Larsen, Clark Spencer, and David Hurst Thomas

1982   *The Anthropology of St. Catherines Island: 4. The St. Catherines Period Mortuary Complex*, 271–342. Anthropological Papers 57. New York: American Museum of Natural History.

Lawrence, J. S.

1955   Rheumatism in Coalminers. Part III: Occupational Factors. *British Journal of Industrial Medicine* 12:249–61.

Lovejoy, C. Owen, Albert H. Burstein, and Kingsbury Heiple
   1976   The Biomechanical Analysis of Bone Strength: A Method and Its Application to Platycnemia. *American Journal of Physical Anthropology* 44:489–506.

Maquet, P.
   1983   What Predisposes for Osteoarthritis: Geometry? *Journal of Rheumatology* 10 (Supplement 9):27–28.

Merbs, Charles F.
   1983   *Patterns of Activity-Induced Pathology in a Canadian Inuit Population.* Archaeological Survey of Canada, Mercury Series 119. Ottawa: National Museum of Man.

Miles, A. E. W.
   1989   *An Early Christian Chapel and Burial Ground on the Isle of Ensay, Outer Hebrides, Scotland, with a Study of the Skeletal Remains.* BAR British Series 212. Oxford: British Archaeological Reports.

Moskowitz, R. W.
   1987   Primary Osteoarthritis: Epidemiology, Clinical Aspects, and General Management. *American Journal of Medicine* 83:5–10.

Nagurka, M. L., and W. C. Hayes
   1980   An Interactive Graphics Package for Calculating Cross-Sectional Properties of Complex Shapes. *Journal of Biomechanics* 13:59–64.

Nordin, Margareta, and Victor H. Frankel
   1980   Biomechanics and Whole Bones and Bone Tissue. In *Basic Biomechanics of the Skeletal System,* edited by Victor H. Frankel and Margareta Nordin, 15–60. Philadelphia: Lea and Febiger.

Ortner, Donald J., and Walter G. J. Putschar
   1985   *Identification of Pathological Conditions in Human Skeletal Remains.* Reprint edition. Contributions to Anthropology no. 28. Washington, D.C.: Smithsonian Institution.

Parrington, Michael, and Daniel G. Roberts
   1990   Demographic, Cultural, and Bioanthropological Aspects of a Nineteenth-Century Free Black Population in Philadelphia, Pennsylvania. In *A Life in Science: Papers in Honor of J. Lawrence Angel,* edited by Jane E. Buikstra, 138–70. Scientific Papers no. 6. Evanston, Ill.: Center for American Archeology.

Pascale, Mark, and William A. Grana
   1989   An Orthopedic Perspective: Does Running Cause Osteoarthritis? *The Physician and Sportsmedicine* 17:156–66.

Radin, Eric L.
   1982   Mechanical Factors in the Causation of Osteoarthritis. *Rheumatology* 7:46–52.
   1983   The Relationship Between Biological and Mechanical Factors in the Etiology of Osteoarthritis. *Journal of Rheumatology* 10 (Supplement 9):20–21.

Robbins, D. M., K. R. Rosenberg, and C. B. Ruff
   1989   Activity Patterns in the Late Middle Woodland, Delaware. *American Journal of Physical Anthropology* 78:290–91.

Rogers, Juliet, Tony Waldron, Paul Dieppe, and Iain Watt
    1987   Arthropathies in Palaeopathology: The Basis of Classification According to
            Most Probable Cause. *Journal of Archaeological Science* 14:179–93.
Ruff, Christopher B.
    1984   Allometry between Length and Cross-Sectional Dimensions of the Femur and
            Tibia in *Homo sapiens sapiens. American Journal of Physical Anthropology*
            65:347–48.
    1987   Sexual Dimorphism in Human Lower Limb Bone Structure: Relationship to
            Subsistence Strategy and Sexual Division of Labor. *Journal of Human Evolu-
            tion* 16:391–416.
    1989   New Approaches to Structural Evolution of Limb Bones in Primates. *Folia
            Primatologica* 53:142–59.
    1991   *Aging and Osteoporosis in Native Americans from Pecos Pueblo, New Mexico.*
            New York: Garland.
    1992   Biomechanical Analyses of Archaeological Human Skeletal Samples. In *Skel-
            etal Biology of Past Peoples: Research Methods,* edited by Shelley R. Saunders
            and M. Anne Katzenberg, 41–62. New York: Wiley-Liss.
Ruff, Christopher B., and Wilson C. Hayes
    1982   Subperiosteal Expansion and Cortical Remodeling of the Human Femur and
            Tibia with Aging. *Science* 217:945–48.
    1983   Cross-Sectional Geometry of Pecos Pueblo Femora and Tibiae—A Biomechani-
            cal Investigation: I. Method and General Patterns of Variation. *American Jour-
            nal of Physical Anthropology* 60:359–81.
Ruff, Christopher B., and Clark Spencer Larsen
    1990   Postcranial Biomechanical Adaptations to Subsistence Strategy Changes on
            the Georgia Coast. In *The Archaeology of Mission Santa Catalina de Guale:
            2. Biocultural Interpretations of a Population in Transition,* edited by Clark
            Spencer Larsen, 94–120. Anthropological Papers 68. New York: American
            Museum of Natural History.
Ruff, Christopher B., Clark Spencer Larsen, and Wilson C. Hayes
    1984   Structural Changes in the Femur with the Transition to Agriculture on the
            Georgia Coast. *American Journal of Physical Anthropology* 64:125–36.
Ruff, Christopher B., William W. Scott, and Allie Y.-C. Liu
    1991   Articular and Diaphyseal Remodeling of the Proximal Femur with Changes
            in Body Mass in Adults. *American Journal of Physical Anthropology* 86:397–
            413.
Schoeninger, Margaret J., Nikolaas J. van der Merwe, Katherine Moore, Julia Lee-Thorp,
        and Clark Spencer Larsen
    1990   Decrease in Diet Quality between the Prehistoric and the Contact Periods. In
            *The Archaeology of Mission Santa Catalina de Guale: 2. Biocultural Inter-
            pretations of a Population in Transition,* edited by Clark Spencer Larsen, 78–
            93. Anthropological Papers 68. New York: American Museum of Natural His-
            tory.

Stewart, T. Dale

1947   Racial Patterns in Vertebral Osteoarthritis. *American Journal of Physical Anthropology* 5:230–31.

1966   Some Problems in Palaeopathology. In *Human Paleopathology,* edited by Saul Jarcho, 43–55. New Haven, Conn.: Yale University Press.

Swanton, John R.

1946   *The Indians of the Southeastern United States.* Bureau of American Ethnology Bulletin 137. Washington, D.C.: U.S. Government Printing Office.

Thomas, David Hurst

1987   *The Archaeology of Mission Santa Catalina de Guale: 1. Search and Discovery,* 47–161. Anthropological Papers 63 (2). New York: American Museum of Natural History.

Walker, Phillip L., and S. E. Hollimon

1989   Changes in Osteoarthritis Associated with the Development of a Maritime Economy among Southern California Indians. *International Journal of Anthropology* 4:171–83.

Webb, Stephen

1989   *Prehistoric Stress in Australian Aborigines: A Palaeopathological Study of a Hunter-Gatherer Population.* BAR International Series 490. Oxford: British Archaeological Reports.

Wells, Calvin

1982   The Human Burials. In *Cirencester Excavations II: Romano-British Cemeteries at Cirencester,* by Alan McWhirr, Linda Viner, and Calvin Wells, 135–202. Cirencester, England: Corinium Museum.

Wood Jones, F.

1910   General Pathology (Including Diseases of the Teeth). In *The Archaeological Survey of Nubia Report for 1907–1908,* vol. 2: *Report on the Human Remains,* edited by G. Elliot Smith and F. Wood Jones, 263–92. Cairo: National Printing Department.

Chapter 6

The Effect of European Contact on the Health of Indigenous Populations in Texas

Elizabeth Miller

The consequences of Columbus' "discovery of America" have long been of interest in anthropology. Contact studies have focused on contrasts between the Old and New World, and the effect of European contact on health, disease, and lifeways (Crosby 1972; Thomas 1989, 1990, 1991; Verano and Ubelaker 1992). Detailed examinations of the timing of contact and New World population decline, strategies of colonization and resistance, patterns of health and sickness, and specific disease processes have been conducted. In particular, investigators have used the occurrence and frequency of pathological conditions (and disorders) such as dental caries, abscesses, linear enamel hypoplasia, and porotic hyperostosis to reconstruct diet, nutrition, effects of changes in subsistence, population size and density, and overall population health (Huss-Ashmore et al. 1982; Larsen 1987a). Within the last 10 years researchers have studied these conditions in skeletal series across North America (cf. Larsen 1984, 1987b, 1990; Larsen and Shavit 1988; Stodder 1990; Walker et al. 1989). The present analysis focuses on the effect of European contact on the health of indigenous populations in Texas.

For this study, skeletal remains of indigenous peoples from two historic and two prehistoric sites were analyzed in an effort to determine overall Native American health in Texas. The goal of this study was not to determine the impact of introduced acute conditions, such as smallpox and measles, nor to answer current questions on the impact of such diseases on population size, but to examine the general well-being of those individuals who survived initial contact in Texas. The questions addressed in this study, then, concerned the evaluation of chronic health conditions that have the potential to compromise the response of the individual to external stressors and to modify the activity patterns and responses at the household and community levels (Stodder and Martin 1992). Reasonable approximations of population health can be obtained by the study of nonspecific pathological conditions, including porotic hyperostosis, cribra orbitalia, generalized periosteal reaction, periodontal infection, caries, abscesses and linear enamel hypoplasia (Goodman 1991; Goodman et al. 1984; Huss-Ashmore et al. 1982; Larsen 1987a). All of these conditions are signs of the struggle of the individual to adapt to stressors (Goodman 1991) and do not indicate specific illnesses. As the response to stress varies with each individual, any single condition cannot be used as a measure of change in health. When the occurrence of the conditions is examined, however, changes in frequency may indicate changes in general population health. These data can then be combined with other data on the physical, biological, and cultural environments to deduce the overall level of health of a population. While it is true that theoretical and methodological problems exist within the field of paleopathology today (Ortner 1991; Palkovich chapter 8 below; Wood et al. 1992), indicators such as these can still provide valuable information on chronic stress when these data are considered within their biological, archaeological, and historic contexts (Ortner 1991).

One aspect not considered in this chapter is the effect of short-term illnesses, which do not manifest skeletally, on overall population health. Endemic diseases were probably enhanced by the change in lifeways associated with European contact, and imported diseases caused many deaths (Verano and Ubelaker 1992). Unfortunately, the only way to see these short-term illnesses skeletally is through demographic analysis of mortality over time, an analysis that was not possible for this chapter due to small sample sizes and lack of fine chronological control. One study of the impact of infectious diseases on the indigenous inhabitants of Texas has been conducted (Ewers 1973), however, and the conclusions of that author are incorporated into this analysis.

In addition to the increasing number and kinds of diseases present in the environment, many other factors must be considered in an analysis such as this. The first of these is the potential stress introduced by contact with nonindigenous animals. There is historic evidence that domesticated animals, primarily horses, cattle, sheep, and goats, were raised in the missions (cf. Casteñeda 1938). These animals were potentially a prime source of zoonotic infections such as tetanus, influenza, and bovine tuberculosis (Van Blerkom 1985). While some of these infections may have skeletal manifestations, many do not. Therefore, in addition to demographic and paleopathological information, historic documentation of farming and ranching activities must be examined to effectively determine overall health in the mission samples.

The decline in health that generally follows a change in subsistence strategy from a mobile to a sedentary one is also important because the missionization process in Texas included the introduction of agriculture and a sedentary lifestyle. People were also forced to relinquish their native religious practices and ideology, and to adopt Catholicism as a way of life. Indigenous groups within the system were persecuted if caught practicing non-Catholic ceremonies (Casteñeda 1938). The changes in technology, diet, and physical, social, and ideological environments likely combined to reduce the general level of health of the population (cf. Goodman 1991; Huss-Ashmore et al. 1982; Larsen 1987a). Other factors directly affecting population health were external variables such as weather, movement of people into or out of an area, and interactions within and between groups.

Indirect and direct contact (both short and long term) are critical variables in this study. Indirect contact with Europeans, through intermediaries, led to the spread of Old World diseases among natives prior to the first direct contact with many groups (Dobyns 1992). This was often followed by a period of direct, but short-term contact between individual groups and European explorers, which was in turn followed by long-term direct contact and the establishment of European missions, forts, and settlements.

None of these potential causes for changes in health can be directly linked with a specific skeletal reaction. This chapter does not attempt to differentiate these causes, but delineates the overall chronic changes in health that have been observed in skeletal samples from Texas.

BACKGROUND

There are at least four Amerindian groups thought to have been present in the areas of the sites used in this study (figure 6.1): Coahuiltecans, Tonkawans, Karankawans and Atakapans. Although the prehistory of these groups in Texas is not well known, they appear to have been highly mobile hunter-gatherers, subsisting on pecans, acorns, mesquite beans, various cacti, deer, javelina, bison and small mammals and reptiles (Bolton 1915; Campbell 1952; Jelks 1953; Sjöberg 1951; Steele 1986a, 1986b; Steele and Hunter 1986; Steele and Mokry 1985; Suhm 1955). The Tonkawa are thought to have utilized bison more heavily than other groups in Texas (Jelks 1953; Suhm 1955), and they, along with the Atakapa, may have traded with the agricultural Caddo to the east (Sjöberg 1951; Suhm 1955). The Karankawa, on the other hand, appear to have relied heavily on marine resources, supplemented with food items from the surrounding grasslands and marshes. Despite these adaptations to differing environments, these four prehistoric groups appear very similar in their lifeways.

As the Spanish moved into Texas, they came in contact with these highly mobile hunter-gatherers. The task of "civilizing" and containing these Amerindians fell to the Catholic Church. Missionaries began serving both the church, in "Christianizing" the Indians, and the state, in containing them and removing them from the path of Spanish intrusion. The missions in Texas were designed as frontier institutions from both a religious and a political standpoint.

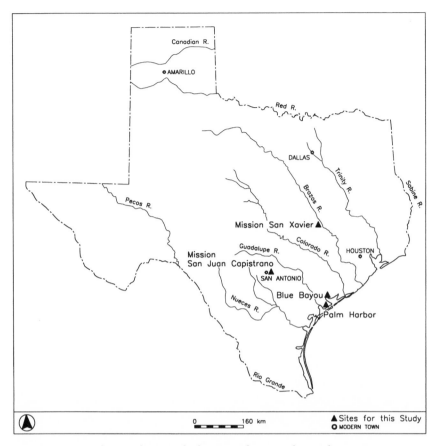

Figure 6.1. Map of Texas showing the location of sites in this study.

They were intended to be temporary settlements for native peoples while the Spanish intruded farther into North America, and they were government agencies designed to extend and hold the so-called civilized territory for Spain (Bolton 1915).

Mission San Juan Capistrano (41BX5; hereafter referred to as San Juan) and Mission San Francisco Xavier de Horcasitas (41MM11; hereafter referred to as San Xavier) were Spanish missions established in central Texas in the mid-1700s. The skeletal series from the two missions differ both in biological affinity and the actual length of European contact.

Mission San Juan was first established in 1716 east of the Angelina River under the name of Mission San José de los Nazones. It was abandoned in 1729 because of the threat of French invasion from Louisiana. Relocation was attempted several times before the new site was finally established on the San

Antonio River in Bexar County. The new mission was opened on March 5, 1731, and renamed San Juan Capistrano. It was secularized in 1794, when the land was given to the families who remained in the mission.

Mission San Xavier is one of three missions in the San Xavier Mission complex. This complex, located in Milam County at the confluence of the San Gabriel River and Brushy Creek, was originally built at the request of representatives of four central Texas groups indigenous to the area.

The first of the three missions, Mission San Xavier was established in 1747. By 1748, however, the number of natives present exceeded the capacity of the mission, and the differing tribal affiliations of the neophytes began to cause conflict. In 1749, Mission San Ildefonso was established to serve four Atakapan groups, while Mission San Xavier continued to house the Tonkawan groups (Bolton 1915). A third mission, Mission Nuestra Señora de la Candelaria, was opened for the Karankawa and other coastal groups sent into central Texas in 1748. The San Xavier missions began to fail after several dry years, and by 1755 all three missions of the San Xavier complex were abandoned (Casteñeda 1932, 1936, 1938).

Agriculture was the primary subsistence strategy in the missions. Maize was grown in all of them, and watermelon, cantaloupe, and squash were cultivated in several as well (Casteñeda 1936, 1938). Cattle were raised on ranches close to and owned by the missions, and beef was used to supplement the agricultural diet. Additional food items were gathered from around the missions, although rarely (Casteñeda 1936), and hunting was apparently allowed on a sporadic basis.

MATERIALS

Samples from both Mission San Juan and Mission San Xavier were analyzed in this study. The sample from Mission San Juan consists of the remains of 92 individuals recovered from 16 interments. This burial population, listed as Coahuiltecan in mission records (Casteñeda 1938), dates to approximately 1760–85. The individuals recovered were probably born within the mission system (Schuetz 1968). The sample contains 25 males, 13 females, and 54 individuals of indeterminate sex. Seventeen of the latter are subadults, while the remainder are either very poorly preserved or represented by only a few elements. Although there is a sex bias in the sample, these skeletal materials appear to be an accurate reflection of the population living in the mission itself. Historic records indicate a predominance of males at San Juan during its operation (Casteñeda 1938). The occurrence of pathological conditions, however, equally affects the males and females recovered. Of the 17 subadults, 10 are infants recovered from a single, secondary interment.

The material recovered from the second historic site, Mission San Xavier, consists of 11 interments, containing the remains of 13 individuals. Mission records are somewhat less clear in this case, but the inhabitants appear to have included Tonkawa, Atakapa, and Karankawa. This sample appears unbiased with regard to the representation of sex, with five males, five females, and three individuals of indeterminate sex (two of whom are infants).

The human material from Blue Bayou, the first prehistoric site to be discussed, was originally analyzed by Comuzzie (1987), and is likely to be representative of the Karankawa. Remains of approximately 45 individuals were analyzed, 22 of whom could be sexed. Of the remaining 23, four are subadults (two are infants) and the rest are too poorly preserved for sex determination. Of the 22 who could be sexed, 12 are male and 10 are female. Analysis of the site indicates that Blue Bayou was an extensive prehistoric cemetery site, only a small portion of which was excavated (Comuzzie 1987; Huebner 1988). This partial recovery could potentially affect the interpretation of these remains (Palkovich chapter 8 below). Blue Bayou is, however, one of the largest mortuary sites excavated on the Texas Gulf Coast, and is more likely to reflect adequately the actual population from which it was drawn than would a smaller, fully excavated site.

Remains of approximately seven individuals were removed from the Palm Harbor site, the second prehistoric site used in this analysis. These individuals are also likely to have been related to the Karankawa. The site was disturbed and the skeletal material was scattered and damaged. The remains removed for examination were inadvertently mixed at the site (Mokry and Fitzpatrick 1980), and are treated as an ossuary sample for this analysis. Only minimal occupational debris was recovered from Palm Harbor, indicating a short-term occupation at the site. Precise dates for the site are being sought. Because of the uncontrolled excavation, however, artifacts that could change this interpretation may have been overlooked. The material was sexed on a bone-by-bone basis: approximately 30 percent of the material is male, 28 percent is female. The remainder of the material cannot be sexed. The remains were originally analyzed by Comuzzie and others (1986) and were reanalyzed for this study.

Methods

The analysis of all the skeletal material used in this study focused on the presence or absence of seven pathological conditions. These conditions were defined using Ortner and Putschar (1981) and Steinbock (1976), and were recorded on a bone-by-bone basis. Dental disorders were defined following Pindborg (1970). The stress markers assessed in this study are as follows: porotic hyperostosis, cribra orbitalia, generalized periosteal reaction, linear enamel hypoplasia, caries, dental abscessing, and periodontal infection.

Patterns of dental wear have been shown to be useful in differentiating hunter-gatherers from agriculturalists (Molnar 1971; Schmucker 1985; Smith 1975). Occlusal surface wear was compared across the four samples primarily because of its correlations with diet, food preparation techniques, and the use of teeth as tools. After dental wear analysis, the seven conditions used as indicators of overall health were assessed. These conditions and the evaluation criteria are described below.

Porotic Hyperostosis and Cribra Orbitalia

Porotic hyperostosis and cribra orbitalia are thought to be skeletal manifestations of anemia, and have long been used as nutritional status indicators (Huss-Ashmore et al. 1982; Kent 1986; Larsen 1984, 1987a; Ortner and Putschar 1981; Steinbock 1976; Stuart-Macadam 1987, 1992). Recent work, however, has led to a reevaluation of these conditions, and they are now thought to be indicative only of general systemic insult (Larsen 1987a; Stuart-Macadam 1992). Porotic hyperostosis was considered present when both thickened diploe and pitting was observed on the parietals. Cribra orbitalia was considered present when symmetrical pores or large, irregular apertures were found in the orbits.

Generalized Periosteal Reaction

Generalized periosteal reaction is also indicative of stress in an individual, and can be caused by many factors. Although periosteal reaction is not in itself a disease, its distribution in an individual can indicate systemic stress and is helpful in determining the health status of a population (Ortner and Putschar 1981; Steinbock 1976). This condition was considered present, and indicative of systemic insult, when it was found on multiple elements and there was no sign of trauma or neoplasm.

Linear Enamel Hypoplasia (LEH)

Linear enamel hypoplasia (LEH) is thought to be the result of stress during enamel formation (Goodman et al. 1980; Rose et al. 1984), and is visible as transverse lines on the teeth. As with the conditions mentioned above, there are multiple causes of LEH. It is, nonetheless, an indication of stress in the individual at an early period in life. LEH was considered present in this study when two or more lines were visible on two or more teeth formed at different times (e.g., an incisor and a canine). Presence of LEH under 10X magnification on different tooth types was considered evidence for systemic stress as opposed to localized trauma (Neiburger 1988).

Periodontal Infection

Periodontal infection, characterized by resorption of 2 mm or more of the alveolar margin from the cementoenamel junction, is generally interpreted as an indicator of oral health (Huss-Ashmore et al. 1982; Milner 1984; Pindborg 1970). The condition was recorded as present when the 2 mm distance was recorded for more than two teeth, and was not associated with localized conditions such as abscessing or chipping. If only one tooth was involved, the condition was not considered systemic (C. G. Turner, personal communication 1989).

Caries

Caries is a disease process characterized by demineralization of enamel through bacterial fermentation of carbohydrates, especially sugars (Larsen 1987a, 1990; Newbrun 1982; Pindborg 1970), and is thought to be indicative of diet. Caries can also be used as an indicator of metabolic stress (Larsen 1987a, 1990). The factors giving rise to the disease include the host (saliva and teeth), the bacteria, and the diet, all of which may have been influenced by European-introduced goods and lifeways. For this study, caries was considered present when visual examination of the teeth indicated the decay process. Only individuals with at least eight teeth recovered were examined for this condition.

Abscessing

Abscessing is closely related to periodontal disease and caries. It is caused by an infection or disturbance in the alveolar margin, and is generally seen skeletally as expansion or perforation of the alveolus. It was considered present when either of these conditions were observed.

All skeletal remains were analyzed as discrete individuals whenever possible, as diagnosis of many conditions relies heavily on the distribution of the disease in the skeleton (Ortner and Putschar 1981; Steinbock 1976). In the case of multiple interments, however, individual analysis was not possible. Since the Palm Harbor material was inadvertently mixed at the site, all material was also analyzed on a bone-by-bone basis following traditional analytical techniques established for ossuary samples (Bass 1971; Brothwell 1981). Simple chi-square tests were then run on the data. The confidence interval was 95 percent in all cases.

Results

Occlusal surface wear, with light and moderate wear occurrences combined, was compared in the two mission samples to determine whether they could be combined for the purposes of this study. The results indicate that wear at Mission San Xavier was more severe than that at Mission San Juan ($X^2 = 17.8$).

Table 6.1. Comparison of mission samples (in %)

Condition	San Juan	San Xavier	Significant (y/n)[a]
Porotic hyperostosis	60	4	n
Cribra orbitalia	32	0	y
Periosteal reaction	82	39	y
Linear enamel hypoplasia	34	63	n
Caries	34	63	n
Abscesses	24	13	n
Periodontal infection	28	50	n

[a]Significant = p<0.05.

The wear is not attributable to age differences within the skeletal series. This disparate wear pattern, along with the different length of operation of the two missions, led to separation of these samples in all subsequent comparisons.

A comparison of occlusal surface wear and the seven pathological conditions in the two prehistoric series showed no significant differences. Thus, these samples were considered similar enough to combine.

The occurrence of the seven skeletal markers was then analyzed in the historic samples. In the comparison between the two mission samples (table 6.1), significantly higher frequencies of cribra orbitalia and periosteal reaction are found in Mission San Juan ($X^2 = 4.19$ for cribra orbitalia and 11.6 for periosteal reaction). The frequency of porotic hyperostosis is also higher in Mission San Juan, but not at the level of statistical significance ($X^2 = 1.10$). As noted above, the prehistoric sample comparison yielded no significant differences for any of the stress indicators (table 6.2), although the actual frequency

Table 6.2. Comparison of prehistoric samples (in %)

Condition[a]	Blue Bayou	Palm Harbor
Porotic hyperostosis	0	0
Cribra orbitalia	0	0
Periosteal reaction	0	43[b]
Linear enamel hypoplasia	0	0
Caries	15	14
Abscesses	8	14
Periodontal infection	19	14

[a]Not significant (p>0.05)

[b]Three individuals exhibited periosteal reaction—in all cases this reaction appears to be due to treponemal infection.

Table 6.3. Comparison of Mission San Juan Capistrano and the combined prehistoric samples (in %)

Condition	San Juan	Prehistoric	Significant (y/n)[a]
Porotic hyperostosis	60	0	y
Cribra orbitalia	32	0	y
Periosteal reaction	82	6	y
Linear enamel hypoplasia	34	0	y
Caries	34	15	n
Abscesses	24	9	n
Periodontal infection	28	18	n

[a]Significant = p<0.05.

of caries and periodontal infection is rather high for a hunter-gatherer sample in Texas.

The last comparisons were between each of the missions and the combined prehistoric skeletal series. The results of these comparisons (tables 6.3 and 6.4) show a higher frequency for all pathological conditions in the mission samples. Statistically significant differences are found in the occurrence of porotic hyperostosis, periosteal reaction, and LEH in both comparisons (X^2 as follows: Mission San Juan/Prehistoric—porotic hyperostosis 14.6, periosteal reaction 66.7, and LEH 8.03, Mission San Xavier/Prehistoric—porotic hyperostosis 6.7, periosteal reaction 9.2, and LEH 13.5). Mission San Juan also shows significant differences in the degree of occlusal surface wear present ($X^2 = 19.55$), and in the frequency of cribra orbitalia ($X^2 = 5.1$), while Mission San Xavier shows a significant difference in the occurrence of caries ($X^2 = 7.5$).

Table 6.4. Comparison of Mission San Xavier and combined prehistoric samples (in %)

Condition	San Xavier	Prehistoric	Significant (y/n)[a]
Porotic hyperostosis	40	0	y
Cribra orbitalia	0	0	n
Periosteal reaction	39	6	y
Linear enamel hypoplasia	63	0	y
Caries	63	15	y
Abscesses	13	9	n
Periodontal infection	50	18	n

[a]Significant = p<0.05.

Discussion

Prehistoric Samples

This analysis suggests that the overall health of hunter-gatherer populations in Texas prior to European contact was generally good. Only the dental disorders of linear enamel hypoplasia, caries, and abscessing are apparent in both prehistoric populations, and all are present only in older individuals. There is no apparent age bias in the prehistoric samples, as adolescents through older adults are affected by these conditions.

Caries usually becomes more frequent with the shift in subsistence from hunting and gathering to agriculture (Larsen 1987a; Larsen et al. 1991; Patterson 1984; Powell 1985; Turner 1979), since cariogenic bacteria thrive on high carbohydrate substrates. Factors such as the physical consistency of food, often determined by the method of preparation, are also associated with caries (Finn and Glass 1975; Patterson 1984; Shaw 1952; Wells 1975).

Although this relationship between diet and carious activity appears to exist, it cannot be assumed that the association is related directly to carbohydrate consumption or to a systemic nutritional effect (Patterson 1984). According to Patterson (1984) and Finn and Glass (1975), it is the form and frequency of carbohydrate consumption, rather than the amount per se, that determines incidence of carious activity. Thick, sticky foods provide the substrate for plaque formation, while foods that are raw and fibrous, even those with high carbohydrate levels, reduce the caries incidence both by their cleansing action and by stimulation of saliva production (Larsen 1987a; Patterson 1984; Turner 1979). Turpin (1985) demonstrated, in at least one Texas sample, that a hunter-gatherer diet rich in sugars and carbohydrates resulted in a caries prevalence at least as high as that in most agricultural populations. In addition, studies conducted on acorns and pecans (Brison 1974; Creel 1986; Ofcarcek and Burns 1971) document that the carbohydrate content of these nuts is as high as that of corn, and both pecans and acorns have been found in Texas archaeological sites.

An alternative explanation for the occurrence of caries in the prehistoric samples is suggested by the work of Pollack and Kravitz (1985, 159), who state that "dental caries is a dietary disease . . . [and] cariogenesis may at least be promoted indirectly by . . . changes in the composition of saliva. Some of these may well be, in part, nutritionally influenced." Any change in diet could, therefore, cause an increase in carious activity, not only through an increase in carbohydrate content of the food but also through a change in the composition of saliva. This change would not take long to affect the caries rate in a population; it has been demonstrated in modern populations that increases in cariogenesis of over 7 percent, attributable to salivary changes, have occurred in less than 36 months (Pollack and Kravitz 1985).

Alveolar abscessing is a pathological condition characterized by destruction of alveolar bone caused by various infectious conditions. It is widespread in many Texas archaeological populations (Patterson 1984; Reinhard et al. 1989). Alveolar abscessing has also been correlated with the adoption of agriculture (Larsen 1987a; Patterson 1984; Powell 1985). Patterson (1984) argues that soft, processed foods reduce cleansing of the teeth, thereby leading to abscessing. Several studies, however, have shown that fibrous, unprocessed foods still allow the buildup of plaque—although to a lesser degree—depending on their carbohydrate and sugar content (Patterson 1984; Turner 1979). A high frequency of abscessing could be found in a hunting and gathering group, as was the case with caries. Since the individuals recovered from both prehistoric sites used in this study probably were subsisting on a high carbohydrate diet (Bolton 1915; Creel 1986), the high frequency of abscessing in the prehistoric skeletal samples is also plausibly explained.

Historic Samples

The comparison between the historic samples also yielded surprising information. Because the occurrence and degree of occlusal surface wear on the dentition differed significantly between the two mission samples, they were not combined into a single sample representative of historic mission populations in Texas. This difference in severity of dental wear between the two mission samples required further analysis.

It has been documented that attrition and abrasion reflect patterns of usage associated with diet and food processing, as well as other cultural practices (Brace and Molnar 1967; Cybulski 1974; Hinton 1981; Molnar 1968, 1970, 1971, 1972). Correlations between diet, food preparation techniques, grit content, and dental wear have also been found by previous authors (Davies 1963; Leigh 1925; Molnar 1971; Taylor 1963; Turner 1979). The importance of wear in archaeological samples is based on this relationship.

Dental wear is considered by many to be a more accurate reflection of subsistence patterns than are fragmentary postcranial remains (cf. Patterson 1984; Schmucker 1985), and several studies have shown that populations practicing a hunter-gatherer subsistence strategy show higher amounts of both attrition and abrasion than those practicing an agricultural strategy (cf. Molnar 1971; Schmucker 1985; Smith 1975).

The statistical difference in dental wear in the two mission samples, combined with the similarity in wear between Mission San Xavier and the prehistoric samples, together with the ethnohistoric information that Mission San Xavier was an active mission for only eight years, suggests that individuals buried at Mission San Xavier practiced a subsistence strategy similar to that of prehistoric hunter-gatherers in Texas for a major part of their adult lives.

The data lead to the further conclusion that those individuals recovered from San Juan spent most of their lives in an agricultural environment, under the direct, daily influence of Europeans (and their diseases).

These conclusions led to a reevaluation of the comparison of the two samples. Rather than being a comparison of two similar mission samples, it became one of two very different populations. The first, Mission San Juan, represents a population that had direct, daily, long-term contact with Europeans and an agricultural subsistence base. Mission San Xavier, on the other hand, represents a primarily hunting and gathering sample, with only a short period of daily contact and agricultural subsistence and an unknown period of indirect contact.

An increase in generalized periosteal infection and in cribra orbitalia is seen from the short-term contact (hunter-gatherer) to the long-term contact (agricultural) samples. This increase in cribra orbitalia should be taken only as a general indicator of stress in the population (Huss-Ashmore et al. 1982; Larsen and Shavit 1988; Milner 1984).

Generalized periosteal reaction is also attributable only to an unknown cause, possibly infectious disease or long-term systemic stress (Huss-Ashmore et al. 1982; Larsen 1987a; Milner 1984). The data suggest, therefore, that chronic stress was more prevalent in the long-term contact sample than in the short-term sample.

Chronic systemic stress can be caused by a multitude of factors, from parasitism to infectious diseases to nutritional deficiencies (Goodman et al. 1984). Several researchers (Cook 1984; Larsen 1987a) have shown that the frequency of subperiosteal bone deposition increases with the shift from a hunting-gathering economy to one based more fully on agriculture. Increases in population density and a change in subsistence strategy took place at both missions in this study. At Mission San Juan, however, these factors operated over the entire life span of the adults in the skeletal assemblage, while at San Xavier they did not.

According to many researchers, a synergistic relationship exists between porotic hyperostosis and infectious disease (Goodman et al. 1984; Huss-Ashmore et al. 1982; Kent 1992; Stuart-Macadam 1987, 1992). The co-occurrence of generalized periosteal infection and porotic hyperostosis is used by these researchers to support this contention. Anemia, which causes porotic hyperostosis in some cases, can inhibit the body's immunological ability (Kent 1992; Ortner and Putschar 1981; Steinbock 1976; Stuart-Macadam 1987, 1992). Conversely, the onset of infection can precipitate anemia (Kent 1992; Stuart-Macadam 1992). Therefore, one might expect to find a significant difference in porotic hyperostosis between the two mission populations, together with the significant difference in periosteal reaction. Such a significant difference did not exist. Porotic hyperostosis, however, can be the result of many factors, including infection, diarrhea, parasitism, and maize dependency (Goodman 1991; Huss-Ashmore et al. 1982; Kent 1992; Larsen 1987a; Ortner and Putschar 1981; Steinbock, 1976; Stuart-Macadam 1987, 1992). Many of these factors could explain the high incidence in both mission samples.

The lack of significant differences in dental disorders between the two mission samples can be easily explained by the relatively high frequency of these conditions in hunter-gatherer samples from central Texas.

Prehistoric and Historic Samples

Through the above methods, the apparently high frequencies of pathological conditions present in the short-term contact, hunter-gatherer population at San Xavier may be plausibly explained. The significant differences between this mission population and the prehistoric hunter-gatherer populations are not as easily inferred. Given the conclusion that the burial sample recovered from Mission San Xavier represents a population of hunter-gatherers who were missionized for only a short period of time, it was not expected to vary significantly from the prehistoric samples. The only major difference between the prehistoric samples and the sample recovered from Mission San Xavier appears to be the European contact. The anomalous status of the San Xavier sample, when compared with the combined prehistoric samples, can be explained by the contact stressors discussed above, with the exception of the change in frequency of linear enamel hypoplasia, a condition formed in childhood. No explanation for this increase was found in the archaeological record.

The differences between the prehistoric samples and the sample recovered from Mission San Juan Capistrano are easily explained by the differing lifestyles. A high frequency of all seven conditions examined in this study was expected. The lack of difference in periodontal infection, abscessing, and caries between the San Juan and prehistoric samples appears to be a reflection of the relatively high frequency of these conditions prehistorically in Texas.

Overall population health, then, appears to have declined in Texas shortly after direct contact with Europeans. However, the difference in length of daily contact expressed by the two missions examined in this study does not appear to have been of great importance. The relatively high rate of porotic hyperostosis, generalized periosteal reaction, and LEH in both mission samples was anomalous when compared to prehistoric populations in Texas, suggesting that both short- and long-term contact had detrimental effects on the health of contacted peoples.

This conclusion is tempered by the possible occurrence of indirect contact between Europeans and indigenous peoples. The extent of this contact, through trade with other groups, war, or any other means, is unknown. There is no mention in Spanish records of any direct contact through trade, although the French, and perhaps the English, may have been trading in Texas on a sporadic basis (Gilmore 1969). The chronic conditions analyzed in this study were just as likely to have been caused by less direct means, such as alteration of the environment for agriculture or the aggregation of people and animals in a central location. No such alteration or aggregation is noted in south-central Texas before Spanish contact.

The transition to agriculture during the missionization process undoubtedly had a major effect on the health of native populations. However, the stressors caused by living in the enclosed environment of a mission, with or without a change in diet, would likely have had a similar effect. One of the primary modifications involved in the adoption of an agricultural way of life is the change from a mobile existence to a sedentary one. This sedentism creates problems in sanitation, disease and parasite control, and ultimately population health. Coupled with the mental stress of the imposition of different religious, political, and social practices, together with a regimentation of lifestyle, this change to a sedentary way of life could have resulted in a decline in health without a change in diet. In this study the effects of contact cannot be separated from the effects of a change in subsistence, although the introduction of agriculture was considered an integral part of the missionization process.

CONCLUSIONS

The initial assumption in the Texas study was that the two mission populations under consideration were similar and could be used to establish a general overview of health patterns at Texas missions. This assumption was challenged by the fact that a significant difference in the amount of occlusal wear existed between the two missions. The difference in wear patterns, and the length of time each mission was in operation, prompted the prediction that the individuals recovered from San Xavier were practicing a hunter-gatherer subsistence strategy for most of their adult lives, while those from San Juan were agricultural for most of their lives.

The San Xavier sample, however, shows incidences of pathological conditions that were apparently anomalous in hunter-gatherer groups in general (Patterson 1984; Powell 1985; Turner 1979). These anomalies are explainable for hunter-gatherer groups, and the possibility that the individuals recovered from San Xavier were hunter-gatherers for most of their adult lives was not precluded.

When compared with data derived from two prehistoric hunter-gatherer populations in Texas, however, the conditions present at San Xavier were again anomalous. Other Texas hunting and gathering groups do not show such high frequencies of these pathological and anomalous conditions. One plausible explanation for these anomalies was the short-term, daily contact with Europeans that occurred at Mission San Xavier. An alternative explanation is that indirect contact with Europeans, or direct contact on a limited, opportunistic basis, occurred. The frequency or amount of this contact is unknown. Ethnohistoric evidence, however, suggests that the Amerindians present at San Xavier were in possession of French rifles when they were contacted by Spanish missionaries (Casteñeda 1938).

The frequency and severity of the seven stress markers at Mission San Juan is high, as was expected. The most likely cause for such high frequencies was European contact. Changes in subsistence strategy and religion were only the beginning of the vast alterations in lifestyle seen after contact in Texas. Along with these changes were exposure to non-native diseases and technology, and changes in the environment caused by this new technology; the decline in health seen at Mission San Juan is easily explained.

In southern North America the effect of Spanish contact on the health of indigenous peoples appears to have been deleterious. In regard to chronic health conditions, either indirect contact had the same effect on populations as direct contact, or short-term contact and long-term contact had roughly the same effect. Although there are significant differences between the missions, these differences are relatively small when compared with the differences between both missions and the prehistoric samples. Contact was deleterious in both cases, although perhaps slightly more so over the long term.

This initial analysis supports other studies in indicating that health status declined with European contact, regardless of prehistoric subsistence strategy. Both agricultural and hunter-gatherer societies appear to be equally affected by European intrusion in the Spanish Borderlands. Further epidemiological and demographic study, in Texas and elsewhere, is now needed to supplement these paleopathological data and test these conclusions.

Acknowledgments

The following individuals allowed the use of their data in this chapter, and provided generous personal help: Clark Larsen, Phillip Walker, Ann Lucy Stodder, and their coworkers. Skeletal material from San Juan Capistrano was provided by the Center for Archaeological Research, University of Texas at San Antonio, and skeletal material from San Francisco Xavier de Horcasitas was provided by the Department of Anthropology, Southern Methodist University.

REFERENCES

Bass, William M.
　1971　*Human Osteology: A Laboratory and Field Manual of the Human Skeleton.* Columbia: Missouri Archaeological Society.
Bolton, Herbert E.
　1915　*Texas in the Middle Eighteenth Century,* 2d edition, 1962. New York: Russell and Russell.
Brace, C. Loring, and Stephen Molnar
　1967　Experimental Studies in Human Tooth Wear: I. *American Journal of Physical Anthropology* 27:213–21.
Brison, F. R.
　1974　*Pecan Culture.* Austin, Tex.: Capital Printing.
Brothwell, Don R.
　1981　*Digging Up Bones.* 3d edition. Ithaca, N.Y.: Cornell University Press.
Campbell, Thomas N.
　1952　The Kent-Crane Site. A Shell Midden on the Texas Coast. *Texas Archaeological and Paleontological Society Bulletin* 23:39–77.
Casteñeda, Carlos E.
　1932　Morfi's History of Texas: A Critical Chronological Account of the Early Exploration, Attempts at Colonization, and Final Occupation of Texas by the Spaniards. Ph.D. diss., Department of Anthropology, University of Texas, Austin.
　1936　*Our Catholic Heritage in Texas, 1519–1936,* vol. 1: *The Mission Era: The Winning of Texas, 1693–1731.* Austin, Tex.: Von Boeckmann-Jones.
　1938　*Our Catholic Heritage in Texas, 1519–1936,* vol. 2: *The Missions at Work, 1731–1761.* Austin, Tex.: Von Boeckmann-Jones.
Comuzzie, Anthony G.
　1987　The Bioarchaeology of Blue Bayou: A Late Prehistoric Mortuary Site from Victoria County, Texas. Master's thesis, Department of Anthropology, Texas A&M University, College Station.
Comuzzie, Anthony G., Marianne Marek, and D. Gentry Steele
　1986　Analysis of Human Skeletal Remains from the Palm Harbor Site (41AS80), a Mortuary Site on the Central Gulf Coast of Texas. *Bulletin of the Texas Archaeological Society* 55:213–49.
Cook, Della C.
　1984　Subsistence and Health in the Lower Illinois Valley: Osteological Evidence. In *Paleopathology at the Origins of Agriculture,* edited by Mark Nathan Cohen and George J. Armelagos, 237–70. Orlando, Fla.: Academic Press.
Creel, Darrel G.
　1986　A Study of Prehistoric Burned Rock Middens in West-Central Texas. Ph.D. diss., Department of Anthropology, University of Arizona, Tucson.
Crosby, Alfred W., Jr.
　1972　*The Columbian Exchange: Biological and Cultural Consequences of 1492.* Westport, Conn.: Greenwood.

Cybulski, Jerome S.
    1974   Tooth Wear and Material Culture: Precontact Patterns in the Tsimshian Area, British Columbia. *Syesis* 7:31–35.

Davies, P. M.
    1963   Social Custom and Habits and Their Effect on Oral Disease. *Journal of Dental Research* 42:209–32.

Dobyns, Henry F.
    1992   Native American Trade Centers as Contagious Disease Foci. In *Disease and Demography in the Americas,* edited by John W. Verano and Douglas H. Ubelaker, 215–22. Washington, D.C.: Smithsonian Institution.

Ewers, John C.
    1973   The Influence of Epidemics on the Indian Populations and Cultures of Texas. *Plains Anthropologist* 18:104–15.

Finn, S. B., and R. B. Glass
    1975   Sugar and Dental Decay. *World Review of Nutritional Dietetics* 22:304–26.

Gilmore, Kathleen
    1969   The San Xavier Missions: A Study in Historical Site Identification. Report no. 16. Unpublished report on file, Texas State Building Commission.

Goodman, Alan H.
    1991   Health, Adaptation, and Maladaptation in Past Societies. In *Health and Past Societies: Biocultural Interpretations of Human Skeletal Remains in Archaeological Contexts,* edited by H. Bush and M. Zvelebil, 31–38. BAR International Series 567. Oxford: British Archaeological Reports.

Goodman, Alan H., George J. Armelagos, and Jerome C. Rose
    1980   Enamel Hypoplasias as Indicators of Stress in Three Prehistoric Populations from Illinois. *Human Biology* 52:515–28.

Goodman, Alan H., Debra L. Martin, George J. Armelagos, and George Clark
    1984   Indications of Stress from Bone and Teeth. In *Paleopathology at the Origins of Agriculture,* edited by Mark Nathan Cohen and George J. Armelagos, 13–49. Orlando, Fla.: Academic Press.

Hinton, R. J.
    1981   Form and Patterning of Anterior Tooth Wear among Aboriginal Human Groups. *American Journal of Physical Anthropology* 54:555–64.

Huebner, Jeffry A.
    1988   The Archaeology of Blue Bayou: A Late Prehistoric and Archaic Mortuary Site, Victoria County, Texas. Master's thesis, Department of Anthropology, University of Texas, San Antonio.

Huss-Ashmore, Rebecca, Alan H. Goodman, and George J. Armelagos
    1982   Nutritional Inference from Paleopathology. In *Advances in Archaeological Method and Theory,* vol. 5, edited by Michael B. Schiffer, 395–474. New York: Academic Press.

Jelks, E. B.
    1953   Excavations at the Blum Rockshelter. *Bulletin of the Texas Archaeological Society* 24:189–207.

Kent, Susan

    1986   The Influence of Sedentism and Aggregation on Porotic Hyperostosis and Anemia: A Case Study. *Man* 21:605–36.

    1992   Anemia Through the Ages: Changing Perspectives and Their Implications. In *Diet, Demography, and Disease: Changing Perspectives on Anemia,* edited by Patricia Stuart-Macadam and Susan Kent, 1–32. New York: Aldine de Gruyter.

Larsen, Clark Spencer

    1984   Health and Disease in Prehistoric Georgia: The Transition to Agriculture. In *Paleopathology at the Origins of Agriculture,* edited by Mark Nathan Cohen and George J. Armelagos, 367–92. Orlando, Fla.: Academic Press.

    1987a   Bioarchaeological Interpretations of Subsistence Economy and Behavior from Human Skeletal Remains. In *Advances in Archaeological Method and Theory,* vol. 10, edited by Michael B. Schiffer, 339–445. San Diego: Academic Press.

    1987b   Bioarchaeological Interpretation and Early Contact Populations on St. Catherines Island, Georgia. *American Journal of Physical Anthropology* 72:222.

    1990   Biocultural Interpretation and the Context for Contact. In *The Archaeology of Mission Santa Catalina de Guale: 2. Biocultural Interpretations of a Population in Transition,* edited by Clark Spencer Larsen, 11–24. Anthropology Papers 68. New York: American Museum of Natural History.

Larsen, Clark Spencer, and Rebecca Shavit

    1988   Dental Evidence for Change in Lifeway Quality: A Case Study from Spanish Florida. *American Journal of Physical Anthropology* 75:236.

Larsen, Clark Spencer, Rebecca Shavit, and Mark C. Griffin

    1991   Dental Caries Evidence for Dietary Change: An Archaeological Context. In *Advances in Dental Anthropology,* edited by Marc A. Kelley and Clark Spencer Larsen, 179–202. New York: Wiley-Liss.

Leigh, R. W.

    1925   Dental Pathology of Indian Tribes of Varied Environmental and Food Conditions. *American Journal of Physical Anthropology* 8:179–99.

Milner, George R.

    1984   Dental Caries in the Permanent Dentition of a Mississippian Period Population from the American Midwest. *Collections of Anthropology* 8:77–91.

Mokry, E. R., and W. S. Fitzpatrick

    1980   Notes on Preliminary Investigations of the Palm Harbor Site, 41AS80, Arkansas County, Texas. Unpublished manuscript on file, Texas Historical Commission, Austin.

Molnar, Stephen

    1968   Experimental Studies in Human Tooth Wear: II. *American Journal of Physical Anthropology* 28:361–68.

    1970   A Consideration of Some Cultural Factors Involved in the Production of Human Tooth Wear. *Stewart Anthropological Society Journal* 2:10–18.

    1971   Human Tooth Wear, Tooth Function, and Cultural Variability. *American Journal of Physical Anthropology* 34:175–89.

    1972   Tooth Wear and Culture: A Survey of Tooth Functions among Prehistoric Populations. *Current Anthropology* 13:511–26.

Neiburger, Ellis J.
  1988   Enamel Hypoplasia—A Poor Indicator of Nutritional Stress. Paper presented at the 57th Annual Meeting of the American Association of Physical Anthropologists, Kansas City, Missouri.

Newbrun, Ernest
  1982   Sugars and Dental Caries: A Review of Human Studies. *Science* 217:418–23.

Ofcarcek, R. P., and E. E. Burns
  1971   Chemical and Physical Properties of Selected Acorns. *Journal of Food Science* 36:576–78.

Ortner, Donald J.
  1991   Theoretical and Methodological Issues in Paleopathology. In *Human Paleopathology: Current Syntheses and Future Options*, edited by Donald J. Ortner and Arthur C. Aufderheide, 5–11. Washington, D.C.: Smithsonian Institution.

Ortner, Donald J., and Walter G. J. Putschar
  1981   *Identification of Pathological Conditions in Human Skeletal Remains.* Contributions to Anthropology no. 28. Washington, D.C.: Smithsonian Institution.

Patterson, David K., Jr.
  1984   *A Diachronic Study of Dental Paleopathology and Attritional Status of Prehistoric Ontario Pre-Iroquois and Iroquois Populations.* Archaeological Survey of Canada, Mercury Series 22. Ottawa: National Museum of Man.

Pindborg, L.
  1970   *Pathology of Dental Hard Tissues.* Philadelphia: W. B. Saunders.

Pollack, R. L., and E. Kravitz
  1985   *Nutrition in Oral Health and Disease.* Philadelphia: Lea and Febiger.

Powell, Mary Lucas
  1985   The Analysis of Dental Wear and Caries for Dietary Reconstruction. In *The Analysis of Prehistoric Diets*, edited by Robert I. Gilbert, Jr., and James H. Mielke, 307–38. Orlando, Fla.: Academic Press.

Reinhard, Karl J., Ben W. Olive, and D. Gentry Steele
  1989   Bioarchaeological Synthesis. In *From the Gulf to the Rio Grande: Human Adaptation in Central, South, and Lower Pecos, Texas*, edited by Robert I. Gilbert, Jr., and James H. Mielke, 307–38. Orlando, Fla.: Academic Press.

Rose, Jerome C., Keith W. Condon, and Alan H. Goodman
  1984   Diet and Dentition: Developmental Disturbances. In *The Analysis of Prehistoric Diets*, edited by Robert I. Gilbert, Jr., and James H. Mielke, 281–305. Orlando, Fla.: Academic Press.

Schmucker, B. J.
  1985   Dental Attrition: A Correlative Study of Dietary and Subsistence Patterns. In *Health and Disease in the Prehistoric Southwest*, edited by Charles F. Merbs and R. J. Miller, 275–323. Arizona State Anthropological Research Paper no. 34. Tempe: Arizona State University.

Schuetz, Mardith K.
  1968   The History and Archaeology of Mission San Juan Capistrano, San Antonio,

Texas. Report no. 10, vol. 1. Unpublished manuscript on file, Texas State Building Commission.

Shaw, J. H.
1952   Nutrition and Dental Caries. In *Survey of the Literature of Dental Caries,* edited by J. Elvehjem and T. King, 415–507. Washington, D.C.: National Academy of Science.

Sjöberg, A. F.
1951   The Bidai Indians of Southwestern Texas. *Southwestern Journal of Anthropology* 7:391–400.

Smith, B. G. N.
1975   Dental Erosion, Attrition, and Abrasion. *Dental Practitioner* 214:347–55.

Steele, D. Gentry
1986a   Analysis of Vertebrate Faunal Remains. In *The Clemente and Herminia Hinojosa Site, 41JW8: A Toyah Horizon Campsite in Southern Texas,* edited by S. L. Black, 108–36. Special Report no. 18. San Antonio: University of Texas Center for Archaeological Research.
1986b   Analysis of Vertebrate Faunal Remains from 41LK201, Live Oak County, Texas. In *Archaeological Investigations at 41LK201, Choke Canyon Reservoir, Southern Texas,* edited by C. L. Highley, 200–249. Choke Canyon Series, vol. 11. San Antonio: University of Texas Center for Archaeological Research.

Steele, D. Gentry, and C. A. Hunter
1986   Analysis of Vertebrate Faunal Remains from 41MC222 and 41MC296, McMullen County, Texas. In *The Prehistoric Sites at Choke Canyon Reservoir, Southern Texas: Results of Phase II Archaeological Investigations,* edited by G. D. Hall, T. R. Hester, and S. L. Black, 452–502. San Antonio: University of Texas, San Antonio.

Steele, D. Gentry, and E. R. Mokry
1985   Archaeological Investigations of Seven Prehistoric Sites along Oso Creek, Nueces County, Texas. *Bulletin of the Texas Archaeological Society* 54:287–308.

Steinbock, R. Ted.
1976   *Paleopathological Diagnosis and Interpretation.* Springfield, Ill.: Charles C. Thomas.

Stodder, Ann Lucy Wiener
1990   Paleoepidemiology of Eastern and Western Pueblo Communities in Protohistoric New Mexico. Ph.D. diss., Department of Anthropology, University of Colorado, Boulder. Ann Arbor, Mich.: University Microfilms.

Stodder, Ann L. W., and Debra L. Martin
1992   Health and Disease in the Southwest before and after Spanish Contact. In *Disease and Demography in the Americas,* edited by John W. Verano and Douglas H. Ubelaker, 55–74. Washington, D.C.: Smithsonian Institution.

Stuart-Macadam, Patricia
1987   Porotic Hyperostosis: New Evidence to Support the Anemia Theory. *American Journal of Physical Anthropology* 74:521–27.

1992   Anemia in Past Human Populations. In *Diet, Demography, and Disease: Changing Perspectives on Anemia,* edited by Patricia Stuart-Macadam and Susan Kent, 151–72. New York: Aldine de Gruyter.

Suhm, D. A.
1955   Excavations at the Collins Site, Travis County, Texas. *Bulletin of the Texas Archaeological Society* 26:7–54.

Taylor, R. M. S.
1963   Cause and Effect of Wear on Teeth. *Acta Anatomica* 53:97–157.

Thomas, David Hurst, ed.
1989   *Columbian Consequences,* vol. 1: *Archaeological and Historical Perspectives on the Spanish Borderlands West.* Washington, D.C.: Smithsonian Institution.
1990   *Columbian Consequences,* vol. 2: *Archaeological and Historical Perspectives on the Spanish Borderlands East.* Washington, D.C.: Smithsonian Institution.
1991   *Columbian Consequences,* vol. 3: *The Spanish Borderlands in Pan-American Perspective.* Washington, D.C.: Smithsonian Institution.

Turner, Christy G., II
1979   Dental Anthropological Indications of Agriculture among the Jomon People of Central Japan. *American Journal of Physical Anthropology* 51:619–36.

Turpin, S. A.
1985   *Seminole Sink: Excavation of a Vertical Shaft Tomb, Val Verde County, Texas.* Texas Archaeological Survey Research Report no. 93. Austin: University of Texas.

Van Blerkom, L. M.
1985   The Evolution of Human Infectious Disease in the Eastern and Western Hemispheres. Ph.D. diss., Department of Anthropology, University of Colorado, Boulder.

Verano, John W., and Douglas H. Ubelaker, eds.
1992   *Disease and Demography in the Americas.* Washington, D.C.: Smithsonian Institution.

Walker, Phillip L., Patricia Lambert, and Michael J. DeNiro
1989   The Effects of European Contact on the Health of Alta California Indians. In *Columbian Consequences,* vol. 1: *Archaeological and Historical Perspectives on the Spanish Borderlands West,* edited by David Hurst Thomas, 349–64. Washington, D.C.: Smithsonian Institution.

Wells, Calvin
1975   Prehistoric and Historic Changes in Nutritional Diseases and Associated Conditions. *Progressive Food and Nutrition Science* 1:729–79.

Wood, James W., George R. Milner, Henry C. Harpending, and Kenneth M. Weiss
1992   The Osteological Paradox: Problems of Inferring Prehistoric Health from Skeletal Samples. *Current Anthropology* 33:343–70.

Chapter 7

Paleoepidemiology of Eastern and Western Pueblo Communities in Protohistoric and Early Historic New Mexico

ANN L. W. STODDER

THE EARLY CONTACT PERIOD IN NEW MEXICO

The intent of this chapter is to examine evidence for health and disease in the Pueblo populations at the time of Spanish contact in northern New Mexico. Results of analysis of skeletal assemblages from two protohistoric villages—San Cristobal, a Tano site in the Galisteo Basin on the eastern fringe of Pueblo territory, and Hawikku, a Zuni site in western New Mexico—are summarized and compared to paleoepidemiological data on prehistoric Pueblos. The contrasting patterns of prehistoric and protohistoric health are interpreted in the context of changing Pueblo adaptations at the end of the prehistoric and during the early Spanish Colonial period, circa 1500–1700.

Contact between Europeans and the Pueblo natives of New Mexico began in 1539 with Marcos de Niza's trip to Zuni. Coronado and his army followed in 1540, and subsequent entradas took place in the 1580s and in 1590–91 (table 7.1). The initial encounters were not friendly; the natives were forced to provision the Spaniards and several pueblos were destroyed by Coronado's party (Hammond and Rey 1940). The chroniclers of these expeditions remarked on the apparent abundance of crops and game, the large size and defensive nature of Pueblo towns, and the robust health of their inhabitants (Hammond and Rey 1940, 1966).

The economic prospects of New Mexico proved a disappointment, but not the potential harvest of souls. In 1598, a small settlement was established on the upper Rio Grande, and the efforts of colonization and conversion began in earnest. The Pueblo Revolt of 1680 temporarily banished the Europeans, but reconquest and recolonization were complete by 1700.

The initial decades of the colony were a time of drought and famine for natives and colonists alike but, by the 1630s, Spanish transportation routes

Table 7.1. Events in sixteenth- and seventeenth-century New Mexico

		Drought	Famine
1512	Cortés landing in Mexico		
	Smallpox pandemic?		
1539	De Niza entrada		
1540	Coronado entrada		
1580-81	Chamuscado, Espejo entradas	x	
1590	Castano de Sosa entrada	x	
1598	Spanish colony founded	x	x
1610	Santa Fe founded	x	x
1612-17	Pecos, Galisteo Basin missions		x
1629-30	Gran Quivira, Zuni missions	x	x
	First recorded epidemics	x	x
1672	Gran Quivira abandoned	x	x
1680	Pueblo Revolt		x
	Reconquest battles		x
1700	Recolonization		

Sources: Dobyns 1983; Espinosa 1988; Hackett 1937; Hammond and Rey 1953, 1966; Hayes 1981; Hodge 1937; Kidder 1924; Scholes 1929, 1935, 1937; Schroeder 1968, 1972, 1984.

from Mexico were improved and a gradual infusion of colonists and mission-aries provided reinforcements (Dozier 1961; Forrestal 1954; Hodge et al. 1945). Franciscans directed the converted Indians in the construction of some 25 churches by 1640. Traditional religious practices were forbidden; kivas were burned. Religious and political factionalism grew within and between Pueb-los. Lands were granted to Spanish ranchers under the Crown's *encomienda* (royal land grant) system, and tribute in the form of labor, corn, buffalo hides, and other products was collected from every Pueblo household within reach (Scholes 1935). Natives supported the colony and the missions.

Trade arrangements between the Eastern Pueblos (northern Rio Grande area) and neighboring Plains peoples were disrupted by Spanish interference, and Plains-Pueblo relations became increasingly hostile (Spielmann 1989). Spielmann (1989) estimates that as much as 20 percent of the dietary protein of eastern frontier Pueblos, like Gran Quivira and Pecos, was provided by meat obtained through trade prior to contact. Due to the Spanish demand for non-subsistence products, however, the focus of trade and, consequently, the qual-ity of diet may have shifted.

A series of localized droughts in the seventeenth century culminated in regional drought and famine in the 1670s (table 7.1). Agriculturalists in the

Southwest were frequently subject to fluctuations in precipitation patterns and temperature regime (Dean et al. 1985; Euler et al. 1979). Demographic flexibility and the maintenance of stored food surplus constituted crucial adaptive mechanisms. Supporting the Spanish colony and missions with labor and products during this drought period could have undermined the Pueblos' ability to maintain the surplus that provided the critical buffer in a marginal environment. Rather than benefiting from new tools, crops, and beasts of burden imported by the Spaniards, it is more likely that the disruption of trade and labor scheduling resulted in food shortages, especially in the northern Rio Grande Valley.

POPULATION DECLINE AND OLD WORLD DISEASE IN THE NORTHERN SOUTHWEST

The majority of church and civil records from the early years of the New Mexico colony were destroyed in the Pueblo Revolt of 1680 and in a later flood (Espinosa 1988; Schroeder 1972). The surviving records do not tell us when Old World diseases first entered the northern area of the Southwest.

The earliest recorded epidemic in New Mexico, believed to have been smallpox (Cook 1946; Forrestal 1954) or scarlet fever (Dobyns 1988), took place in the 1630s—well after initial contact. Dobyns (1966, 1983, 1988) proposes that at least two waves of epidemic disease reached the Pueblo people prior to direct contact between Pueblos and Europeans, and that several more swept through during the early 1600s. Records from the Jesuit missions of northern and northwestern Mexico in the 1600s indicate that smallpox, measles, typhus, and other diseases spread ahead of the mission frontier, sometimes completely depopulating villages of the Tepehuan, Opata, Tarahumara, Yaqui, and other tribes (Reff 1985, 1987, 1992).

Prior to direct Spanish-Pueblo contact, or during the period of intermittent contact between Pueblos and the various exploratory parties, epidemics of Old World disease are hypothesized to have spread northward along trade networks that extended from central Mexico to the Zuni pueblos in the west and Pecos in the east (Dobyns 1992; Upham 1986, 1992; Upham and Reed 1989). According to this scenario the large, prosperous, and healthy Pueblo settlements described in the early Spanish chronicles are presumed to be only remnants of those that existed prior to the European presence in the New World.

Demographic disruptions and depopulation took place throughout the 1600s and continued after the revolt and recolonization (Bancroft 1889; Forrestal 1954; Kessell 1979; Palkovich 1985; Wilcox 1981). Migrations and settlement shifts occurred on local and regional scales (Schroeder 1972, 1979). Schroeder (1972) estimates that as many as half of the Rio Grande pueblos were abandoned by 1640, and many more settlements, including San Cristobal and

Hawikku, were abandoned after the 1680 Pueblo Revolt (Espinosa 1988; Ferguson 1981; Mera 1940). Multiple skirmishes and battles in the late 1600s finally led to the reconquest of the northern Rio Grande Valley and the re-settlement of the colony. In the manner typical of Spanish colonial reduction policy, the Pueblo population was aggregated into fewer, more isolated settle-ments (Wilcox 1981). Multiple epidemics are recorded for the eighteenth cen-tury, beginning with smallpox at Nambe in 1719 and including major out-breaks of measles in 1728–29 and smallpox in 1733–34 and 1781 (Chavez 1957; Simmons 1966; Stodder 1990).

Disease, famine, warfare, and migration all contributed to decline in the native population. Both the timing and extent of pre- and postcontact popula-tion reduction are subjects of controversy that must be resolved through addi-tional controlled field study of regional and community population dynamics starting at the intrasite level.

Based on a review of ethnohistoric accounts and population estimates us-ing a constant percentage of occupied rooms per site and number of persons per room, Upham (1992, 229–30) estimates the A.D. 1500 population of the Rio Grande Valley Pueblos at 131,750, and the Zuni Pueblos at 24,662. Creamer's (1990, 1992) ongoing study of multicomponent sites, however, con-firms that not all room blocks were occupied in the fifteenth and sixteenth centuries. This study suggests smaller momentary population estimates than those based on total site area.

The rate of population decline was clearly rapid after contact and coloniza-tion, but the timing is uncertain. Upham (1992, 233) estimates a 50 percent reduction in Pueblo populations between 1500 and 1600, due to (undocu-mented) epidemics. Ubelaker (1988, 292) estimates the steepest population decline, about 35 percent, between 1600 and 1700. Pueblo population size reached its nadir of 12,000 to 13,000 in about 1750 (Simmons 1979).

Paleoepidemiology of the Protohistoric Pueblos: Background

The health impact of economic and demographic disruption, and of conflict with Europeans, non-Pueblo native groups, and among Pueblos, is reflected in the data from protohistoric skeletal assemblages. Paleoepidemiological data from sites occupied during the 1300s through the late protohistoric and early contact periods (circa 1680) are available for Gran Quivira, Pecos, and San Cristobal in the east, and the Zuni village of Hawikku in the west (figure 7.1). Pecos Pueblo was occupied until 1838 (Kidder 1924). Hawikku and San Cristobal were abandoned at about the time of the Pueblo Revolt (Nelson 1914; Smith et al. 1966), and Gran Quivira was abandoned shortly before the revolt in 1672 (Hayes 1981).

Some of the data on skeletal remains from Gran Quivira (Swanson 1976;

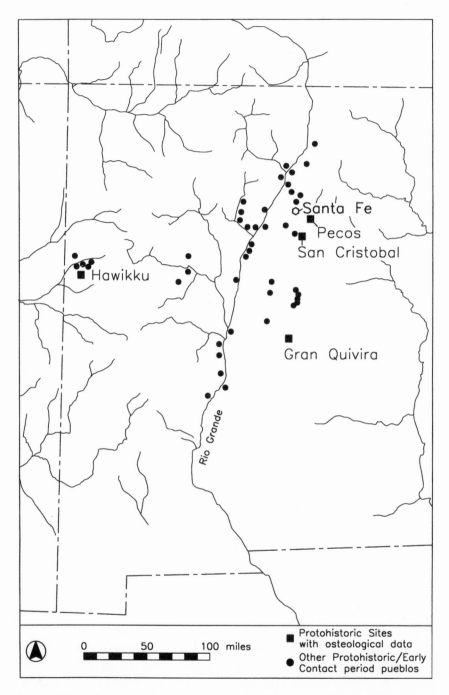

Figure 7.1. Protohistoric and early contact period pueblos in New Mexico (adapted from Hammond and Rey 1953).

Turner 1981) and Pecos (Hooton 1930) distinguish between pre- and postcontact components in the burial assemblages and allow us to examine diachronic changes in samples of datable individuals from these sites. San Cristobal and Hawikku were excavated early in this century, and neither project resulted in a comprehensive publication (cf. Nelson 1914; Smith et al. 1966). Hodge and his coworkers recorded 679 burials and 317 cremations during their 1930s excavation of Hawikku (Smith et al. 1966), with a total of 261 burials collected. Of these, 70 individuals can be dated on the basis of artifactual or architectural associations, and an additional 51 on the basis of mortuary patterns. Of the datable individuals studied, 71 percent date to the post-1475 component of the site (Stodder 1990).

Excavation at San Cristobal by Nelson (1914, 1916) and Sullivan (unpublished field notes) recorded 492 burials, of which 277 were collected. Of the collected burials, 185 (67 percent) can be confidently assigned to pre- or postcontact periods based on site unit and stratigraphic provenience data in field notes, and on Nelson's brief reports (1914, 1916). These assemblages can reasonably be considered to represent samples of the populations residing at these sites after 1475 to about 1680. Of the analyzed burials that can be dated based on artifact association or architectural context, 86 percent of those from Hawikku and 72 percent from San Cristobal date to A.D. 1475 or later (Stodder 1990).

Comparisons of paleoepidemiological data from protohistoric Pueblos with data from prehistoric (Anasazi) skeletal assemblages suggest that some aspects of health changed significantly over time (Stodder and Martin 1992). In addition, the rates and age-specific patterns of certain skeletal stress indicators differ significantly between the protohistoric assemblages from San Cristobal and Hawikku. The health differences between contemporaneous peoples in the Eastern Pueblos (represented by San Cristobal, Gran Quivira, and Pecos) and Western Pueblos (represented by Hawikku) further underscore the need for detailed, multidisciplinary study of the varied experiences of native peoples in the late prehistoric and early contact eras in the New World.

As discussed by Palkovich (chapter 8 below), it is crucial that we attend to the archaeological and biological contexts of skeletal data. To evaluate the biological impact of European contact on native populations in the Southwest, we must understand both the similarities and differences between prehistoric and protohistoric health and demography. Long-term continuity is evident in many aspects of Pueblo subsistence and settlement but, in terms of disease loads suggested by skeletal pathology, the protohistoric populations are more similar epidemiologically to large, sedentary, Midwestern populations than they are to earlier Southwestern populations (Stodder 1990). Just as the ethnographic present is not the proper model for reconstructing the organization of precontact Pueblos (Wilcox and Masse 1981), our investigation and gradual understanding of the impact of European contact must derive from the protohistoric and not the prehistoric context.

PALEOEPIDEMIOLOGY OF THE PROTOHISTORIC PUEBLOS: DATA

Several categories of data are presented here in order to examine similarities and differences in health patterns suggested by Southwestern skeletal samples: dental pathology, developmental arrest, evidence for iron deficiency anemia, skeletal infection, and traumatic injury. Much of the prevalence data cited here came from multiple sources as a way of discerning general trends in health status. In future studies the trends identified here need to be tested using data from archaeological sites with better chronological control.

Dental Pathology

The prevalence of dental caries (percentage of adults with one or more carious teeth) reported in the literature on prehistoric Southwestern skeletal assemblages ranges from 9 percent to 15 percent in Basketmaker (A.D. 400–700) and early Pueblo (A.D. 700–1100) populations (Berry 1983) to as much as 85 percent involvement in later Pueblo (A.D. 1100–1300) adults from Chaco Canyon (Akins 1986). The average rate of caries reported for 11 prehistoric site assemblages is about 34 percent (Stodder and Martin 1992). As shown in table 7.2, protohistoric (A.D. 1300–1600) populations exhibit uniformly high caries rates: between 53 percent and 85 percent of adults in these skeletal samples exhibit carious teeth. The caries rate is a broad indicator of dental health and the data here do not control for age differences in the samples. Young adults in a high attrition environment have higher caries rates than older adults in whom occlusal wear obliterates enamel (Stodder 1987).

The rate of dental abscessing ranges from 44 percent to 58 percent in adults from protohistoric populations, a substantial increase over prehistoric skeletal series, which average about 28 percent abscess involvement (Stodder and Martin 1992). The slight increase in caries rates in the post- versus precontact Gran Quivira components and in caries and abscess rates in Pecos adults suggests a higher carbohydrate (and presumably lower meat) component in Eastern Pueblo diets after contact. Faunal remains from Gran Quivira also support a shift in the pattern of resource exploitation after European contact. Fewer bison were consumed, while the consumption of locally available large game did not increase concomitantly (Spielmann 1989). Further study of age-controlled skeletal samples is needed to assess possible differences in dental health among these populations, and to investigate their meaning with respect to dietary differences at specific localities.

Table 7.2. Prevalence of caries and abscesses in adults from protohistoric and historic Pueblo skeletal samples

Locality	Date/stage	Caries		Abscesses	
		n	%	n	%
San Cristobal	PIV-1680	136	57	136	46
Hawikku	PIV-1680	98	53	95	58
Gran Quivira	1315-1550	51	69		
	1550-1672	41	85		
	1315-1672	92	81	111	66
Pecos	1300-1550	126	48	126	41
	1550-1600	59	61	68	44
	1600-1800	68	43	68	46

Note: PIV = Pueblo IV, A.D. 1300-1600.

Sources: San Cristobal, Hawikku: Stodder 1990; Gran Quivira: Swanson 1976; Pecos: Hooton 1930.

Developmental Arrest

The frequency and age patterns of developmental arrest and recovery during childhood at Hawikku and San Cristobal are documented in the dentition by enamel hypoplasias and in the skeleton by transverse radiopaque lines (Harris Lines). The presence of hypoplasias—pits or grooves on the surface of the dental enamel (figure 7.2)—were recorded in the permanent and deciduous incisors and the permanent canines of 111 individuals from Hawikku and in 146 individuals from San Cristobal. The presence and location of transverse radiopaque lines were observed in anterior-posterior x-rays of the distal growth portion of the tibiae of 38 children and young adults (ranging in age from 6 months to 22 years) from Hawikku and in 42 individuals from San Cristobal. The methods used to estimate the etiological age of hypoplasias and transverse lines—the age at which the markers of developmental arrest were formed—roughly follow the methods of Goodman et al. (1980) and Hummert and Van Gerven (1985), and are described elsewhere (Stodder 1990).

Dental Enamel Hypoplasia. Prehistoric Anasazi from Black Mesa (Martin et al. 1991) and the Mesa Verde region (Stodder 1987) exhibit typical peaks in enamel hypoplasia formation at 2.5 to 3 years in the incisors and 4 to 4.5 years in canines (table 7.3). At Hawikku and San Cristobal distinctive peaks of hypoplasia formation occurred during infancy. Later weaning and longer birth intervals in protohistoric populations are suggested by the 3- to 3.5-year peak in hypoplasia formation. A later, post-weaning peak in developmental arrest is indicated for children from Hawikku at age 4.5 to 5 years. Hypoplasias indi-

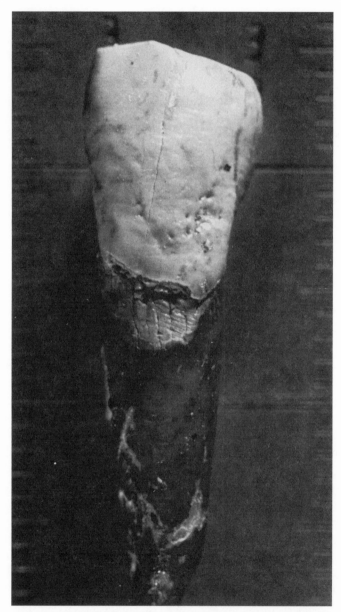

Figure 7.2. Dental enamel hypoplasia in an Anasazi individual from Two Raven House, Mesa Verde National Park (site 5MV1645).

Table 7.3. Peak ages of enamel hypoplasia formation in permanent incisors and canines in four Southwestern skeletal assemblages

Age	B	1	2	3	4	5	6
Black Mesa (n = 55)				xxxx	xxxx		
Mesa Verde Region (n = 168)				xxxx	xxxx		
San Cristobal (n = 146)		xxxx		xxxx	xxxx		
Hawikku (n = 115)		xxxx		xxxx	xxxx		

Sources: Black Mesa: Martin et al. 1991; Mesa Verde Region: Stodder 1987; San Cristobal and Hawikku: Stodder 1990.

cating prenatal or neonatal developmental arrest are present in 6 of the 20 Hawikku infants with well-preserved deciduous incisors and in 1 of 33 San Cristobal infants.

Individuals from Hawikku exhibit significantly more hypoplasias than those from San Cristobal in terms of the number of defects per individual ($p<0.001$, Student's t-test), and the proportion of the sample exhibiting defects in the deciduous ($p>0.02$, chi-square test) and permanent ($p<0.05$, chi-square test) anterior dentition (Stodder 1990).

Transverse Radiopaque Lines. More frequent developmental arrest in Hawikku children during the prenatal and infancy periods is also suggested by the appearance of growth arrest lines in radiographs of distal tibiae. Two percent of the x-rayed sample from San Cristobal and 18 percent of the Hawikku sample exhibit lines formed prenatally ($p<0.05$, chi-square test). The mean number of lines per individual does not differ in the two site samples, but the age distribution of lines does differ.

Peak ages of line formation in the San Cristobal sample occur at infancy, weaning, and adolescence. These are ages of rapid growth at which there is high susceptibility to growth arrest through a variety of physiological and psychological insults. Other studies of Southwestern skeletal samples report peak line formation at ages 2 to 4 years (Hinkes 1983; Stodder 1987; Woodall 1968). Hawikku children also experienced growth arrest and recovery at these developmental stages, but they exhibit peaks in line formation at ages 7 and 10. These lines may reflect spurts of catch-up growth at ages when the frequency of skeletal infection declines substantially in Hawikku subadults. A cultural explanation is also possible. Zuni boys are initiated into the Kachina Society through a two-stage process at ages 5 to 9 and 10 to 14 (Tedlock 1979). A similar practice at protohistoric Hawikku of imposing two discrete periods of acute stress might contribute to the unusual pattern in the Hawikku sample.

Difficulty in interpreting patterns in growth arrest line formation and their apparent lack of correspondence to other indicators of skeletal stress have long been observed (e.g., Goodman et al. 1984; Magennis 1989). In the protohistoric pueblos the greater frequency of lines in the Hawikku sample may be interpreted as evidence of more growth arrest and relatively poorer health than the San Cristobal sample. This interpretation is in agreement with the higher rates of hypoplasias and of subadult skeletal infections in the Hawikku sample. Alternatively, the greater frequency of lines could suggest better health among the Hawikku children indicated by more frequent recovery from growth arrest incidents and more growth spurts than the San Cristobal children. However, there is no significant difference in the adult stature of males or females from San Cristobal and Hawikku.

Anemia

Two types of cranial lesions are indicative of iron deficiency anemia in skeletal assemblages from the Southwest. Porotic hyperostosis (figure 7.3) is characterized by porosity on the external surface of the frontal, parietal, and occipital regions of the cranium, and cribra orbitalia (figure 7.4) by pitting in the roofs of the eye orbits (Carlson et al. 1974; Steinbock 1976). These lesions are formed when the diploe of the cranium is expanded due to proliferation of bone marrow in anemia. In extreme cases the outer table of the bone is destroyed, leaving the spongy, trabecular bone exposed. Although commonly recorded separately, the orbital and postorbital lesions are believed to have the same etiology (Lallo et al. 1977; Mensforth et al. 1978; Stuart-Macadam 1987a, 1987b). In the present study they are considered together under the general term porotic hyperostosis.

The etiology of iron deficiency anemia in prehistoric Southwestern populations is most often related to the low available iron component in corn (El-Najjar 1976; El-Najjar et al. 1975; El-Najjar et al. 1976), the dietary staple. However, the rate of porotic hyperostosis in an assemblage does not serve as a simple index of corn consumption or of agricultural intensity. Several other factors are recognized in the etiology of anemia. The specific technique used in corn processing may enhance or reduce the availability of iron, zinc, and other nutrients (Calloway et al. 1974; Katz et al. 1974; Stodder 1987; Walker 1985). Hygiene, population density, and house type, as well as the use of reservoirs for domestic water storage and the presence of domesticated dogs and turkeys in human settlements, all probably influenced the levels of endemic infection, parasitism, and anemia in prehistoric Pueblo communities (Kunitz and Euler 1972; Reinhard 1988). The anemia that resulted in porotic hyperostosis may not have had the same underlying etiology in all communities. Etiological factors in anemia differ between age groups as well (Palkovich 1987; Stodder 1988, 1990).

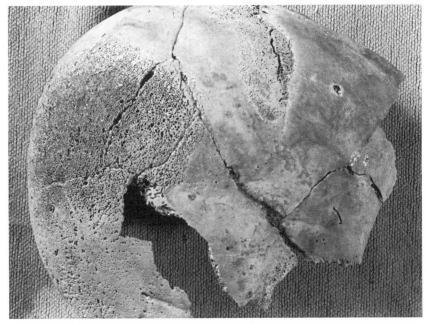

Figure 7.3. Porotic hyperostosis on the left parietal of an Anasazi infant from Mug House, Mesa Verde National Park (site 5MV1229).

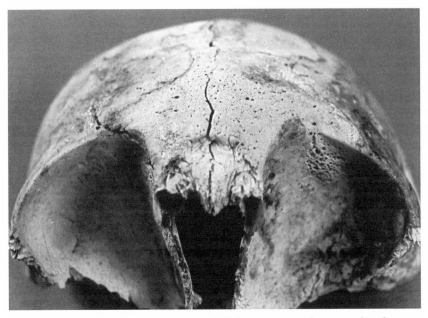

Figure 7.4. Cribra orbitalia in an Anasazi child from Mesa Verde National Park.

High frequencies of porotic hyperostosis are commonly observed in sub-adults from Southwestern skeletal assemblages. Rates reported for children 0 to 10 years old from prehistoric sites range from low prevalences—15 percent at Grasshopper Pueblo (n = 367; Hinkes 1983), 22 percent at Arroyo Hondo (n = 54; Palkovich 1987), and 18 percent at Gran Quivira (El-Najjar et al. 1975)—to near ubiquity—75 percent at Canyon de Chelly (n = 65; El-Najjar, Lozoff, et al. 1975), 85 percent at Black Mesa (n = 55; Martin et al. 1991), and 87 percent in the Mesa Verde area (n = 80; Stodder 1987). At 87 percent and 74 percent, the San Cristobal and Hawikku children have high rates of ane-mia, but not the highest reported.

Peak ages of unremodeled porotic hyperostosis differ among subadults from different skeletal samples. The highest frequency of unremodeled lesions—77 percent in the San Cristobal sample (n = 66) and 89 percent in the Hawikku sample (n = 40)—occurs in 1-to-3-year-olds, the typical age of greatest iron deficiency anemia in childhood (Dallman et al. 1980). Porotic hyperostosis co-occurs with skeletal infection in 9 percent of San Cristobal subadults and in 33 percent of Hawikku subadults, suggesting a different balance among etiologi-cal factors, including differences in diet and infectious disease, underlying ane-mia in subadults from these two communities.

Skeletal Infection

Rates of infection (excluding dental infections) reported in prehistoric South-western skeletal samples range from 2 percent to 23 percent (table 7.4). Hawikku has the highest rate of infection at 36 percent. When infections secondary to traumatic injury are excluded, the rate is 31 percent for the Hawikku sample and 21 percent for San Cristobal. Tuberculosis and treponemal infection, both endemic in the prehistoric Southwest (Baker and Armelagos 1988; El-Najjar 1979; Merbs 1989; Merbs and Miller 1985), appear to have been present in the Hawikku and San Cristobal populations in addition to nonspecific conditions like periostitis (figure 7.5).

Five adults and possibly as many as three children from San Cristobal, and one adult and possibly one child from Hawikku had tuberculosis (figures 7.6, 7.7, and 7.8). All of the adult tuberculosis cases at San Cristobal were recov-ered from a single site unit, Midden E. This midden was one of seven extra-mural burial areas at the site (Nelson 1914). The subadult cases are from the adjacent midden, Midden D (figure 7.9). Both middens date from the later component of the site. The apparent spatial and temporal clustering of the tuberculosis cases suggests the possibility of an epidemic wave of tuberculosis during the later stages of the site's occupation.

A significantly greater prevalence of infection, characterized predominantly by osteolytic or destructive (rather than osteoblastic or proliferative) lesions

Table 7.4. Frequencies of skeletal infections reported in Southwestern skeletal samples

Locality	n	Date/stage	%	Source
Navajo Reservoir	82	BMIII-PII	2	Berry 1983
Dolores	64	BMIII-PII	11	Stodder 1987
Black Mesa	173	PI-PII	23	Martin et al. 1991
Chaco Canyon	135	PI-PIII	17	Akins 1986
Salmon Ruin	97	PII	6	Berry 1983
Grasshopper	442	1275-1400	12	Berry 1983
Point of Pines	117	1000-1450	13	Berry 1983
Paa'ko	57	PIII-PIV	4	Ferguson 1980
Arroyo Hondo	101	PIV	13	Palkovich 1980
San Cristobal	210	PIV-H	23	Stodder 1990
Hawikku	142	PIV-H	36	Stodder 1990

Stages: Basketmaker III: A.D. 400-700; Pueblo I: 700-900; Pueblo II: 900-1100; Pueblo III: 1100-1300; Pueblo IV: 1300-1600; Historic: 1540-.

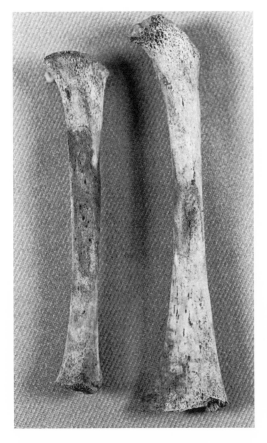

Figure 7.5. Periostitis in the long bones of a 1- to 2-year-old child from Hawikku (USNM 314,341).

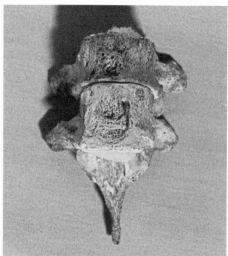

Left: Figure 7.6. Tuberculous lesions in the thoracic vertebrae of a young adult female, approximate age 19–22 years, from Hawikku (USNM 308,636).

Below: Figure 7.7. Psoas abscess on the right hip bone, tuberculosis (USNM 308,636).

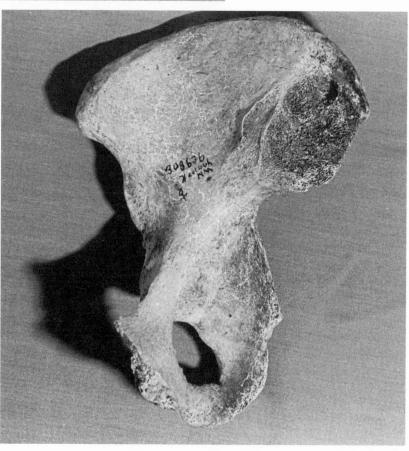

Figure 7.8. Rib lesions, tuberculosis (USNM 308,636).

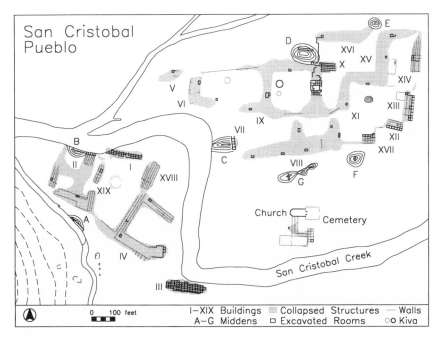

Figure 7.9. San Cristobal pueblo (adapted from Nelson 1914).

typical of tuberculosis and other mycobacterial diseases, occurs in the San
Cristobal burials compared to those from Hawikku (table 7.5). Estimates of
the percentage of all tuberculosis cases represented by those cases displaying
skeletal involvement range from 1 percent (Daniel 1981) to 7 percent (El-Najjar
1979), but generally range between 5 percent and 7 percent (Steinbock 1976).
Counting only the five adult cases and using a fairly conservative estimate
that these represent 5 percent of the tuberculosis cases in the community, as
many as 100 individuals—about 8 percent of the estimated (momentary) population of the historic portion of San Cristobal (1,310 individuals)—could have
had tuberculosis (Stodder 1990).

Tuberculosis has been observed in skeletal remains of at least 11 individuals from prehistoric sites in the Southwest (El-Najjar 1979; Merbs 1989; Stodder
1990) and in individuals from Gran Quivira (Coyne 1981) and Pecos Pueblo
(Hooton 1930) as well. Tuberculosis is a highly communicable, opportunistic
disease able to persist in small populations. Its frequency rapidly increases in
times of warfare, famine, and population displacement (Youmans 1979, 358)
and it is a frequent sequel to epidemics of smallpox and other diseases (Mercer
1986). The frequency of tuberculosis may have increased substantially during
the repeated droughts, famines, and migrations of the early contact period
(see table 7.1).

The overall rate of skeletal infection (table 7.5) is significantly ($p < 0.001$,
chi-square test) higher, by 29 percent, in Hawikku than in San Cristobal children. Infection is most common in the first year of life at Hawikku, affecting
75 percent of individuals who died before 1 year of age. In the San Cristobal
sample those aged 2 to 5 years have the highest frequency of infection (36
percent). Infants from both sites exhibit widespread infection. After infancy,
however, infections in the San Cristobal sample are primarily localized (except disseminated lesions in adults with tuberculosis), while Hawikku children and adults maintain a high rate of systemic infection (table 7.5). The
tibia is the most commonly affected bone in both samples, but infection involving the radius and ulna are more common in San Cristobal subadults while
the tibia, humerus and femur are the predominant sites of infection at Hawikku
(Stodder 1990).

While the rates of infection in subadults and adults from San Cristobal are
essentially equal, infection is 25 percent more frequent in subadults than in
adults from Hawikku ($p < 0.01$, chi-square). Rates of infection among adults
from the two sites are also very similar (table 7.5). Systemic periostitis—in-
flammation of skeletal elements in more than one body segment (lower limb,
upper limb, axial skeleton)—affects 15 percent of the Hawikku sample and
accounts for 40 percent of the skeletal infections. Only 3 percent of the individuals from San Cristobal exhibit systemic periostitis (table 7.5). This con-

Table 7.5. Skeletal infection in the Hawikku and San Cristobal skeletal samples

PREVALENCE OF INFECTION:

		San Cristobal			Hawikku	
	n	no. infected	% infected	n	no. infected	% infected
Subadults	67	15	22	57	29	51
Adults	143	33	23	85	22	26
Total	210	48	23	142	51	36

TYPE AND FREQUENCY OF INFECTION:[a]

	San Cristobal		Hawikku	
	% of infection (n = 55)	% of sample (n = 210)	% of infection (n = 55)	% of sample (n = 143)
Local periostitis	42	11	44	17
Systemic periostitis	11	3	40	15
Treponematosis	5	1	5	4
Local osteolytic	20	5	4	3
Tuberculosis	15	4	4	1
Osteomyelitis	4	1	2	1

[a]Local infections are defined here as those evident in one body segment; systemic infections affect skeletal elements in more than one segment.

trasts to the greater frequency of osteolytic skeletal lesions and of recognizable tuberculosis cases in the San Cristobal sample.

Both the age distribution and nature of skeletal infections appear to differ fundamentally in the skeletal samples from these sites. The contrasting patterns of skeletal infection in the two communities suggest that infectious disease at Hawikku, although more prevalent, was less likely to cause mortality after infancy. An endemic treponemal syndrome like that identified in the Moundville (Powell 1988) and Hardin village (Cassidy 1972) populations in the eastern United States might account for this pattern at Hawikku. Three adults from Hawikku exhibit chronic bilateral infection and remodeling of the tibiae with deformation of the shafts. Moodie (1923, plates 88, 89, 93–95) identified two adults from San Cristobal as exhibiting syphilitic osteitis in the long bones. A third adult appears to display treponemal infection in the long bones (Stodder 1990). No cranial vault or facial lesions characteristic of treponematosis were observed in either skeletal assemblage. None of the cases fits Hackett's (1976) "diagnostic criteria" for treponemal infections and can only be placed in his category of "diagnostic criteria on trial."

While both tuberculosis and treponematosis appear to have been present in the San Cristobal and Hawikku populations, the overall patterns of skeletal infection and lesion types suggest that tuberculosis may have been more common at San Cristobal, and the possible treponemal condition more prevalent at Hawikku. Regardless of the specific kinds of disease present in these assemblages, it is important to recognize that the health status among these presumably contemporaneous and culturally quite similar communities does not appear to have been uniform. This observation suggests that we should be wary of interpretations of the early contact period that posit the same endemic health context and responses to contact in all New World populations, or even those within a culture area.

Cranial Trauma

The rates of cranial trauma (table 7.6) are significantly higher in the Hawikku, San Cristobal, and postcontact (1550–1600 and 1600–1800) Pecos adults than in prehistoric skeletal assemblages (only the rates at Hawikku and Paa'ko do not differ significantly according to chi-square tests). Cranial trauma rates are even higher in adult males—20 percent at San Cristobal and 17.5 percent at Hawikku. Cranial trauma in the Pecos series increased significantly after 1550—from 3 percent to 16 percent.

These data probably include some accidental injury, but they clearly reflect the prevalence of violence and warfare in the later prehistoric and protohistoric Pueblos. Archaeological data suggest the presence of considerable warfare in the northern Rio Grande Valley prior to contact (Haas and Creamer 1990; Nelson 1914; Schaafsma 1990). Ethnohistoric records describe multiple battles and smaller-scale confrontations between Pueblos and Spaniards before the 1680 Pueblo Revolt, and evidence of inter-Pueblo conflict both before and after the revolt. The Spanish presence exacerbated existing conflicts within and between Pueblos, and between Pueblos and non-Pueblo native peoples.

CONCLUSION

Paleoepidemiological data from protohistoric Pueblo skeletal assemblages indicate that rates of infectious disease, developmental arrest, and traumatic injury increased during this era of demographic, economic, and social disruption. Life tables for Hawikku (n = 821) and San Cristobal (n = 492) suggest relatively low life expectancy—19 years at San Cristobal and 17 years at Hawikku (Stodder 1990).

Higher relative fertility in the protohistoric versus prehistoric Pueblo populations is suggested by D30+/D5+ ratios that are 0.3303 and 0.4455 for San Cristobal and Hawikku respectively, compared to 0.5362 for Arroyo Hondo, 0.5555 for Point of Pines, and 0.5687 for the Black Mesa skeletal sample

Table 7.6. Rates of cranial trauma reported in adults from Southwestern skeletal assemblages

Locality	n	Stage/date	Cranial trauma %	Reference
Chaco Canyon	85	PI-II	1	Akins 1986
Paa'ko	57	PIII-IV	3	Ferguson 1980
Arroyo Hondo	47	PIV	0	Palkovich 1980
Tijeras	64	PIV	2	Ferguson 1980
Cochiti	122	PIV	2	Heglar 1974
Hawikku	93	PIV-H	12	Stodder 1990
San Cristobal	131	PIV-H	15	Stodder 1990
Pecos	204	1425-1550	3	Hooton 1930
Pecos	93	1550-1600	8	Hooton 1930
Pecos	88	1600-1800	16	Hooton 1930

Stages: Pueblo I: A.D. 700–900; Pueblo II: 900–1100; Pueblo III: 1100–1300; Pueblo IV: 1300–1600; Historic: 1540–.

(Stodder 1990). A decrease in the ratio of the number of individuals who died after age 30 to those who died after age 5 indicates an increase in birth rate (Buikstra et al. 1986; Larsen et al. 1990). Juvenile mortality, however, also appears to have been higher and birth intervals longer at San Cristobal and Hawikku (Stodder 1990), offsetting the apparent increase in fertility in these populations.

Tuberculosis and treponematosis, endemic in the prehistoric Southwest, may have increased in prevalence and severity in communities with compromised host resistance, particularly during periods of drought and famine when the problems of poor agricultural productivity were exacerbated by the tribute and labor demands of the Spaniards. Eastern Pueblos like San Cristobal, Gran Quivira, and Pecos, closer to the center of Spanish activity, may have suffered more nutritional stress due to food shortages, as well as conflict with Spaniards and hostile non-Pueblo peoples.

While it is clear that native population declined dramatically after contact, the questions of precontact epidemics and population decline remain to be addressed with systematic archaeological data for the Pueblo region. The number of postcontact occupied settlements continued to decline after contact, but ethnohistoric census figures from certain pueblos have been interpreted as indicating stabilization of population size in the late 1600s (Kessell 1979; Wilson 1985; Zubrow 1974). This pattern suggests that simultaneous processes of site abandonment, migration, and the maintenance of localized populations through aggregation at certain settlements all occurred within the general trend of regional population decline. The careful assessment of the growth and decline of specific settlements and settlement clusters is crucial for our understanding of population dynamics and also for the interpretation of paleode-mographic data from skeletal remains.

Mortuary data from contact-period sites also require systematic study. Changes in the use of cremation at Gran Quivira and at Hawikku have been interpreted as evidence of in-migration (Hayes 1981) and long-distance trade influence (Smith et al. 1966). Cremation as a disease-oriented method of dis-posal has not been seriously considered. Inhumation in trash middens is com-mon throughout Southwestern prehistory and is the dominant method of inhumation at many protohistoric- and contact-period sites. Mass or multiple burials that could be attributed to pre- or postcontact epidemics have not yet been identified, but the differential age distributions of burial assemblages from the middens at San Cristobal (Stodder 1990) and the concentration of tuberculosis cases in Midden E suggest that middens or cemetery deposits should be approached with the possibility of corporate interment in mind.

The clarification of pre- versus postcontact components of settlements and of skeletal populations is needed to further define the bioarchaeological and demographic parameters of the protohistoric Pueblos. Linking these data with the sparse documentation from the early contact period and later census and historical epidemiology records will provide a long-term picture of population dynamics and native health in the northern Southwest.

Acknowledgments

Research on human remains from San Cristobal and Hawikku was supported by a Richard H. Lounsbury Fellowship for Predoctoral Research at the Ameri-can Museum of Natural History, by the University of Colorado Graduate Foun-dation, and by Sigma Xi.

References

Akins, Nancy J.
    1986   A Biocultural Approach to Human Burials from Chaco Canyon, New Mexico. Reports of the Chaco Center no. 9. Santa Fe, N.M.: National Park Service.
Baker, Brenda J., and George J. Armelagos
    1988   The Origin and Antiquity of Syphilis. Current Anthropology 29:703–37.
Bancroft, Hubert H.
    1889   History of Arizona and New Mexico. San Francisco: History Company.

Berry, David R.
    1983   Disease and Climatological Relationship among Pueblo III–Pueblo IV Anasazi
            of the Colorado Plateau. Ph.D. diss., University of California, Los Angeles.
Buikstra, Jane E., Lyle W. Konigsberg, and Jill Bullington
    1986   Fertility and the Development of Agriculture in the Prehistoric Midwest.
            American Antiquity 51:528–46.
Calloway, Doris H., R. D. Giauque, and F. M. Costa
    1974   The Superior Mineral Content of Some American Indian Foods in Compari-
            son with Federally Donated Counterpart Commodities. *Ecology of Food and
            Nutrition* 3:203–11.
Carlson, David S., George J. Armelagos, and Dennis P. Van Gerven
    1974   Factors Affecting the Etiology of Cribra Orbitalia in Prehistoric Nubia. *Jour-
            nal of Human Evolution* 3:405–10.
Cassidy, Claire M.
    1972   A Comparison of Nutrition and Health in Pre-Agricultural and Agricultural
            Amerindian Skeletal Populations. Ph.D. diss., University of Wisconsin. Ann
            Arbor, Mich.: University Microfilms.
Chavez, Fray Angelico
    1957   *Archives of the Archdiocese of Santa Fe.* Publications of the Academy of Ameri-
            can Franciscan History, Bibliographic Series, vol. 8. Washington, D.C.: Acad-
            emy of American Franciscan History.
Cook, Sherburne F.
    1946   The Incidence and Significance of Disease among the Aztecs and Related Tribes.
            Hispanic American Historical Review 26:213–38.
Coyne, Sheila A.
    1981   Variations and Pathologies in the Vertebral Columns of Gran Quivirans. In
            Contributions to Gran Quivira Archeology, edited by Alden C. Hayes, 151–
            55. Publications in Archeology no. 17. Washington, D.C.: National Park Ser-
            vice.
Creamer, Winifred
    1990   The Study of Prehistoric Demography in the Northern Rio Grande Valley,
            A.D. 1450–1680. Paper presented at the 59th Annual Meeting of the American
            Association of Physical Anthropologists, Miami.
    1992   Developing Complexity in the American Southwest: A Model for the Rio
            Grande Valley. Paper presented at the 57th Annual Meeting of the Society for
            American Archaeology, Pittsburgh.
Dallman, Peter R., Martti A. Siimes, and Abraham Stekel
    1980   Iron Deficiency Anemia in Infancy and Childhood. *American Journal of Clini-
            cal Nutrition* 33:86–118.
Daniel, Thomas M.
    1981   An Immunochemist's View of the Epidemiology of Tuberculosis. In *Prehis-
            toric Tuberculosis in the Americas,* edited by Jane E. Buikstra, 35–48. Scien-

tific Papers no. 5. Evanston, Ill.: Northwestern University Archeological Program.

Dean, Jeffrey S., Robert C. Euler, George J. Gumerman, Fred Plog, Richard H. Hevly, and Thor N. V. Karlstrom
    1985   Human Behavior, Demography, and Paleoenvironment on the Colorado Plateaus. *American Antiquity* 50:537–54.

Dobyns, Henry F.
    1966   Estimating Aboriginal American Population 1: An Appraisal of Techniques with a New Hemispheric Estimate. *Current Anthropology* 7:395–416.
    1983   *Their Number Become Thinned: Native American Population Dynamics in Eastern North America.* Knoxville: University of Tennessee Press.
    1988   Discussant. The Southwest Symposium. Arizona State University, Tempe.
    1992   Native American Trade Centers as Contagious Disease Foci. In *Disease and Demography in the Americas,* edited by John W. Verano and Douglas H. Ubelaker, 215–22. Washington, D.C.: Smithsonian Institution.

Dozier, Edward P.
    1961   Rio Grande Pueblos. In *Perspectives in Native American Indian Culture Change,* edited by Edward H. Spicer, 94–186. Chicago: University of Chicago Press.

El-Najjar, Mahmoud Y.
    1976   Maize, Malaria, and the Anemias in the Pre-Columbian New World. *Yearbook of Physical Anthropology* 20:329–37.
    1979   Human Treponematosis and Tuberculosis: Evidence from the New World. *American Journal of Physical Anthropology* 51:599–618.

El-Najjar, Mahmoud Y., Betsy Lozoff, and Dennis J. Ryan
    1975   The Paleoepidemiology of Porotic Hyperostosis in the American Southwest: Radiological and Ecological Considerations. *American Journal of Roentgenology, Radium Therapy and Nuclear Medicine* 125:918–24.

El-Najjar, Mahmoud Y., Dennis J. Ryan, Christy G. Turner, II, and Betsy Lozoff
    1976   The Etiology of Porotic Hyperostosis among the Prehistoric and Historic Anasazi Indians of the Southwestern United States. *American Journal of Physical Anthropology* 44:477–88.

Espinosa, J. Manuel
    1988   *The Pueblo Revolt of 1696.* Norman: University of Oklahoma Press.

Euler, Robert C., George J. Gumerman, Thor N. V. Karlstrom, Jeffrey S. Dean, and Richard H. Hevly
    1979   The Colorado Plateaus: Cultural Dynamics and Paleoenvironment. *Science* 205:1089–1101.

Ferguson, Cheryl
    1980   Analysis of Skeletal Remains. In *Tijeras Canyon: Analyses of the Past,* edited by Linda S. Cordell, 121–48. Albuquerque: University of New Mexico Press.

Ferguson, T. J.

1981   The Emergence of Modern Zuni Culture and Society: A Summary of Zuni Tribal History, A.D. 1450–1700. In *The Protohistoric Period in the North American Southwest, A.D. 1450–1700*, edited by David R. Wilcox and W. Bruce Masse, 336–53. Anthropological Research Paper no. 24. Tempe: Arizona State University.

Forrestal, P.

1954   *Benavides' Memorial of 1630*. Washington, D.C.: Academy of American Franciscan History.

Goodman, Alan H., George J. Armelagos, and Jerome C. Rose

1980   Enamel Hypoplasias as Indicators of Stress in Three Prehistoric Populations from Illinois. *Human Biology* 52:515–28.

1984   The Chronological Distribution of Enamel Hypoplasias from Prehistoric Dickson Mounds Populations. *American Journal of Physical Anthropology* 65:259–66.

Haas, Jonathan, and Winifred Creamer

1990   The Irritating Role of Warfare in the Pueblo III Period. Paper presented at the Conference on Pueblo Cultures in Transition: A.D. 1150–1350 in the American Southwest, Crow Canyon Archeological Center, Cortez, Colorado.

Hackett, C. J.

1976   *Diagnostic Criteria of Syphilis, Yaws and Treponarid (Treponematoses) and of Some Other Diseases in Dry Bones*. Berlin: Springer-Verlag.

Hackett, Charles W.

1937   *Historical Documents Relating to New Mexico, Nueva Vizcaya, and Approaches Thereto, to 1773*, vol. 3. Washington, D.C.: Carnegie Institute.

Hammond, George P., and Agapito Rey

1940   *Narratives of the Coronado Expedition, 1540–1542*. Coronado Historical Series, vol. 1. Albuquerque: University of New Mexico Press.

1953   *Don Juan de Oñate, Colonizer of New Mexico*. Albuquerque: University of New Mexico Press.

1966   *The Rediscovery of New Mexico, 1580–1594*. Albuquerque: University of New Mexico Press.

Hayes, Alden C., ed.

1981   *Contributions to Gran Quivira Archeology*. Publications in Archeology no. 17. Washington, D.C.: National Park Service.

Heglar, Roger

1974   The Prehistoric Population of Cochiti Pueblo and Selected Interpopulation Biological Comparisons. Ph.D diss., University of Michigan.

Hinkes, Madeline J.

1983   Skeletal Evidence of Stress in Subadults: Trying to Come of Age at Grasshopper Pueblo. Ph.D. diss., University of Arizona. Ann Arbor, Mich.: University Microfilms.

Hodge, Frederick W.
    1937   *History of Hawikuh.* Los Angeles: Southwest Museum.
Hodge, Frederick W., George P. Hammond, and Agapito Rey
    1945   *Fray Alonso Benavides' Revised Memorial of 1634.* Albuquerque: University of New Mexico Press.
Hooton, Earnest A.
    1930   *The Indians of Pecos Pueblo.* New Haven, Conn.: Yale University Press.
Hummert, James R., and Dennis P. Van Gerven
    1985   Observations on the Formation and Persistence of Radiopaque Transverse Lines. *American Journal of Physical Anthropology* 66:297–306.
Katz, S. H., M. L. Hediger, and L. A. Valleroy
    1974   Traditional Maize Processing Techniques in the New World. *Science* 184:765–73.
Kessell, John L.
    1979   *Kiva, Cross, and Crown.* Washington, D.C.: National Park Service.
Kidder, Alfred V.
    1924   *An Introduction to the Study of Southwestern Archaeology.* New Haven, Conn.: Yale University Press.
Kunitz, Stanley J., and Robert C. Euler
    1972   *Aspects of Southwestern Paleoepidemiology.* Anthropological Research Reports no. 2. Prescott, Ariz.: Prescott College Press.
Lallo, John W., George J. Armelagos, and Robert P. Mensforth
    1977   The Role of Diet, Disease, and Physiology in the Origin of Porotic Hyperostosis. *Human Biology* 49:471–83.
Larsen, Clark Spencer, Margaret J. Schoeninger, Dale L. Hutchinson, Katherine F. Russell, and Christopher B. Ruff
    1990   Beyond Demographic Collapse: Biological Adaptation and Change in Native Populations of La Florida. In *Columbian Consequences,* vol. 2: *Archaeological and Historical Perspectives on the Spanish Borderlands East,* edited by David Hurst Thomas, 409–28. Washington, D.C.: Smithsonian Institution.
Magennis, Ann L.
    1989   Growth and Transverse Line Formation in Contemporary Children. *American Journal of Physical Anthropology* 78:266.
Martin, Debra L., Alan H. Goodman, George J. Armelagos, and Ann L. Magennis
    1991   *Black Mesa Anasazi Health: Reconstructing Life from Patterns of Death and Disease.* Occasional Paper no. 14. Carbondale: Center for Archaeological Investigations, Southern Illinois University.
Mensforth, Robert P., C. Owen Lovejoy, John W. Lallo, and George J. Armelagos
    1978   The Role of Constitutional Factors, Diet and Infectious Disease in the Etiology of Porotic Hyperostosis and Periosteal Reactions in Prehistoric Infants and Children. *Medical Anthropology* 2:1–59.
Mera, Harry P.
    1940   *Population Changes in the Rio Grande Glaze-Paint Area.* Technical Series Bulletin no. 9. Santa Fe, N.M.: Laboratory of Anthropology.

Merbs, Charles F.
    1989   Patterns of Health and Sickness in the Precontact Southwest. In *Columbian Consequences,* vol. 1: *Archaeological and Historical Perspectives on the Spanish Borderlands West,* edited by David Hurst Thomas, 41–55. Washington, D.C.: Smithsonian Institution.
Merbs, Charles F., and Robert J. Miller, eds.
    1985   *Health and Disease in the Prehistoric Southwest.* Anthropological Research Paper no. 34. Tempe: Arizona State University.
Mercer, A. J.
    1986   Relative Trends in Mortality from Related Respiratory and Airborne Infectious Diseases. *Population Studies* 40:129–45.
Moodie, Roy L.
    1923   *Paleopathology: An Introduction to the Study of Ancient Evidences of Disease.* Urbana: University of Illinois Press.
Nelson, Nels C.
    1914   *Pueblo Ruins of the Galisteo Basin, New Mexico.* Anthropological Papers 15(1). New York: American Museum of Natural History.
    1916   Chronology of the Tano Ruins, New Mexico. *American Anthropologist* 18:159–80.
Palkovich, Ann M.
    1980   *Pueblo Population and Society: The Arroyo Hondo Skeletal and Mortuary Remains.* Santa Fe, N.M.: School of American Research Press.
    1985   Historic Population of the Eastern Pueblos: 1540–1910. *Journal of Anthropological Research* 41:401–26.
    1987   Endemic Disease Patterns in Paleopathology: Porotic Hyperostosis. *American Journal of Physical Anthropology* 74:527–38.
Powell, Mary Lucas
    1988   *Status and Health in Prehistory: A Case Study of the Moundville Population.* Washington, D.C.: Smithsonian Institution.
Reff, Daniel T.
    1985   The Demographic and Cultural Consequences of Old World Disease in the Greater Southwest, 1520–1660. Ph.D. diss., University of Oklahoma. Ann Arbor, Mich.: University Microfilms.
    1987   The Introduction of Smallpox in the Greater Southwest. *American Anthropologist* 89:704–8.
    1992   Contact Shock in Northwestern New Spain, 1518–1764. In *Disease and Demography in the Americas,* edited by John W. Verano and Douglas H. Ubelaker, 265–76. Washington, D.C.: Smithsonian Institution.
Reinhard, Karl J.
    1988   Cultural Ecology of Prehistoric Parasitism on the Colorado Plateau as Evidenced by Coprology. *American Journal of Physical Anthropology* 77:355–66.
Schaafsma, Polly
    1990   War Imagery and Magic: Petroglyphs at Comanche Gap, Galisteo Basin, New

Mexico. Paper presented at the 55th Annual Meeting of the Society for American Archaeology, Las Vegas.

Scholes, France V.

1929   Documents for the History of the New Mexico Missions in the Seventeenth Century. *New Mexico Historical Review* 4:45–58.

1935   Civil Government and Society in New Mexico in the Seventeenth Century. *New Mexico Historical Review* 10:71–111.

1937   *Church and State in New Mexico, 1610–1650.* Historical Society of New Mexico Publications in History, vol. 11. Albuquerque: University of New Mexico Press.

Schroeder, Albert H.

1968   Shifting for Survival in the Spanish Southwest. *New Mexico Historical Review* 43:291–310.

1972   Rio Grande Ethnohistory. In *New Perspectives on the Pueblos*, edited by Alfonso Ortiz, 42–70. Albuquerque: University of New Mexico Press.

1979   Pueblos Abandoned in Historic Times. In *Southwest*, edited by Alfonso Ortiz, 236–54. *Handbook of North American Indians*, vol. 9, William C. Sturtevant, general editor. Washington, D.C.: Smithsonian Institution.

1984   The Protohistoric and Pitfalls of Archaeological Interpretation. *Papers of the Archaeological Society of New Mexico* 9:133–39.

Simmons, Marc

1966   New Mexico's Smallpox Epidemic of 1780–1781. *New Mexico Historical Review* 41:319–24.

1979   History of Pueblo-Spanish Relations to 1821. In *Southwest*, edited by Alfonso Ortiz, 178–93. *Handbook of North American Indians*, vol. 9, William C. Sturtevant, general editor. Washington, D.C.: Smithsonian Institution.

Smith, Watson, Richard B. Woodbury, and Nathalie F. S. Woodbury, eds.

1966   *The Excavation of Hawikuh by Frederick Webb Hodge. Report of the Hendricks-Hodge Expedition.* Contributions of the Museum of the American Indian, Heye Foundation, vol. 20. New York: Museum of the American Indian.

Spielmann, Katherine A.

1989   Colonists, Hunters, and Farmers: Plains-Pueblo Interaction in the Seventeenth Century. In *Columbian Consequences*, vol. 1: *Archaeological and Historical Perspectives on the Spanish Borderlands West*, edited by David Hurst Thomas, 101–13. Washington, D.C.: Smithsonian Institution.

Steinbock, R. Ted

1976   *Paleopathological Diagnosis and Interpretation.* Springfield, Ill.: Charles C. Thomas.

Stodder, Ann Lucy Wiener

1987   The Physical Anthropology and Mortuary Practice of the Dolores Anasazi: An Early Pueblo Population in Local and Regional Perspective. In *Dolores Archaeological Program Supporting Studies: Settlement and Environment,* compiled by Kenneth Lee Petersen and Janet D. Orcutt, 309–504. Denver: U.S. Bureau of Reclamation Engineering and Research Center.

1988   The Status of Bioarchaeological Research in the American Southwest. Paper presented at the 53rd Annual Meeting of the Society for American Archaeology, Phoenix.

1990   Paleoepidemiology of Eastern and Western Pueblo Communities in Protohistoric New Mexico. Ph.D. diss., Department of Anthropology, University of Colorado, Boulder.

Stodder, Ann L. W., and Debra L. Martin

1992   Native Health and Disease in the Southwest before and after Spanish Contact. In *Disease and Demography in the Americas,* edited by John W. Verano and Douglas H. Ubelaker, 55–74. Washington, D.C.: Smithsonian Institution.

Stuart-Macadam, Patricia

1987a   A Radiographic Study of Porotic Hyperostosis. *American Journal of Physical Anthropology* 74:511–20.

1987b   Porotic Hyperostosis: New Evidence to Support the Anemia Theory. *American Journal of Physical Anthropology* 74:521–26.

Swanson, Cheryl E.

1976   Dental Pathologies in the Gran Quivira Population. Master's thesis, Arizona State University, Tempe.

Tedlock, Dennis

1979   Zuni Religion and World View. In *Southwest,* edited by Alfonso Ortiz, 499–508. *Handbook of North American Indians,* vol. 9, William C. Sturtevant, general editor. Washington, D.C.: Smithsonian Institution.

Turner, Christy G., II

1981   The Arizona State University Study of Gran Quiviran Physical Anthropology. In *Contributions to Gran Quivira Archeology,* edited by Alden C. Hayes, 119–21. Publications in Archeology no. 17. Washington, D.C.: National Park Service.

Ubelaker, Douglas H.

1988   North American Indian Population Size, A.D. 1500 to 1985. *American Journal of Physical Anthropology* 77:289–94.

Upham, Steadman

1986   Smallpox and Climate in the American Southwest. *American Anthropologist* 88:115–28.

1992   Population and Spanish Contact in the American Southwest. In *Disease and Demography in the Americas,* edited by John W. Verano and Douglas H. Ubelaker, 223–36. Washington, D.C.: Smithsonian Institution.

Upham, Steadman, and Lori Stephens Reed

1989   Regional Systems in the Central and Northern Southwest: Demography, Economy, and Sociopolitics Preceding Contact. In *Columbian Consequences,* vol. 1: *Archaeological and Historical Perspectives on the Spanish Borderlands West,* edited by David Hurst Thomas, 57–76. Washington, D.C.: Smithsonian Institution.

Walker, Phillip L.

1985   Anemia among Prehistoric Indians of the American Southwest. In *Health and Disease in the Prehistoric Southwest,* edited by Charles F. Merbs and Robert J. Miller, 139–64. Anthropological Research Paper no. 34. Tempe: Arizona State University.

Wilcox, David R.

1981   Changing Perspectives on the Protohistoric Pueblos, A.D. 1450–1700. In *The Protohistoric Period in the North American Southwest, A.D. 1450–1700,* edited by David R. Wilcox and W. Bruce Masse, 378–409. Anthropological Research Paper no. 24. Tempe: Arizona State University.

Wilcox, David R., and W. Bruce Masse

1981   A History of Protohistoric Studies in the North American Southwest. In *The Protohistoric Period in the North American Southwest, A.D. 1450–1700,* edited by David R. Wilcox and W. Bruce Masse, 1–27. Anthropological Research Paper no. 24. Tempe: Arizona State University.

Wilson, John P.

1985   Before and after the Pueblo Revolt: Population Trends, Apache Relations and Pueblo Abandonments in Seventeenth Century New Mexico. *Papers of the Archaeological Society of New Mexico* 11:113–20.

Woodall, J. Ned

1968   Growth Arrest Lines in Long Bones of the Casa Grande Population. *Plains Anthropologist* 13:152–66.

Youmans, Guy P.

1979   *Tuberculosis.* Philadelphia: W. B. Saunders.

Zubrow, Ezra B.

1974   *Population, Contact and Climate in the New Mexican Pueblos.* Anthropological Papers no. 24. Tucson: University of Arizona Press.

PART THREE

Theoretical Perspectives and Prospects

The previous chapters discuss case studies from specific regions in the Spanish Borderlands. This last section of the volume, in contrast, is devoted to theoretical issues and prospects for future bioarchaeological research concerning depopulation after European contact.

Several authors in the preceding chapters (e.g., Kealhofer chapter 4; Miller chapter 6; Stodder chapter 7) note the difficulties in comparing biological and cultural data derived from sites excavated with disparate methods or research goals. In chapter 8, Ann Palkovich confronts this problem directly. Using examples from the American Southwest, she argues that direct comparisons of demographic characteristics and skeletal indicators of stress between assemblages mask specific contexts of localized population dynamics and biological responses to stress. This position seemingly questions the validity of conclusions drawn from the type of skeletal samples and data sets presented in previous chapters. Palkovich's approach is contrary to studies of depopulation that deduce broad conclusions or generalizations from direct comparisons of specific data sets.

How, then, can we evaluate the impact of European contact on Native American populations? Palkovich calls for "context-embedded analyses" in which careful consideration is given to the biocultural context of cemetery data and the specific biological context of skeletal responses to disease and nutritional stress. Her challenge is not unheeded by contributors to this volume, who take care to assess biases in their samples and ground their evaluations in local cultural and biological contexts.

Milner's summary (chapter 9) of current problems and prospects for contact-era research indicates just how much has been learned in the last decade. Research in the Spanish Borderlands has contributed substantially to our understanding of heterogeneity in social organization, population distribution, and the cultural and biological responses to contact and colonization in the New World. From this deeper appreciation new questions arise that prompt ongoing reevaluations of our method and theory. Kealhofer and Baker (chapter 10) stress the importance of questioning our methods and assumptions about depopulation and demographic collapse.

The chapters in this volume clearly indicate that demographic change and biological response were not uniform, but resulted from a complex interplay of multiple variables—only one of which was introduced disease.

Chapter 8

Historic Depopulation
in the American Southwest

Issues of Interpretation and Context-Embedded Analyses

Ann M. Palkovich

Prehistoric Amerindian groups are a study of contrasts. Agriculturally based village life for these groups was as varied as the environmental conditions and cultural diversity documented for the protohistoric period. Biocultural change was affected directly by the nature and extent of such diversity; and diversity is grounded in the contexts in which particular groups exist, persist, and change. The search for widely applicable explanations of biocultural change among protohistoric Amerindians clearly must find a way to preserve the significance and integrity of the prehistoric biocultural diversity. An understanding of the disease impact of European contact on the structure of indigenous North American populations, therefore, must be cast as a context-embedded analysis—defined broadly as a myriad of grounded contexts (both archaeological and historical) that are applicable to each group.

Several reexaminations of the processes of depopulation in North America (Dobyns, 1966, 1983; Kintigh 1988; Palkovich 1994; Ramenofsky 1987; Reff 1985, 1991; Thomas 1989; Upham 1986, 1992; Verano and Ubelaker 1992) support the view that epidemics of introduced diseases initially were a sixteenth-century phenomenon. These studies suggest that historical accounts of Amerindian groups record populations already ravaged by novel pathogens and experiencing catastrophic cultural and social disruptions prior to direct contact. These investigations raise a central issue: How and why did certain groups (and not others) persist despite the potentially devastating demographic and epidemiologic effects of novel diseases? Ramenofsky (1987) and others (e.g., Upham 1986, 1992) challenge us to address the general issue of disease processes among highly diverse cultural groups occupying broadly differing environmental settings.

Demographic Reconstructions and
Context-Embedded Analyses

The depopulation of North America is one of several issues for which archaeology provides the primary source of answers. Archaeological studies of protohistoric demography are ambitious and potentially provide significant insights into the nature of rapid biocultural change. Such archaeological studies also lead to the persistent, nagging problem: At what are we really looking?

Broadly based observations and conclusions have been proposed to describe and explain the factors that underlie biocultural processes (e.g., Cohen 1989). These explanations depend on human remains recovered archaeologically to reconstruct, directly and indirectly, demographic and epidemiologic change. While such generalized conclusions provide a rough approximation of the scale and scope of the problem being observed, Ramenofsky, Upham, and others correctly suggest that variations among populations tend to get masked in the broad sweep of data. Direct regional comparisons of demographic characteristics (as reconstructed from age profiles of cemeteries) and epidemiologic impact (as reconstructed from incidence of skeletal pathology) are not appropriate levels of analysis (contra Cohen 1989, 120). Such analyses overlook crucial data characteristics that are necessarily grounded in specific contexts, such as regional population dynamics and underlying biological synergisms. Patterns of skeletal lesions do not directly measure or reflect the characteristics and trends of disease impact for each group or region. Cemetery-specific age profiles do not directly measure or reflect generalizable mortality trends. Thus, epidemiologic and demographic models that attempt to describe catastrophic demographic collapse do not directly correlate with the archaeological data available for Amerindian populations.

Context is the key to interpreting both the broad and the specific patterns reflected in these data. It is essential to consider carefully both the wider biocultural context of these once-living populations (and its implications for epidemiology) and the specific biological context of the various indicators of disease, that is, pathogen-specific patterns of skeletal lesions and generalized osseous responses to disease stress.

Context-embedded analyses of regionally based data provide a useful means of evaluating various patterns of demographic impact during the contact and postcontact periods in North America. A context-embedded analysis allows us to interpret a set of data and draw general inferences from it by first basing the data set in its specific context. In many respects this approach is antithetical to some previous interpretations of the depopulation of North America in which broad conclusions were derived from direct comparisons among specific data sets. It has been long recognized, however, that "inferences to the best explanation" depend on the relevant contexts from which a particular data set is derived (Kelley and Hanen 1988).

In experimental research (such as experiments conducted by biologists or psychologists), contexts are controlled by creating particular conditions and assumptions under which an experiment is run. With identical contexts (or as identical as can be achieved experimentally), the criteria of reproducible conditions are met and, thus, direct comparisons of data sets are accommodated. In the world of quasi-experimental research and inductive-abductive inference, which we face with archaeological data, identical contexts and controlled conditions do not exist. What appear to be identical data sets (e.g., similar frequencies of skeletal pathology or similar mortality rates), in fact, may represent vastly different processes or underlying conditions if the contexts are unknown or unspecified. The evaluation of data sets within specific, appropriate contexts, therefore, becomes a central element of interpreting archaeologically derived data about depopulation.

For archaeological data, "context" encompasses three elements. First, the specific historical context must be specified, including not only the historical particulars of a group but also environmental and social factors. Information on settlement patterns, population distribution and density, subsistence patterns, and environmental variation is essential to estimating the population and the social context of these behaviors. In order to estimate and differentiate the nature and extent of processes of demographic collapse versus depopulation, such demographic preconditions—the situation prior to contact—must be estimated. In addition, estimates of overall health-disease patterns before contact must then be considered against this general context.

Second, the context of the archaeological series must be considered. Many researchers interested in the problem of Native American depopulation note that the available archaeological data were collected over the past 70 years to address research problems other than those related to rapid population changes. It is essential to keep in mind that what we can say about a particular data set is shaped in very distinct ways by what data were available, what data were actually obtained, and how these data were collected. This is of particular importance when considering the archaeological data available for prehistoric, protohistoric, and historic Amerindian groups. While, in many cases, the late prehistoric context of population density and distribution may be estimated reasonably with the available data, drastic changes in population size and distribution have not been considered specifically for the relatively short span of several hundred years from the fifteenth to the eighteenth century. What kinds of data are actually available and what they reflect as a reliable and valid sample from which to infer depopulation processes must be considered carefully. For example, it is necessary to establish the extent to which any given skeletal sample is a valid, reliable cross section of the interments at the site from which they were recovered. Questions such as how the skeletal sample was collected, the possibility of infant-juvenile underenumeration, and temporal or social-status bias in the recovered sample must all be considered before comparisons can be made.

Analyses of compromised collections often reflect our sole or largest skeletal assemblage for some prehistoric groups. Far from completely ignoring these data, it is possible to adapt the grounded methods of naturalistic inquiry (Lincoln and Guba 1985). Most useful are suggestions that the most credible explanations be sought for the existing data. While the data lack empirical integrity, making direct comparisons to other populations (termed "transferability") difficult to justify, it may be possible to demonstrate patterned coherence within the data set, given explicitly defined constraints. This, then, provides some focal points of patterned comparisons in a general sense (e.g., see Hinkes 1983).

Finally, the biological context of the available data must be considered. Some researchers propose that direct comparisons of data sets (such as incidence of particular types of skeletal pathology) can be made between regions and world areas in order to infer general conclusions about disease processes (see Cohen 1989). In this respect, skeletal series are treated as experimental or clinical data sets in which contexts are closely controlled. Data sets, therefore, are assumed to be comparable. In such nonexperimental situations, however, comparability of data sets cannot be assumed. Even experimental biological and medical researchers have long questioned the assumed homogeneity of biological responses and assumed general patterns of human response to disease (e.g., Woodhead et al. 1988).

The incidence pattern of observed skeletal pathology does not afford a direct means of comparing different populations. Responses to stress significantly vary among different demographic, dietary, and health conditions. Also, within a population, individuals are not equally susceptible to diseases. Factors such as age, previous immunological insults, chronic disease states, and nutritional status render some individuals at risk; that is, more likely to experience morbidity and/or mortality from a given pathogen. In addition, thresholds of response in the skeletal system to pathogens and other stressors have not yet been studied in any detail. Given equivalent exposures to a particular disease, greatly differing skeletal responses may occur among individuals. Within a population, primary and secondary responses to pathogens may also be evident.

Analysis of lesions for each skeletal sample thus requires a detailed evaluation of the incidence patterns of each pathology. For example, primary response to tuberculosis in a previously unexposed population will likely result in high initial mortality from the disease and a very low secondary disease response that appears skeletally. A previously exposed population will incur fewer initial deaths due to some acquired immunity in the group and will show a much higher incidence of secondary skeletal lesions. In this case the skeletal lesion pattern is the same, but the underlying epidemiological insult is vastly different (Palkovich 1981).

Acknowledging that simple comparisons of lesion incidence among skeletal samples are insufficient to interpret the biocultural consequences of Native American depopulation draws us into another, deeper problem: understanding the physiological basis of skeletal pathology itself. Investigating the underlying epidemiological context of observable skeletal lesions, both disease-specific and generalized skeletal responses to stress, represents the most significant development in paleopathological studies in the past decade. Some paleopathologists are now mastering the intricacies of bone biochemistry and physiology as they relate to normal growth, development, and aging, as well as the nature, formation, and patterning of osseous lesions (e.g., Baker 1992).

For example, Stuart-Macadam (1985, 1987a, 1987b) examined the patterning of porotic lesions in documented, living individuals. While most of our earlier notions of the significance of these lesions have been confirmed, important details of the associations among porotic lesions at different anatomical sites are finally being established (also see Hill and Armelagos 1990). It is now possible to demonstrate physiologically which lesion patterns among different skeletal samples are epidemiologically comparable, thus providing a truer picture of similar patterns of biological stress in different groups.

Our understanding of another long-established skeletal measure of biological stress, Harris lines—transverse radiopacities thought to indicate incidents of growth arrest and resumption—recently has been challenged. Harris lines have become a standard means of establishing the extent and patterning of a group's underlying biological stress. Magennis (1990) demonstrates that Harris line formation is a localized tissue phenomenon related to growth. Using documented, longitudinal data from living subjects, she provides the first clear evidence that line formation is as frequent and random in healthy individuals as in those experiencing some sort of biological, physiological, or psychological stress. Therefore, the utility of Harris lines as a nonspecific indicator of stress in undocumented samples must be reassessed.

The issues raised here that are relevant to examinations of biocultural dynamics utilizing the archaeological record are not novel. These factors individually have been the focus of debate and discussion over the years (e.g., Goodman et al. 1984; Huss-Ashmore et al. 1982; Palkovich 1978). In a context-embedded analysis, however, these factors are central to data analysis and interpretation. Cross-cultural comparisons of protohistoric groups are possible only once context-embedded patterns of demographic and epidemiologic response are established.

The Eastern Pueblos of New Mexico: A Case Study

To illustrate the ways in which these various data contexts shape our interpretations, I wish to explore briefly aspects of the Eastern Pueblos of New Mexico as a case study of demographic change along the Spanish Borderlands.

Prehistoric Context

The prehistoric context of Eastern Pueblo populations is a central concern in interpreting processes of historic depopulation in this region. Environmental fluctuations in this desert area have long shaped the demographic characteristics of groups occupying northern New Mexico. At the time of contact the American Southwest was occupied by a variety of successful maize agriculturalists. The shift to agricultural economies among the Anasazi encompasses two broad cultural phases: Basketmaker and Pueblo. The Basketmaker period (beginning in the first century A.D.) generally is characterized by semipermanent villages and a mixed subsistence economy. Groups were still dependent largely on hunting and gathering with some incipient food production. A slow shift occurred toward greater dependence on agricultural resources and the construction of more permanent settlements near the end of the Basketmaker period (roughly A.D. 700–750). There is widespread homogeneity in the material culture throughout the Anasazi region during Basketmaker times, but cultural experimentation and local environmental differences are manifest in a great diversity of architectural styles, ceramic types, and burial practices during the following Pueblo phase.

Eastern Pueblo settlement patterns generally reflect more occupations, larger village settlements, regional cultural diversity, and full-fledged dependence on agriculture (Glassow 1972; Lipe 1978; Martin and Plog 1973). It is generally believed that the population increased throughout the Pueblo period in eastern New Mexico. However, large-scale migrations, smaller-scale shifts in local populations, and sequential use of and rebuilding of sites confound our ability to establish reliable population growth rates (see Nichols and Powell 1987; Palkovich 1984, 1985).

Cyclical environmental conditions in the desert Southwest have been considered a primary cause of shifting prehistoric settlement patterns, particularly during the Basketmaker and Pueblo periods (Dean et al. 1985; Euler et al. 1979; Irwin-Williams and Haynes 1970; Jorde 1977). The history of occupation in the Southwest can be read as a series of strategies designed to adapt to specific conditions. Each strategy, however, provided only a temporarily successful, and usually still marginal, existence for human groups.

A detailed case study of Pueblo Arroyo Hondo in northern New Mexico demonstrates that fluctuations in dietary adequacy appear to have been intimately associated with cycles of concurrent short-term and long-term drought conditions (Rose et al. 1981; Wetterstrom 1986). The productivity of both natural and cultivated plant species at Arroyo Hondo was dependent upon and highly sensitive to local rainfall patterns. Short-term drought conditions reduced the productivity of species already experiencing the limits of marginal growing conditions, and long-term droughts could significantly damage soils and substantially alter the composition of plant communities (Rose et al. 1981; Wetterstrom 1986). Large-scale population movements in northern New Mexico prior to the settlement of Arroyo Hondo suggest that the instability of the environment frequently upset established subsistence patterns. Intensive agricultural practices and population aggregation in large villages located in primary zones of agricultural production like Arroyo Hondo were insufficient buffers against the vagaries of rainfall patterns. What were marginal protein-calorie diets in average years were virtually starvation diets in drought years (Wetterstrom 1986). Thus, buffering mechanisms of settlement patterns and hierarchical subsistence strategies could not always soften the biological impact of poor diets. The Pueblos of eastern New Mexico were groups under the constant threat of starvation and associated nutritional morbidity-mortality stress.

Population Patterns

Historic accounts and archaeological research (Berry 1982; Dickson 1975, 1980; Plog 1984; Powell 1983) appear to record continual shifts in Pueblo population density and distribution up through European contact. Few large Pueblo settlements existed immediately prior to the sixteenth century. Populations usually were clustered in small settlements scattered throughout the areas best suited for agriculture. These settlement clusters shifted in apparent response to the cyclical rainfall patterns and, thus, agricultural potential among the various regions. Ironically, it is not until after the Pueblo Revolt of 1680 and Spanish reconquest of this region in 1692 that the Pueblo population was concentrated and resettled into larger villages, potentially a major factor in promoting the epidemic outbreaks that were to occur in the subsequent centuries.

An analysis of the available historic estimates of the Eastern Pueblo populations (Palkovich 1985) demonstrates that the counts are inconsistent, incomparable, and often simply inaccurate. The rate of change in population size charted from these data show dramatic fluctuations, suggesting the true rate of demographic decrease is masked by census difficulties, social disruptions, indigenous warfare, and other factors. Also, epidemic outbreaks that were documented historically do not clearly coincide with substantial population reductions. The long-established pattern of shifts in settlement concentrations responding to fluctuating environmental conditions cannot be distinguished clearly from disease losses in the historic period. It is likely that epidemic depopulation, as well as the social disruption caused by the Pueblo Revolt, exacerbated rather than initiated such settlement shifts.

The historic-environmental context for the precontact Eastern Pueblos is one of small, shifting settlements living on the subsistence edge. While a trend toward depopulation is apparent between the 1500s and the nineteenth century, altered age patterns and causes of mortality after contact likely served to intensify the preexisting shifts in settlement patterns. Though it complicates our ability to evaluate the historic population dynamics of these groups, this long-established pattern of settlement shifts and demographic reorganization may have served to maintain Pueblo demographic viability by sustaining breeding cohorts and social integrity in the face of new, historically introduced, biological and social disruptions. Cultural flexibility to adapt to an unpredictable environment may have provided a means for the Eastern Pueblos to persist, despite depopulating epidemic disease, while other Native American groups were biologically and socially devastated (Palkovich 1985). Spanish reliance on the Pueblos for survival, as suggested by Ramenofsky (1987), is likely related to the marginal existence possible in this desert environment.

Archaeological Context

The context of data collection for the historic Pueblos of New Mexico must be considered on two levels—the archaeological data that immediately predate European contact and the protohistoric-historic data that are available. Of major concern in the archaeological record for the Pueblo IV period (just prior to historic contact) is that the recovered skeletal collections, used to reconstruct the health-disease status of these precontact groups, are biased significantly. For example, paleodemographic reconstructions of Pecos Pueblo, one of the major villages occupied in the sixteenth and seventeenth centuries, could potentially serve as an important reference series for the late prehistoric period. Unlike most Pueblo sites in the Southwest, the skeletal preservation at Pecos— even for infants and children—as originally reported by Kidder (1958, 284) is excellent. The datable skeletal sample (based on associations of seriated ceramics in graves), however, is seriously biased. Over 70 percent of the recovered interments from Pecos are undatable. Particularly troubling is the large portion (71 percent) of individuals less than 10 years of age that is undatable

(Palkovich 1983). Therefore, diachronic studies of health-disease conditions in the most susceptible age groups are not possible.

At Pecos, and likely at many other sites as well, differential treatment at death and its effect on the archaeological recovery of individuals and on demographic reconstructions has not been considered. Ceramics at Pecos were selectively interred with some individuals and not others; only 573 of the 1,824 interments (31.4 percent) recovered from the site could be dated. It has been demonstrated that the subset of dated individuals is not representative of the entire skeletal series (Palkovich 1983). Thus, the skeletal sample is biased in some unreconstructable way. In general, the validity and reliability of skeletal series representing individual sites has not been established. This renders direct comparisons of the incidence of various skeletal pathologies tenuous at best.

Infant underenumeration is commonly reported for late prehistoric Pueblo skeletal series. While such underenumerations are usually attributed to preservation problems, the location of excavations at a particular site and the extent of these excavations also may have affected the recovery of infant and child interments. Prehistoric Pueblo groups commonly interred infants in subfloor pits, yet published reports suggest that these archaeological contexts were not systematically explored at many sites. Also, spatio-temporal shifts in burial locations (subfloor pits versus plazas versus trash middens) have been noted at various pueblo sites (e.g., Palkovich 1980).

Demographic Reconstructions

Demographic reconstructions of the population at various Eastern Pueblo sites during the historic period must be examined carefully as well. Even if the casual observations of travelers to the region are eliminated and only formal census data considered, several problems persist. Not all pueblos were visited in the sixteenth century. Combined population estimates for the region may be low, but an overall figure of 60,000 individuals at the time of contact for all Eastern Pueblos (Hammond and Rey 1938) is commonly cited and appears to be consistent with the archaeological estimates of the human carrying capacity for this region (Kroeber 1939; Zubrow 1975). Archaeological surveys designed to identify specifically which sites were occupied at contact and the size of their populations will serve to clarify these historic estimates (Creamer 1990).

Sincere attempts to provide accurate counts of the indigenous population during the seventeenth and eighteenth centuries were biased by a variety of factors. Only those estimates provided by Fray Bartolomé Marquez in 1664 are likely to be reliable. As far as we know, Marquez actually visited all the pueblos he reported and tried to provide an accurate accounting of the population (Scholes 1929). Comparing Marquez's total estimate of 16,442 to Castañeda's similarly based estimate over 100 years earlier suggests a relatively stable overall Eastern Pueblo population size during this time. Other population estimates (including those citing 60,000 individuals as the Eastern Pueblo census at the time of contact) are not necessarily based on the same set of villages or on actual counts (rather than estimates). Widespread epidemics apparently had not yet devastated these populations.

The Pueblo Revolt of 1680 dramatically changed the nature of Eastern Pueblo population and village life forever. Reconquered in 1692 by de Vargas, many Pueblo Indians were killed in retaliation for the Spanish deaths 12 years earlier. Settlements were burned and many Indians taken captive. De Vargas frequently noted in his journal that pueblos were found recently abandoned. At least 10 pueblos previously documented by the Spanish were abandoned or destroyed in the aftermath of the revolt. Only two pueblos, Acoma and Isleta, can be identified unequivocally as occupying the same settlement before and after the revolt. Population estimates for the rest of the seventeenth century are unreliable or unavailable (Hammond and Rey 1938).

By the eighteenth century historic population estimates are complicated by census procedures. Population figures for this time reflect the location of major churches and the surrounding *visita* pueblos (settlements within the jurisdiction of a particular mission but without resident clergy) of each mission. Census figures were commonly reported for a church and its visita settlements combined, rather than for each individual pueblo. Since the location of the major churches with resident missionaries and the visitas associated with each church changed over time, overall population estimates by the missionaries are likely to be representative, while estimates for any given pueblo do not necessarily reflect the same settlement unit from year to year.

By the nineteenth century census data problems are compounded by inconsistencies in documenting who are Indians. Often only men or adults or baptized individuals in residence at the time of the census were counted. It is likely that discrepancies in census figures at the time are as attributable to Indians joining "wild" tribes as to health problems. In fact, American Indian agents were keenly aware of "special mortality" such as epidemics, and they attempted to document epidemic outbreaks and restrict their spread to other pueblos.

The first documented epidemic for Eastern Pueblos was recorded by Fray Juan de Prada in 1638. In general, the incidence and spread of epidemic disease among the Eastern Pueblos is poorly documented. A major smallpox epidemic, probably encompassing all the pueblos, occurred in 1781 and reportedly killed 5,025 of the 9,104 Pueblo inhabitants counted in that year (Bancroft 1962). However, reports from the nineteenth-century Indian agents indicate that sporadic outbreaks, particularly of smallpox and influenza, occurred most frequently and with devastating effects on a pueblo-to-pueblo basis rather than as general epidemics (cf. Kealhofer chapter 4 above). Even by this late date, after the Spanish resettlement during the seventeenth century, the pueblos were distinct settlements often separated by hundreds of miles. It is not surprising that local epidemics could occur without widely affecting the rest of the villages.

Most telling in an analysis of the demographic trends for the seventeenth and eighteenth centuries is the relationship of epidemic outbreaks to overall population size. Population estimates for the years or periods immediately following epidemic outbreaks do not consistently reflect comparable declines. Yet, the population figures in subsequent years inconsistently reflect both declines and increases in the rate of change in the population.

For the Pueblos, population movements and resettlements did not originate with the historic period as Dobyns (1983, 310–11) suggests. Such population movements already existed as a response to environmental and subsistence instability. Depopulation likely just heightened the frequency and incidence of these resettlements. Establishing the beginnings and pattern of depopulation among the Eastern Pueblos, therefore, is a task complicated by prehistorically established patterns of shifting settlements and inconsistent historic population estimates.

Biological Context

The biological context of archaeologically recovered skeletal series for the Eastern Pueblos presents another intriguing problem of interpretation. It is well established that many Southwestern populations experienced long-standing dietary stress (e.g., Berry 1983; El-Najjar 1974; Hinkes 1983; Ryan 1977; Stodder chapter 7 above). Endemically inadequate diets affected those individuals most susceptible to malnutrition—infants and young children. This pattern has been interpreted as widespread throughout sequential prehistoric periods in the Southwest. Additionally, it has been suggested (though not explored in any detail for prehistoric Pueblo populations) that high childhood mortality may result in increased survivorship in subsequent adult age classes (Palkovich 1980). Apparently, those individuals who survive the disease and nutritional stresses of childhood are biologically best able to cope with similar stresses as adults (Lovejoy et al. 1977; Meindl and Swedlund 1977). As a result, populations in which mortality is concentrated in the younger age classes may experience increased survivorship among young adults, unlike populations with low or moderate levels of childhood mortality. Such explanations have been offered for the erratic age profiles often noted for Pueblo skeletal series (e.g., Palkovich 1980).

A closer examination of incidence patterns of skeletal pathology and age patterns of mortality begins to suggest the fundamental importance of contextualizing biological data. As an example, the widespread prevalence of porotic hyperostosis is often cited as evidence of the singular importance of nutritional stress among infants and children in prehistoric Pueblo groups. Though confounded by the difficulties of biased skeletal samples and infant underenumeration at many sites, diachronic comparisons of the incidence of porotic hyperostosis (and occasionally related porotic lesions) are presented as a rough measure of the extent of dietary stress in a given group. These comparisons begin to break down, however, when the details of these lesion patterns are explored further.

For example, porotic skeletal lesions attributable to iron-deficiency anemia are commonly observed in these Southwestern populations. Infants over the age of 6 months through children 2–3 years of age are implicated as the age group with peak incidence of these lesions. This is typically true for clinically documented cases of iron-deficiency anemia.

However, the age-of-onset pattern of these lesions is often overlooked. Specifically, this characterization does not account for those individuals less than 6 months of age who show these lesions yet clinically are not supposed to develop them. It has been suggested for these early age-of-onset individuals that inadequate diets are not only affecting young children but pregnant females as well. Malnourished pregnant females are more likely to have low birthweight neonates. Such low birthweight infants have smaller blood volumes as well as lower body weight, and thus greatly reduced blood stores of iron. So, endemically inadequate diets acting synergistically with immediately acquired infection and limited iron stores (not necessarily the weaning diet in young children) are the probable major underlying cause for the unusually early onset of iron-deficiency anemia documented at some Eastern Pueblo sites (Palkovich 1985; cf. Stuart-Macadam 1992). A simple comparison of incidence patterns of nutrition-related pathology may thus yield misleading results.

Earlier studies of Southwestern populations that document the incidence of porotic hyperostosis among juveniles (e.g., Berry 1983; El-Najjar 1974; Hinkes 1983; Ryan 1977) lump individuals younger than 6 months at the time of death with children 2–3 years of age at the time of death. Incidence of porotic hyperostosis categorized in this fashion will confound the interpretation of stress among juveniles by obscuring differences in etiology. In some cases it may not be possible to separate these groups for demographic analysis due to infant underenumeration or poor preservation. Such skeletal series are not directly comparable to those for which these age groups can be analyzed separately. In each instance the analysis of each site proceeds from archaeological and temporal context to the skeletal series. Only once individual data sets can be demonstrated to reflect comparable information can regional assessments be attempted.

Endemic malnutrition had a significant impact on these populations. Ironically, it has also been suggested that populations already experiencing significant health stress may be better able to cope with novel pathogens. Individuals most likely to survive the severe physiological rigors of endemic malnutrition may be those most likely to survive other disease insults as well. At the time of contact, Eastern Pueblo groups living in small, dispersed villages may have been somewhat buffered from the rapid spread of novel epidemic pathogens and better able biologically to cope with the aftermath of such diseases.

CONCLUSION

The depopulation of the Eastern Pueblos of the American Southwest immediately prior to European contact illustrates the importance of a context-embedded analysis in bioarchaeology. For the Eastern Pueblo populations three aspects of this embedded analysis require special attention. First, skeletal series recovered from various late prehistoric and historic Eastern Pueblo sites do not necessarily provide reliable and valid paleodemographic reconstructions. Changes in interment practices, infant enumeration, and choice of excavation areas within each site require that these skeletal series be evaluated individually for potential archaeological biases (e.g., Miller chapter 6 above; Stodder chapter 7 above). Second, incidence of some skeletal lesions (e.g., porotic hyperostosis) is intimately related to local dietary and health conditions and is not generalizable for either the Eastern Pueblos or the American Southwest as a whole. Such lesion patterns must be interpreted for each site prior to broad comparisons. Finally, census figures available for the historic period are imprecise and at times contradictory. The overall population estimate of 60,000 individuals for the Eastern Pueblos at the time of European contact and population dynamics throughout the historic period require careful verification by archaeological data. Despite the varied problems of reliability and validity for the available archaeological and documentary data, several general conclusions may be drawn.

The population of the Eastern Pueblos clearly was reduced after European contact. Population density and distribution, and the rigors of the unforgiving environment in which these Pueblo groups lived, all suggest that a continual depopulation occurred historically over the course of several centuries. There is no evidence to suggest a demographic collapse. To the contrary, it is reasonable to hypothesize at this point that the long-established pattern of settlement shifts and demographic reorganization in response to the vagaries of the environment may have served to maintain Pueblo demographic viability in the face of new biological and social disruptions. The demographic and organizational flexibility to adapt to an unpredictable environment may have provided a means for the Eastern Pueblos to persist, despite depopulating epidemic disease. The persistence of the Pueblos may be attributed to the severe constraints placed on all groups, indigenous Pueblo and intruding Spanish alike, by the environment. In this case the potential effect of depopulation cannot be divorced from the preceding decades of survival patterns. Considerable research will be required to test the proposition of Pueblo persistence as a consequence of environmentally imposed restraints that were then overlain by novel biological and social conditions.

The picture we will build of the depopulation of North America must be based on fully documented, detailed case studies that carefully evaluate the available data in context-embedded analyses. We cannot draw broad conclusions from simple comparisons, such as skeletal lesion incidence. Such attempts may be misleading and will tend to mask both subtle and substantial differences. A focus on context allows the following: the limitations of the archaeological record and the appropriate reconstructions of the available data to be noted on a case-by-case basis; the implications of environmental and resulting subsistence differences among groups to be explored; the implications of population distributions and densities to be fully understood and significant temporal changes to be charted; what appear on the surface to be similar data patterns to be fully explicated and contrasted; and the essential studies of the underlying nature of epidemiological evidence as reflected in skeletal pathology to be understood fully for the first time as documented processes of the living human physiological system and its age variants.

The answer to the challenge posed by Ramenofsky (1987) and others—explaining the puzzling details of the depopulation of North America, the timing of disease contact, the differential population survival, and the nature of adaptive rebound—lies in how we contextualize our data. Detailed case studies and regional assessments represent the appropriate level of analysis and provide our clearest avenue for a fuller understanding of these phenomena.

REFERENCES

Baker, Brenda J.
    1992   Collagen Composition in Human Skeletal Remains from the NAX Cemetery (A.D. 350–550) in Lower Nubia. Ph.D. diss., University of Massachusetts. Ann Arbor, Mich.: University Microfilms.
Bancroft, Hubert H.
    1962   *History of Arizona and New Mexico: 1530–1888*. In *The Works of Hubert H. Bancroft*, vol. 17. 1889. Reprint, Albuquerque: Horn and Wallace.

Berry, David R.
   1983   Disease and Climatological Relationship among Pueblo III–Pueblo IV Anasazi of the Colorado Plateau. Ph.D. diss., University of California, Los Angeles.
Berry, Michael S.
   1982   *Time, Space and Transition in Anasazi Prehistory.* Salt Lake City: University of Utah Press.
Cohen, Mark Nathan
   1989   Paleopathology and the Interpretation of Economic Change in Prehistory. In *Archaeological Thought in America,* edited by C. C. Lamberg-Karlovsky, 117–32. Cambridge: Cambridge University Press.
Creamer, Winifred
   1990   The Study of Prehistoric Demography in the Northern Rio Grande Valley, A.D. 1450–1680. Paper presented at the 59th Annual Meeting of the American Association of Physical Anthropologists, Miami.
Dean, Jeffrey S., Robert C. Euler, George J. Gumerman, Fred Plog, Richard H. Hevly, and Thor N. V. Karlstrom
   1985   Human Behavior, Demography and Paleoenvironment on the Colorado Plateaus. *American Antiquity* 50:537–54.
Dickson, D. Bruce, Jr.
   1975   Settlement Pattern Stability and Change in the Middle Northern Rio Grande Region, New Mexico. *American Antiquity* 40:159–71.
   1980   *Prehistoric Pueblo Settlement Patterns: The Arroyo Hondo, New Mexico, Site Survey.* Arroyo Hondo Archaeological Series, vol. 2. Santa Fe, N.M.: School of American Research Press.
Dobyns, Henry F.
   1966   Estimating Aboriginal American Population 1: An Appraisal of Techniques with a New Hemispheric Estimate. *Current Anthropology* 7:395–449.
   1983   *Their Number Become Thinned: Native American Population Dynamics in Eastern North America.* Knoxville: University of Tennessee Press.
El-Najjar, Mahmoud Y.
   1974   People of Canyon de Chelly: A Study of Their Biology and Culture. Ph.D. diss., Arizona State University, Tempe.
Euler, Robert C., George J. Gumerman, Thor N. V. Karlstrom, Jeffrey S. Dean, and Richard H. Hevly
   1979   The Colorado Plateaus: Cultural Dynamics and Paleoenvironment. *Science* 205:1089–1101.
Glassow, Michael A.
   1972   Changes in the Adaptations of Southwestern Basketmakers: A Systems Perspective. In *Contemporary Archaeology,* edited by Mark P. Leone, 289–302. Carbondale: Southern Illinois University Press.
Goodman, Alan H., Debra L. Martin, George J. Armelagos, and George Clark
   1984   Indications of Stress from Bone and Teeth. In *Paleopathology at the Origins of Agriculture,* edited by Mark Nathan Cohen and George J. Armelagos, 13–49. Orlando, Fla.: Academic Press.

Hammond, George P., and Agapito Rey

  1938   *New Mexico in 1602: Juan de Montoya's Relation of the Discovery of New Mexico.* Berkeley, Calif.: Quivira Society.

Hill, M. Cassandra, and George J. Armelagos

  1990   Porotic Hyperostosis in Past and Present Perspective. In *A Life of Science: Papers in Honor of J. Lawrence Angel,* edited by Jane E. Buikstra, 52–63. Scientific Papers no. 6. Evanston, Ill.: Center for American Archeology.

Hinkes, Madeline J.

  1983   Skeletal Evidence of Stress in Subadults: Trying to Come of Age at Grasshopper Pueblo. Ph.D. diss., University of Arizona. Ann Arbor, Mich.: University Microfilms.

Huss-Ashmore, Rebecca, Alan H. Goodman, and George J. Armelagos

  1982   Nutritional Inference from Paleopathology. In *Advances in Archaeological Method and Theory,* vol. 5, edited by Michael B. Schiffer, 395–474. New York: Academic Press.

Irwin-Williams, Cynthia, and C. Vance Haynes

  1970   Climatic Change and Early Population Dynamics in the Southwestern United States. *Quaternary Research* 1:59–71.

Jorde, L. B.

  1977   Precipitation Cycles and Cultural Buffering in the Prehistoric Southwest. In *For Theory Building in Archaeology,* edited by Lewis Binford, 385–96. New York: Academic Press.

Kelley, Jane, and Marsha Hanen

  1988   *Archaeology and the Methodology of Science.* Albuquerque: University of New Mexico Press.

Kidder, Alfred V.

  1958   *Pecos, New Mexico: Archaeological Notes.* Papers of the Robert S. Peabody Foundation for Archaeology no. 5. Andover, Mass.: Phillips Academy.

Kintigh, Keith

  1988   Protohistoric Transitions in the Western Pueblo Area. Paper presented at the Southwest Symposium, Arizona State University, Tempe.

Kroeber, Alfred L.

  1939   *Cultural and Natural Areas of Native North America.* University of California Publications in American Archaeology and Ethnology no. 38. Berkeley: University of California Press.

Lincoln, Yvonna, and Egon Guba

  1985   *Naturalistic Inquiry.* Beverly Hills, Calif.: Sage.

Lipe, William

  1978   The Southwest. In *Ancient Native Americans,* edited by Jesse D. Jennings, 327–401. San Francisco: Freeman.

Lovejoy, C. Owen, Richard S. Meindl, Thomas R. Pryzbeck, Thomas S. Barton, Kingsbury G. Heiple, and David Kotting

  1977   Paleodemography of the Libben Site, Ottawa County, Ohio. *Science* 198:291–93.

Magennis, Ann L.
  1990   Growth and Transverse Line Formation in Contemporary Children. Ph.D. diss.,
          University of Massachusetts. Ann Arbor, Mich.: University Microfilms.
Martin, Paul S., and Fred Plog
  1973   *The Archaeology of Arizona*. Garden City, N.Y.: Doubleday.
Meindl, Richard S., and Alan C. Swedlund
  1977   Secular Trends in Mortality in the Connecticut Valley, 1700–1850. *Human
          Biology* 49:389–414.
Nichols, Deborah L., and Shirley Powell
  1987   Demographic Reconstructions in the American Southwest: Alternative Be-
          havioral Means to the Same Archaeological Ends. *The Kiva* 52(3):193–207.
Palkovich, Ann M.
  1978   A Model of the Dimensions of Mortality and Its Application to Paleo-
          demography. Ph.D. diss., Northwestern University. Ann Arbor, Mich.: Uni-
          versity Microfilms.
  1980   *Pueblo Population and Society: The Arroyo Hondo Skeletal and Mortuary
          Remains*. Arroyo Hondo Archaeological Series, vol. 3. Santa Fe, N.M.: School
          of American Research Press.
  1981   Tuberculosis Epidemiology in Two Arikara Skeletal Samples: A Study of Dis-
          ease Impact. In *Prehistoric Tuberculosis in the Americas*, edited by Jane E.
          Buikstra, 161–75. Scientific Papers no. 5. Evanston, Ill.: Northwestern Uni-
          versity Archeological Program.
  1983   A Comment on Mobley's "Demographic Structure of Pecos Indians." *Ameri-
          can Antiquity* 48:142–47.
  1984   Agriculture, Marginal Environments and Nutritional Stress in the Prehis-
          toric Southwest. In *Paleopathology at the Origins of Agriculture*, edited by
          Mark Nathan Cohen and George J. Armelagos, 425–38. Orlando, Fla.: Aca-
          demic Press.
  1985   Historic Population of the Eastern Pueblos: 1540–1910. *Journal of Anthropo-
          logical Research* 41:401–26.
  1994   Historic Epidemics of the Eastern Pueblos. In *In the Wake of Contact: Bio-
          logical Responses to Conquest*, edited by Clark Spencer Larsen and George R.
          Milner, 87–95. New York: Wiley-Liss.
Plog, Stephen
  1984   Regional Perspectives on the Western Anasazi. *American Archaeology* 4:162–
          70.
Powell, Shirley
  1983   *Mobility and Adaptation: The Anasazi of Black Mesa*. Carbondale: Southern
          Illinois University Press.
Ramenofsky, Ann F.
  1987   *Vectors of Death: The Archaeology of European Contact*. Albuquerque: Uni-
          versity of New Mexico Press.
Reff, Daniel T.
  1985   The Demographic and Cultural Consequences of Old World Disease in the

Greater Southwest, 1520–1660. Ph.D. diss., University of Oklahoma. Ann Arbor, Mich.: University Microfilms.

1991   *Disease, Depopulation, and Culture Change in Northwestern New Spain, 1518–1764.* Salt Lake City: University of Utah Press.

Rose, Martin R., Jeffrey S. Dean, and William J. Robinson

1981   *The Past Climate of Arroyo Hondo, New Mexico, Reconstructed from Tree Rings.* Arroyo Hondo Archaeological Series, vol. 4. Santa Fe, N.M.: School of American Research Press.

Ryan, Dennis J.

1977   The Paleopathology and Paleoepidemiology of the Kayenta Anasazi Indians in Northeastern Arizona. Ph.D. diss., Arizona State University. Ann Arbor, Mich.: University Microfilms.

Scholes, France V.

1929   Documents for the History of the New Mexico Missions in the Seventeenth Century. *New Mexico Historical Review* 4:45–71.

Stuart-Macadam, Patricia

1985   Porotic Hyperostosis: Representative of a Childhood Condition. *American Journal of Physical Anthropology* 66:391–98.

1987a   A Radiographic Study of Porotic Hyperostosis. *American Journal of Physical Anthropology* 74:511–20.

1987b   Porotic Hyperostosis: New Evidence to Support the Anemia Theory. *American Journal of Physical Anthropology* 74:521–26.

1992   Anemia in Past Human Populations. In *Diet, Demography, and Disease: Changing Perspectives on Anemia,* edited by Patricia Stuart-Macadam and Susan Kent, 151–72. New York: Aldine de Gruyter.

Thomas, David Hurst, ed.

1989   *Columbian Consequences,* vol 1: *Archaeological and Historical Perspectives on the Spanish Borderlands West.* Washington, D.C.: Smithsonian Institution.

Upham, Steadman

1986   Smallpox and Climate in the American Southwest. *American Anthropologist* 88:115–28.

1992   Population and Spanish Contact in the American Southwest. In *Disease and Demography in the Americas,* edited by John W. Verano and Douglas H. Ubelaker, 223–36. Washington, D.C.: Smithsonian Institution.

Upham, Steadman, and Lori Stephens Reed

1989   Regional Systems in the Central and Northern Southwest: Demography, Economy, and Sociopolitics Preceding Contact. In *Columbian Consequences,* vol. 1: *Archaeological and Historical Perspectives on the Spanish Borderlands West,* edited by David Hurst Thomas, 57–76. Washington, D.C.: Smithsonian Institution.

Verano, John W., and Douglas H. Ubelaker, eds.

1992   *Disease and Demography in the Americas.* Washington, D.C.: Smithsonian Institution.

Wetterstrom, Wilma
    1986   *Food, Diet, and Population at Prehistoric Arroyo Hondo Pueblo, New Mexico.*
              Arroyo Hondo Archaeological Series, vol. 6. Santa Fe, N.M.: School of Ameri-
              can Research Press.
Woodhead, A. D., Michael Bender, and Robin Leonard
    1988   *Phenotypic Variation in Populations.* New York: Plenum.
Zubrow, Ezra B.
    1975   *Prehistoric Carrying Capacity: A Model.* Menlo Park, Calif.: Cummings.

Chapter 9

Prospects and Problems in Contact-Era Research

GEORGE R. MILNER

The impact of European colonization on native North American peoples and their cultures has long been an active area of research among biological anthropologists, archaeologists, and historians. The symposium organized by Baker and Kealhofer for the 1990 annual meeting of the American Association of Physical Anthropologists was just one of several such sessions held in recognition of the quincentenary of Columbus' first landfall in the Americas (e.g., Larsen and Milner 1994; Thomas 1989, 1990, 1991; Verano and Ubelaker 1992). For better or worse, commemorative events have a tendency to call forth such scholarly attention. In this instance, much can be gained by the critical appraisal of controversial issues surrounding the nature, magnitude, and timing of cultural and demographic collapse in North America and, often, the persistence of Indian groups in the face of unprecedented challenges to survival.

Taken together, the articles in this volume demonstrate that considerably more can be said about the early contact period than was possible a decade or so ago. Nevertheless, as Baker and Kealhofer point out in chapter 1, there remains the need for a more sophisticated integration of biological and cultural information when addressing the demographic and social consequences of contact between the peoples of the Old and New Worlds. Scholars must broaden the scope of their studies to include more than the immediate impact of novel pathogens on their human hosts. Several contributions to this volume clearly show a broader appreciation of introduced diseases as only one of the factors, although a very important one, that contributed to Native American population loss and relocation, as well as cultural change and subsequent reorganization along greatly modified lines.

The necessity of studying the nature of accommodation to radically different socioeconomic pressures and the challenges of new diseases is raised in several chapters. This largely neglected but important counterpoint to what is typically, and accurately, described as cultural and demographic catastrophe invites further work.

SPANISH BORDERLANDS

The chapters can be divided on the basis of the geographical areas of interest, either the eastern or western Spanish Borderlands. Differences between the two regions in terms of physical and biotic settings, as well as cultural traditions, are readily apparent, and each broadly defined area was by no means internally homogeneous. Nevertheless, much remains the same in terms of basic issues: the dating, amount, and rate of population loss, and the degree of continuity or discontinuity in regional cultural sequences and human occupation. From my perspective, oriented as it is toward the Eastern Woodlands, I find interesting parallels in current research efforts in the Southwest and Southeast that focus on the contact era. Both areas are afforded the briefest of historical documentation by the Spanish in the early to mid-sixteenth century. Early accounts include those from the well-known and simultaneous de Soto and Coronado expeditions, both failures in the eyes of the Spanish. This leaves modern researchers with little except archaeological and osteological data with which to evaluate the cultural, population, and health changes and accommodations to the social and biological phenomena set in motion by the European presence in the Americas.

Archaeologists in both regions are struggling with problems associated with implementing regional projects, developing fine-grained local chronologies, estimating demographic trends over great spans of time, and explaining fluctuating population histories within complex sociopolitical landscapes. Biological anthropologists are similarly seeking to document variability in late prehistoric health and to examine changes in disease patterns after A.D. 1492. There is ample, although largely unexplored, ground for collaborative efforts on issues of common concern.

The recent survey work in the Chickasaw region of Mississippi by Johnson and Lehmann underscores points that are increasingly being emphasized by Southeastern researchers (e.g., Anderson 1994; Milner 1990; Peebles 1987). Quite simply, late prehistoric sociopolitical and demographic landscapes were both varied and continually changing. We cannot assume that the Southeast, or any other such broadly defined geographical area, was culturally homogeneous or that the distribution of people remained fixed over time. Fluctuating population histories and changes in sociopolitical organization in particular regions were commonplace prior to contact, and they often occurred in time frames measured by generations, not hundreds of years. The investigation of the post-Columbian era is not simply a process of identifying which Old World influences affected a static Native American world. Changes in the early postcontact era were played out against a complex mosaic of volatile socio-political relationships, organizationally distinct societies, and regions of different population distributions and densities.

COLLAPSE

There is no consensus of opinion regarding the extent of postcontact demographic collapse and cultural change, when it occurred, or how it took place. Much of this debate hinges on widely divergent opinions regarding the size of late prehistoric populations, their spatial distribution, and the degree of contact among members of separate middle-range societies. Recent estimates for North America, excluding most or all of Mexico, range from about 2 to 18 million (Dobyns 1983, 42; Ubelaker 1976, 1988). The highest estimate is based on Dobyns' (1966, 1983) belief that newly introduced high-mortality diseases spread frequently and essentially uniformly throughout broad geographical areas, ranging to entire continents. Pervasive pathogen transmission resulted in the rapid and widespread decimation of Native Americans and correspondingly profound changes in their ways of life. Other population estimates range from Kroeber's (1939, 134) now dismissed low figure of about 1 million to Thornton's (1987, 32) and Ramenofsky's (1987, 162) higher estimates of over 7 and 12 million, respectively.

Several points of disagreement lie behind the wide discrepancy in authoritative estimates of precontact population size. The more important areas of controversy include the following: the veracity of early historical records, especially those used to derive population estimates; the level of mortality that accompanied specific disease episodes, particularly the appropriateness of mortality estimates from known situations when projected onto distinctly different sociopolitical and ecological settings; the possibility of population recovery, most importantly in the more remote parts of the Americas; and the nature of pathogen transmission among heterogeneous host populations that featured varying degrees of intergroup contact. Several of these issues have been the focus of recent scholarship, whereas others are rarely addressed. All such topics, however, require systematic study.

Kealhofer argues effectively that we should not assume that the biological and cultural impact of epidemic diseases on Native Americans and their cultures was uniform. Demographic collapse of a sudden and catastrophic nature is differentiated from more gradual but no less significant depopulation. By making that distinction, she rightly stresses the complex, context-specific nature of demographic and cultural change. Also emphasized are the imperfectly understood and interrelated factors that contributed to varied histories of transformation, including accommodation, during historic times. The work of other contributors to this volume, especially Palkovich, shares this general theme.

Baker and Kealhofer rightly point to major problems with the application of so-called depopulation ratios for estimating precontact population size from counts of historic people or villages, which are themselves crude approximations. When applied to North American protohistoric populations, these estimates of mortality are based on, at best, spongy information from societies in the colonized parts of the Americas. Contributors to this volume are not alone in questioning the applicability of depopulation ratios to societies that differed dramatically in such critical dimensions as population density, organizational complexity, and the nature of relations within and between social groups. Furthermore, it cannot be assumed that there was underlying uniformity in host susceptibility to novel pathogens.

To address these issues it is essential that we learn more about heterogeneity in contact-era social organization and population distribution. As Johnson and Lehmann point out in their Mississippi study, the likelihood of transmitting communicable diseases and, hence, the spread of pathogens through broad geographical areas would have been strongly influenced by the spatial arrangement of people and the nature and regularity of contacts between communities. A demographic landscape with wide, unpopulated, and irregularly traversed stretches between separate societies would have impeded the spread of introduced communicable diseases through the Spanish Borderlands and beyond. An uneven spread of newly introduced, high-mortality, communicable diseases with some areas spared for a time is consistent with archaeological findings elsewhere in the Eastern Woodlands (Snow and Lanphear 1988; Ward and Davis 1991). Their argument stands in marked contrast to the position promoted by ethnohistorian Henry Dobyns (1983), who maintains that high-mortality epidemics swept both frequently and uniformly through vast portions of the Americas. A 1492 North American Indian population of 18 million was thereby reduced through multiple epidemics to only a small fraction of its previous size during the sixteenth century. The debate is not over the spread of newly introduced diseases beyond areas of direct contact but over the areal scope and evenness of pathogen distribution across physically, socially, and demographically diverse landscapes. I happen to agree with these authors, and a number of other researchers, that the high estimates of Dobyns (1983) and others are vastly inflated.

Nevertheless, researchers are still left with two critical unresolved problems: how are we to recognize when and where epidemics struck, and how do we measure their short and long-term social and demographic consequences? Hill reviews how mortuary remains, including skeletons, can be used to monitor changes in ways of life. Variability in mortuary behavior that includes artifactual content, burial position, interment facility, grave location, and corpse treatment, along with age and sex information, can be used for this purpose.

Mass burials may be one indication of epidemic-related death. Such interments, however, are made for many reasons, as all archaeologists know. Differentiation among the various reasons for multiple interments rests on contextual and skeletal information acquired through careful excavation.

Looking at age-at-death distributions might be another way to identify anomalous mortality episodes, especially if the epidemic victims were buried in a separate cemetery or otherwise distinguished by unusual mortuary practices. While holding some promise, it is certainly true that much more work needs to be done by osteologists to develop the means of determining whether a particular accumulation of skeletons represents an unbiased sample of the deaths expected in traditional societies and of differentiating the multiple factors, including epidemics, that contribute to atypical mortality distributions (Johansson and Horowitz 1986; Milner et al. 1989; Paine 1989). There is certainly no unanimity of opinion among paleodemographers over the configuration of normal age-at-death distributions for prehistoric populations represented by archaeological remains (Howell 1982; Johansson and Horowitz 1986; Lovejoy et al. 1977; Mensforth 1990; Milner et al. 1989; Paine 1989; Sattenspiel and Harpending 1983). Some factors contributing to atypical mortality distributions may be of biological significance, others of cultural interest, and the remainder are a function of observational bias, sampling error, differential preservation, or excavation methods.

Finally, several contributors remind us that skeletal lesions are of no help in identifying instances where death occurred as a result of an acute crowd infection that swept rapidly through a community. Smallpox, which can affect the juvenile skeleton, is a possible exception for the survivors of this disease (see Ortner and Putschar 1985, 227–28). Of more interest is the effect of a novel disease that results in rapid death without recognizable bone involvement on the paleopathologist's evaluation of the supposed health of past communities. Such interpretations are necessarily derived from hard tissue lesions displayed by skeletons. The evaluation of such accumulations of skeletons is not a straightforward task. The sudden death of a significant part of a community, including a disproportionate number of its most susceptible members, will affect the proportions of nonsurvivors with and without osseous lesions entering the mortuary sample, as well as the relative frequencies of lesions that were either remodeled or active at the time of death. For example, the mortuary sample might well contain a higher proportion than usual of individuals lacking any sign of pathological bony involvement. On the other hand, individuals suffering from active osseous lesions presumably would have experienced some elevated susceptibility to the challenge of a new communicable disease. For these people, lowered resistance to novel pathogens increased their risk of death. The effects of these processes on studies based on non-survivors—that is, inferences derived from skeletal lesion frequencies in cemetery samples—are not at all clear.

VIOLENT CONTACT

Convincing evidence for trauma inflicted by metal weapons has been discussed by Hutchinson (1990) for recently excavated skeletons from Tatham Mound in Florida. It has also been argued that many of the individuals buried at the King site in northwestern Georgia were victims of de Soto's soldiers (Blakely and Mathews 1990; Detweiler-Blakely 1988; Mathews 1988). Needless to say, these possibilities should, and do, attract considerable attention among both scholars and the general public (for the latter, see Blakely 1989).

I do not intend to be an apologist for the sixteenth-century Spanish who cut a wide swath through Southeastern Indian societies. There are major flaws, however, in the King site scenario of many Spanish-caused deaths (Milner et al. 1994). The King site periostitis total is reported as including many examples of bone responses to wounds suffered when fighting the Spanish (Blakely and Mathews 1990; Detweiler-Blakely 1988). Such bone involvement, however, is notoriously nonspecific. The generalized nature of bony responses to precipitating stimuli is particularly problematic when interpretations rest on the osteologist's ability to link rapidly remodeling and healed osseous reactions to the trauma caused by metal-edged weapons (as opposed to other objects). As far as injuries that supposedly led to immediate death are concerned, recent examinations of the available bones from the site call into question whether any of these people were killed by being struck with sharp-edged metal weapons such as swords. Many agents can damage archaeological bone and produce an array of osseous defects that are unrelated to the life histories of the individuals interred in a cemetery. The King site specimens display the usual damage attributable to rodents, roots, and excavators.

HEALTH

Several chapters focus on the challenges to their health faced by Native Americans in the post-1492 era. Hill notes a dramatic increase in porotic hyperostosis lesion frequencies and the severity of bone involvement in the late protohistoric period of Alabama. These findings are interpreted as nutritional stress complicated by infection that was the result of multiple factors acting together to the detriment of the Indians of this region.

Paleopathological evidence assembled by Miller and Stodder is also interpreted as indicating a deterioration in health during the contact era among the western populations. Moreover, the direct and indirect effects of Old World peoples on the health of Native Americans were not uniform. It is gratifying to see that multiple hard tissue indicators of disease experience, both dental and skeletal, were examined. Stodder also points out that it is likely that unprecedented cultural changes affected host resistance to indigenous diseases. Monitoring the factors precipitating changes in the health of populations that practiced different ways of life and who were exposed to different communicable diseases is clearly a complex process, a point also stressed by other contributors to this volume.

Several osteologists raise, perhaps unintentionally, an especially intractable problem with the existing paleopathological literature. Quite simply, the extrapolation from frequencies of skeletal lesions to the prevalence of conditions in once-living populations is not a straightforward task.

Researchers over the past two decades have worked hard at developing the means of identifying the social structure indicated by mortuary remains, of determining skeletal age and sex, of differentiating the characteristic signatures of several disease processes, and of measuring disease experience using a broad array of hard tissue morphological characteristics. Several of the contributors to this volume provide useful discussions of these issues.

Other fundamental concerns, however, have been largely neglected. First, we must refine our ability to identify whether an accumulation of skeletons from an archaeological site approximates an age-at-death distribution that could conceivably have been drawn without significant bias from the deaths expected to occur in a premodern society. Second, evaluations of the demographic structure of accumulations of skeletons should be routinely incorporated as integral parts of paleopathological analyses. The age structure of a skeletal sample will affect lesion frequencies for many conditions, as has been noted by a number of osteologists. Third, osteologists are only beginning to explore what is actually indicated by hard tissue lesion frequencies. Counts of bone lesions are assuredly not the same as prevalence figures in once-living populations if the condition increased the likelihood of death. This discrepancy is because a cemetery, by definition, contains nonsurvivors; there is a decidedly, although unknown, nonrandom entry into the sample; and this group is highly selected for lesions related in any way to the risk of death (Wood et al. 1992). Moreover, there is no straightforward way to transform lesion prevalence figures from clinical settings to expected lesion frequencies in nonsurvivor samples (skeletons), as some researchers elsewhere have done, unless we also know the effect of that condition on the age-specific risk of death. Incidentally, when referring to archaeological skeletons in this context, I intentionally use the word "accumulation," instead of the more common "population." This word choice emphasizes the need to come to grips with the nature of mortality samples before attempting to make statements regarding the disease characteristics of the target population, a once-living community.

Accommodation

The study by Larsen and coworkers of skeletons from southern Atlantic coastal sites is an especially important step furthering our understanding of the adjustments made by Native Americans following contact with Old World peoples. The nature of accommodations to a new sociopolitical arena and different subsistence and settlement patterns, especially as reflected in workload, is shown by alterations in bone strength and osteoarthritis from the mechanical wear-and-tear of joints. Male and female shifts over time in body size, long bone cross-sectional area and shape, and the arthritic involvement of the bone surfaces and margins of several joints are sometimes parallel and at other times divergent. Their study underscores the importance of breaking down samples by sex and examining multiple skeletal features when reconstructing past ways of life. The focus on accommodation in the face of unprecedented challenges to survival deserves more attention by other researchers.

The southern Atlantic coastal materials are unique in their temporal span coupled with fine chronological and contextual controls. I look forward to seeing the results of continuing research by Larsen and his coworkers as it unfolds in the future.

Conclusion

Finally, I should underscore a point made throughout this volume. It is commonplace to make a distinction between the protohistoric and historic periods in terms of pertinent sources of data. Clearly, the only way we will learn about the protohistoric period is through additional archaeological and osteological studies. Much is made in some circles about the availability of written records documenting many aspects of the early historic period. Several of the studies in this volume demonstrate just how very thin those records actually are, particularly when we are interested in past ways of life and human responses to altered settings.

Overall, the authors of these chapters have provided provocative contributions that address one of the most dramatic, but still poorly understood, episodes in Native American cultural and demographic trajectories. The chapters are a fine beginning to a barely charted field of scholarship. Additional information about the profound demographic and cultural changes of the contact period, as well as the accommodations to dramatically altered social and biotic (including disease) environments, will only be forthcoming through the combined efforts of biological anthropologists and archaeologists.

REFERENCES

Anderson, David G.
1994   *The Savanna River Chiefdoms.* Tuscaloosa: University of Alabama Press.
Blakely, Robert L.
1989   A Coosa Massacre. *Archaeology* 42(3):30.
Blakely, Robert L., and David S. Mathews
1990   Bioarchaeological Evidence for a Spanish-Native American Conflict in the Six-
        teenth-Century Southeast. *American Antiquity* 55:718–44.
Detweiler-Blakely, Bettina
1988   Stress and the Battle Casualties. In *The King Site: Continuity and Contact in
        Sixteenth-Century Georgia,* edited by Robert L. Blakely, 87–98. Athens: Uni-
        versity of Georgia Press.
Dobyns, Henry F.
1966   Estimating Aboriginal American Population 1: An Appraisal of Techniques
        with a New Hemispheric Estimate. *Current Anthropology* 7:395–449.
1983   *Their Number Become Thinned: Native American Population Dynamics in
        Eastern North America.* Knoxville: University of Tennessee Press.
Howell, Nancy
1982   Village Composition Implied by a Paleodemographic Life Table: The Libben
        Site. *American Journal of Physical Anthropology* 59:263–69.
Hutchinson, Dale L.
1990   Postcontact Biocultural Change: Mortuary Site Evidence. In *Columbian Con-
        sequences,* vol 2: *Archaeological and Historical Perspectives on the Spanish
        Borderlands East,* edited by David Hurst Thomas, 61–70. Washington, D.C.:
        Smithsonian Institution.
Johansson, S. Ryan, and S. Horowitz
1986   Estimating Mortality in Skeletal Populations: Influence of the Growth Rate
        on the Interpretation of Levels and Trends During the Transition to Agricul-
        ture. *American Journal of Physical Anthropology* 71:233–50.
Kroeber, Alfred L.
1939   *Cultural and Natural Areas of Native North America.* Publications in Ameri-
        can Archaeology and Ethnology no. 38. Berkeley: University of California
        Press.
Larsen, Clark Spencer, and George R. Milner, eds.
1994   *In the Wake of Contact: Biological Responses to Conquest.* New York: Wiley-
        Liss.
Lovejoy, C. Owen, Richard S. Meindl, Thomas R. Pryzbeck, Thomas S. Barton, Kingsbury
        G. Heiple, and David Kotting
1977   Paleodemography of the Libben Site, Ottawa County, Ohio. *Science* 198:291–
        93.
Mathews, David S.
1988   The Massacre: The Discovery of De Soto in Georgia. In *The King Site: Conti-*

nuity and Contact in Sixteenth-Century Georgia, edited by Robert L. Blakely, 101–16. Athens: University of Georgia Press.

Mensforth, Robert P.

1990   Paleodemography of the Carlston Annis (Bt-5) Late Archaic Skeletal Population. *American Journal of Physical Anthropology* 82:81–99.

Milner, George R.

1990   The Late Prehistoric Cahokia Cultural System of the Mississippi River Valley: Foundations, Florescence, and Fragmentation. *Journal of World Prehistory* 4:1–43.

Milner, George R., Dorothy A. Humpf, and Henry C. Harpending

1989   Pattern Matching of Age-at-Death Distributions in Paleodemographic Analysis. *American Journal of Physical Anthropology* 80:49–58.

Milner, George R., Clark Spencer Larsen, Dale L. Hutchinson, and Matt Williamson

1994   Conquistadors, Excavators, or Rodents? Paper presented at the Southeastern Archaeological Conference, Lexington, Kentucky.

Ortner, Donald J., and Walter G. J. Putschar

1985   *Identification of Pathological Conditions in Human Skeletal Remains.* Reprint edition. Contributions to Anthropology no. 28. Washington, D.C.: Smithsonian Institution.

Paine, Richard R.

1989   Model Life Table Fitting by Maximum Likelihood Estimation: A Procedure to Reconstruct Paleodemographic Characteristics from Skeletal Age Distributions. *American Journal of Physical Anthropology* 79:51–61.

Peebles, Christopher S.

1987   The Rise and Fall of the Mississippian in Western Alabama: The Moundville and Summerville Phases, A.D. 1000 to 1600. *Mississippi Archaeology* 22:1–31.

Ramenofsky, Ann F.

1987   *Vectors of Death: The Archaeology of European Contact.* Albuquerque: University of New Mexico Press.

Sattenspiel, Lisa, and Henry C. Harpending

1983   Stable Populations and Skeletal Age. *American Antiquity* 48:489–98.

Snow, Dean R., and Kim M. Lanphear

1988   European Contact and Indian Depopulation in the Northeast: The Timing of the First Epidemics. *Ethnohistory* 35:15–33.

Thomas, David Hurst, ed.

1989   *Columbian Consequences,* vol. 1: *Archaeological and Historical Perspectives on the Spanish Borderlands West.* Washington, D.C.: Smithsonian Institution.

1990   *Columbian Consequences,* vol. 2: *Archaeological and Historical Perspectives on the Spanish Borderlands East.* Washington, D.C.: Smithsonian Institution.

1991   *Columbian Consequences,* vol. 3: *The Spanish Borderlands in Pan-American Perspective.* Washington, D.C.: Smithsonian Institution.

Thornton, Russell

    1987   *American Indian Holocaust and Survival: A Population History since 1492.* Norman: University of Oklahoma Press.

Ubelaker, Douglas H.

    1976   Prehistoric New World Population Size: Historical Review and Current Appraisal of North American Estimates. *American Journal of Physical Anthropology* 45:661–65.

    1988   North American Indian Population Size, A.D. 1500 to 1985. *American Journal of Physical Anthropology* 77:289–94.

Verano, John W., and Douglas H. Ubelaker, eds.

    1992   *Disease and Demography in the Americas.* Washington, D.C.: Smithsonian Institution.

Ward, H. Trawick, and R. P. Stephen Davis, Jr.

    1991   The Impact of Old World Diseases on the Native Inhabitants of the North Carolina Piedmont. *Archaeology of Eastern North America* 19:171–81.

Wood, James W., George R. Milner, Henry C. Harpending, and Kenneth M. Weiss

    1992   The Osteological Paradox: Problems of Inferring Prehistoric Health from Skeletal Samples. *Current Anthropology* 33:343–70.

Chapter 10

Counterpoint to Collapse
Depopulation and Adaptation

LISA KEALHOFER AND BRENDA J. BAKER

In the first volume of *Columbian Consequences,* Thomas (1989, 11) called for multiple perspectives in considering why some Native American groups maintained their cultural identities "while others disappeared virtually overnight," and what role disease and demographic collapse played in the process. In the final volume, however, multiple perspectives converged into a "new demographic paradigm" that "demonstrates catastrophic depopulation," as defined by Dobyns (1991, 543–45) and others. If we accept this "new demographic paradigm," or universal population collapse, then we are prevented from considering multiple perspectives, multiple causes of depopulation, and multiple biocultural responses to contact. Ironically, in the same volume Ramenofsky (1991, 437) laments, "we have barely begun to outline the nature, magnitude, or direction of change that occurred throughout the Contact period," due to a lack of theory "that addresses 'why' kinds of questions." While both a lack of data and a lack of theory have limited our ability to understand protohistoric processes, the "new demographic paradigm" assumes the answers to demographic or biological questions are known, rather than encouraging the study of the variable and complex cultural and biological changes that occurred during and after the protohistoric period.

One purpose of this volume is to promote biocultural studies of Native American responses to European contact by pointing out both the data we have and the many lacunae that still exist. Specifically, we believe there is a need to focus on questions of depopulation and disease-driven demographic collapse. In contrast to many recent discussions of this subject (e.g., Dobyns 1991; Dunnell 1991; Ramenofsky 1987; Stannard 1991), the contributors to this volume did not investigate indigenous biological and cultural change based on the notion that epidemic diseases rapidly swept across the New World, decimating populations and destroying cultural and biological continuity within extant groups (cf. Thomas 1991, xix). Instead, the authors sought to explore biocultural change, considering evidence for adaptation and resilience as well as for cultural and demographic collapse. As the data begin to accumulate, here and elsewhere (e.g., Larsen and Milner 1994; Verano and Ubelaker 1992), it is clear that a coherent, all-encompassing explanation for Native American response to European contact does not exist; rather, the complexity and diversity of responses become more apparent. Clearly, not only are multiple perspectives still needed in this analysis, but we need to accumulate many more data sets to sample the complexity of indigenous reactions to European contact.

The analyses presented in this volume demonstrate a diverse and sometimes conflicting set of approaches for investigating demographic, biological, and cultural changes and their causes. Many other approaches are possible that would further complement these studies. A crucial factor for future investigations of the variables responsible for biocultural change is a fine-grained chronology and sequence of settlement pattern changes (both intra- and intersite) within a particular region. These sequences determine the degree of resolution possible for identifying relationships between variables such as mortuary patterning and indicators of health. The lack of fine-grained chronological resolution in many data sets (cf. Hill chapter 2 above; Stodder chapter 7 above) makes the role of direct versus indirect contact in biocultural and demographic transformation ambiguous. Many of the biological and cultural patterns seen in the protohistoric period have late prehistoric precursors (e.g., Miller chapter 6 above). In the last 10 years finely dated settlement pattern data have slowly increased, as demonstrated here in several chapters (e.g., Johnson and Lehmann chapter 3 above; cf. Creamer 1990; Snow 1995).

While building a solid regional chronology and sequence of settlement pattern changes, data pertaining to biocultural change must be collected from a problem-oriented perspective. Bioarchaeological data collected without a theoretical issue shaping the data collection process are rarely sufficient for answering the questions currently being addressed by researchers. As discussed below, this problem was common in California and many other areas where large skeletal assemblages were excavated prior to the development of current issues and methods of analysis in physical anthropology and bioarchaeology. Many contemporary CRM projects often continue to pattern their data collection on these outmoded issues and paradigms and, consequently, do not gather sufficient or useful data for addressing issues such as demographic change, epidemic disease, and biocultural adaptation. Studying the bioarchaeology of the contact period in California (and many other states) is severely constrained by the prohibition on excavating mortuary sites, as well as by lack of funding. Walker and others have completed excellent studies on contact-period skeletal assemblages; however, their results are constrained by the lack of chronological and spatial data provided by previous archaeologists (Walker and Johnson 1992; Walker et al. 1989).

The archaeological and osteological data needed to evaluate the issues we seek to investigate are currently few, but a variety of projects across the Borderlands are seeking to remedy this problem (e.g., Creamer 1992). The authors here present data that were collected to address specific local issues. Nevertheless, these data can be used to construct a case for the need to expand archaeological and bioarchaeological research on cultural and demographic change at the time of contact. Their data show that we cannot casually accept universal demographic collapse but must investigate each region and culture for reactions to contact. For example, in northeastern Mississippi, Johnson and Lehmann (chapter 3 above) used settlement pattern data to question the relationship between European contact and depopulation. They correlated their settlement pattern data with soil type and stream order to show that major demographic and subsistence shifts predated the contact period. Settlement dispersal reflected significant economic and cultural change, but did not indicate demographic decline in the protohistoric period. Based on settlement pattern data, Creamer (1990) and Palkovich (chapter 8 above) both suggest ongoing demographic migrations and transformations throughout the Pueblo periods (before and after contact) in the Southwest (cf. Lycett 1989, 121). Many of the shifts in settlement, including abandonment, in the Eastern Pueblos prior to the 1680 Pueblo Revolt were part of a continuing long-term oscillation in regional populations (Palkovich chapter 8 above). The complexity of the timing in local settlement pattern changes in the Southwest precludes any simplistic link between European contact and depopulation. In nearby Sonora (northern Mexico), McGuire and Villalpando (1989) note settlement data provide evidence for demographic collapse prior to contact. These studies demonstrate the significance of settlement pattern data for resolving the relationship between site size and location changes in demographic terms.

Changes in mortality and health patterns, and the imprint of epidemic-based demographic decline, must be correlated with the detailed settlement data and chronology. Clearly, population movement, such as dispersal or migration, severely affects the interpretation of mortuary-based demographic reconstructions. These settlement data, however, have rarely been collected for most of the Borderlands, and often only detailed analyses of sites and site subsamples are possible. Comparing health indicators in skeletal data from prehistoric and historic sites, Miller (chapter 6 above) suggests that the degradation in health seen in historic mission groups in central Texas was induced by changes in settlement pattern and subsistence, as well as by stressors such as epidemic disease, introduced by direct European contact. This finding is comparable to Mission period California (Cook 1943, 1978; Cook and Borah 1979;

Kealhofer chapter 4 above; Walker et al. 1989). Stodder's analysis (chapter 7 above) of two large late prehistoric to early historic skeletal assemblages from the Western Pueblos demonstrates the considerable underlying biological variability in culturally similar groups. Although chronological resolution is not precise, the health status of the two groups in the protohistoric period seems predicated on health patterns in the late prehistoric period rather than determined solely by European contact. This is not a surprising conclusion, but it is not one frequently pursued.

In the Southeast clear differences in mortuary traditions over time encouraged Hill (chapter 2 above) to question what caused these changes. The societal transformation during the protohistoric period negatively affected health, but it is as yet unclear whether the changes in settlement pattern, burial practices, and the increase in dependence on maize were set in motion prior to—or as a consequence of—European contact. Other groups in the Southeast responded very differently to contact. Milanich (1990, 9) noted the Calusa of Florida survived 150 years of contact relatively intact, only to demographically succumb in the eighteenth century—a pattern very different from the Timucua to the north.

The detailed analysis by Larsen, Ruff, and Griffin (chapter 5 above) of late prehistoric to historic period biomechanical changes in skeletal assemblages from coastal Georgia and Florida provides an excellent example of the complex biological changes initiated with European contact, including the divergence in workload, type of work, as well as in the quantity and quality of diet. Based on their data, activity levels declined during the historic period, although both body size and age at death increased for the contact-period skeletal assemblages. Their focus on adaptation counters the prevailing emphasis on demographic collapse.

The biological studies introduce specific and highly informative evidence for changing adaptations in the protohistoric and historic periods. These data, however, need to be understood within the framework of the regional settlement pattern and chronology. While many other comparable situations occur, this need for detailed context is particularly clear in the review of the archaeological and mortuary data available from California (Kealhofer chapter 4 above). While a massive amount of osteological information is available, little of it has the corresponding chronological or settlement pattern data necessary to address problems of demographic change.

Together, the chapters in this volume clearly demonstrate that the cultural and biological changes identified in the archaeological record were not synchronized across the Spanish Borderlands; neither were they unidirectional. Rapid, massive depopulation does not seem to have swept through the Spanish Borderlands in the sixteenth century based on the data presented. Although

Thornton and coworkers (1991, 28) suggest that American indigenous populations were equally susceptible to Old World pathogens, the considerable variability in population density, settlement pattern, sociopolitical complexity, and health status of Spanish Borderlands groups in the late prehistoric period indicates this was unlikely (cf. Blakely and Detweiler-Blakely 1989; Milner chapter 9 above; Zubrow 1990). Highly stressed populations, with higher infant mortality and lower life expectancies, were undoubtedly more susceptible to European pathogens, as Thornton and coworkers (1991) themselves demonstrate.

Evidence from historical documents has been used to identify epidemic-based demographic collapse all over the New World (e.g., Dobyns 1966, 1983, 1989; Hann 1988; Reff 1987, 1991). Numerous accounts of indigenous societies in the sixteenth to nineteenth centuries, however, describe many areas as having well-populated, surplus-producing, integrated cultures (e.g., Brown 1967; Krech 1983; Reff 1991). Often, in areas where local statistics are available for deaths, the pattern does not correspond to profiles of epidemic mortality (Jackson 1983; Palkovich chapter 8 above). Depopulation in many areas was related to massive relocation projects carried out by the Spanish (e.g., Griffen 1969; 1981, 51). After a region was depopulated, mobile groups, such as the Apache, often expanded into the void, specifically adapting to the economic niche of the colonial periphery. Thus, the demographic changes and declines on a regional level were highly complex and tied to multiple variables that included, but were not reducible to, disease.

The changing political and economic status of Spain from the sixteenth to nineteenth centuries, including eighteenth-century Bourbon reform, was critical in altering the pattern of frontier interaction and exploitation (Bannon 1974). Contact in the Southeast was dissimilar to that in the greater Southwest. Nor were the experiences in California similar to Texas or New Mexico (cf. Kealhofer chapter 4 above; Miller chapter 6 above; Stodder chapter 7 above). Not only were the agents different, but so were their goals and methods. Much more research is needed to investigate the ramifications of the changing tactics of colonial powers, and the impact of these policies on the choices made by indigenous groups and their cultural and biological survival. This research would complement the burgeoning studies of the changing strategies used by Native Americans to deal with the Europeans.

Evaluations of the precontact population size of the Americas are inextricably tied to depopulation arguments. As discussed in chapter 1, the use of depopulation ratios ignores the environmental, cultural, and biological diversity so clearly demonstrated by the contributors to this volume. Modeling of epidemic population loss and recovery by Thornton and his coworkers (1991) shows how problematic demographic reconstructions based on "working backwards" from nadir populations to precontact populations can be. Thornton and coworkers (1991, 38–41) note that the primary causes of depopulation were "indirect," related both to the side effects (social, economic, and biological) of epidemics and to the psychological and cultural reaction to contact (see also Crosby 1976). Historically, demographic recovery from loss due to repeated epidemics was common (Johansson 1982, 140; Thornton et al. 1991, 29). Therefore, the reason why indirect causes made such a significant contribution to population decline in much of the Americas must be investigated. Why did secondary, long-term population decline continue in many areas long after epidemics swept through? Stannard (1991, 532) defined a similar issue, separating initial epidemic loss from subsequent demographic decline, and suggested that secondary factors arising from European diseases caused increased sterility, spontaneous abortion, subfecundity, and infant mortality. Stannard (1991, 532–33) believes these factors to be responsible for the cases of long-term, steady demographic decline and, more particularly, an inability to recover demographically from epidemic loss.

Long-term population decline may have been more closely linked to direct contact and direct imposition of European culture (specifically economic and political systems), than to the spread of epidemic diseases (Jackson 1985; Krech 1983; Reff 1987). For example, Krech (1978, 711; 1983) found little evidence of disease-driven demographic decline in northern Athapaskan groups until the nineteenth century, when political and social upheaval increased dramatically with direct contact. Interactions between Native American cultures and colonists were historically and environmentally shaped; despite this local specificity, the variables involved were *not* unique. The process of depopulation and recovery can be studied based on the preconditions, as Harris (1991) emphasizes. The chronologically sensitive archaeological evidence that is available supports this supposition (e.g., Hann 1986; Johnson and Lehmann chapter 3 above; Perttula 1991). Major demographic change in the Southwest was irrevocable with missionization in the seventeenth century (Reff 1991, 228–29). Similarly, the direct intrusion of large-scale resettlement and subsistence shifts in the mission areas of California and Texas created biological, social, and cultural disruption, dramatically altering subsequent fertility, mortality, and nutrition (Cook and Borah 1979; Ewers 1973; Miller chapter 6 above; Reff 1991). Groups that experienced indirect contact often underwent extensive but more gradual transformations (e.g., Ewers 1973; Harvey 1967). Delayed contact, such as that experienced by the central California groups, often proved to be even more devastating than earlier incursions nearby (Hurtado 1988; Thornton 1987).

Recently, the variability in regional depopulation has been tied to aboriginal settlement patterns and mobility (Ramenofsky 1990). Ramenofsky (1990),

Perttula (1991), and Ewers (1973) all suggest that sedentary groups were more susceptible to demographic loss than mobile hunter-gatherers. This recalls Steward's (1955) suggestion that more complex societies were the most politically fragile and, therefore, more susceptible to deculturation with European contact. Ramenofsky (1990, 40–41) also identifies the degree of settlement nucleation versus dispersal and the proximity of settlements to communication routes as additional, critical factors in the degree and rate of depopulation. While settlement patterning is only one variable (albeit a crucial one) that contributed to biocultural responses, Ramenofsky's study begins to address the underlying biological, cultural, and environmental variability influencing the course of biocultural change after European contact.

Palkovich's (chapter 8) plea for context-embedded analysis is reiterated here. Our understanding of the contact period in the Americas must develop from regional, diachronic analyses of environment, culture, and biology, as well as the relationship of these variables to the larger colonial economic and political milieu. Few such studies have as yet been completed, although several are currently underway (e.g., Creamer 1990; Palkovich chapter 8 above; Perttula 1991).

The goal of this volume has been to encourage researchers to focus on more detailed studies of the cultural, biological, and demographic impact of European contact and colonization. The paradigm for interpreting the protohistoric period has shifted several times, and we have attempted to demonstrate the need for it to shift yet again, toward a more defined, problem- and data-oriented study of specific regions. Kroeber (1925) and other contemporary ethnographers (e.g., Steward 1938; Stewart 1941) assumed that, despite the evidence for upheaval and cultural loss, their informants provided a clear window on the prehistoric cultures of North America. Beginning in the 1960s, Dobyns (1966, 1983, 1991) presented an opposing view: imported European diseases killed more than 90 percent of the Native American population of the New World and, by the early twentieth century, indigenous cultures bore little relationship to their precontact ancestors. The implications of this view are enormous for interpreting ethnographic, historical, and archaeological data (cf. Dunnell 1991).

As we gain more knowledge of the past, it is clear that neither of these views is entirely true or false. Both schools of thought have selectively used the data available to construct a relationship between the past and present. The studies in this volume often support Dobyns' arguments for severe demographic disruption; however, several key issues remain in question. The timing and rate of demographic decline is extremely variable between culture areas, as is the correlation between disease and demographic decline. Only more in-depth, problem-oriented analyses will allow us to understand the complex destructive and adaptive processes that occurred in indigenous societies after European contact.

Demographic collapse has enormous implications for our basic methodology and interpretations in anthropology and archaeology (cf. Dunnell 1991). If there are major cultural and biological discontinuities in the record, then survivors' accounts cannot be used as indicative of predisaster behavioral and cultural patterns (Dunnell 1991, 569–70). A tiny group of survivors is neither biologically nor culturally representative of the original population. Dunnell (1991, 569–70) and Dobyns (1991, 545) both seriously question the validity of early historic accounts and ethnographic data, and Dobyns (1991, 554) expresses further skepticism about our ability to know the past through such techniques as ethnoarchaeology.

Questioning our methodology and assumptions is vital for improving the confidence of our inferences about the past. However, ethnoarchaeology and ethnohistory do not define linear, or one-to-one (isomorphic) relationships between past and present, between trait and cultural institution. Ethnoarchaeology does not equate the ethnographic present with the past (cf. Dunnell 1991, 568; e.g., Binford 1987; Hillier and Hanson 1984; Hodder 1987; Kealhofer and Epstein 1990; Kramer 1982; Redman 1991). Different types of data and approaches are necessary counterbalances for understanding the processes that operated in the past and explaining change in the archaeological record. Whether or not specific New World cultures were intact at the time of direct contact, many viable cultures were extant. Provided we understand the context in which the data were collected, they can often be used in the analysis of cultural relationships pertinent in the past, present, and future.

The historical, biological, and cultural relationships of postcontact cultures to their precontact counterparts should not only be open to question, but it should be one of the most important questions that New World ethnohistorians and bioarchaeologists are asking (particularly due to the need to attribute modern cultural affiliation to past remains as required by NAGPRA). If we negate the relationship between precontact and postcontact data sets, we negate our ability to study cultural and biological change. The implications are not only methodological but political. Negating the relationship between modern and precontact cultures denies the cultural identity of indigenous groups today. It is unlikely that the relationship between modern and precontact Europeans would be questioned, yet European societies were also dramatically transformed by contact. This comparison highlights the implied imperialism in questioning any continuity between past and present Native American cultures. As Harris (1991, 582) notes, epidemics and depopulation are not unique, but part of human ecology. The biological and cultural perturbations caused by disease espisodes need to be studied as part of the larger socio-natural system (see McGlade 1995).

In conclusion, the chapters in this volume are a step toward a more balanced view of the cultural and biological changes that ensued from European contact. Together, they demonstrate the need for more complete data sets for evaluating issues of demographic change. Demographic collapse is a seductive conclusion, not only since it can be easily pulled out in any corner of the New World, but particularly because there is no unified counterargument. We contend that this is the point—there are no universal, easy solutions to understanding contact-period biology or culture change. We cannot say that if demographic collapse did not occur then "x" or "y" did occur. Rather, we must define the parameters and see how they are combined to create equations with unique cultural and biological outcomes. Our hope is that future research will address the specific regional, archaeological, and biological contexts for change during the late prehistoric and protohistoric periods, opening the door to a better understanding of culture change and biological adaptation.

References

Bannon, John Francis
   1974   *The Spanish Borderlands Frontier, 1513–1821.* Albuquerque: University of New Mexico Press.
Binford, Lewis
   1987   Researching Ambiguity: Frames of Reference in Site Structure. In *Method and Theory for Activity Area Research,* edited by Susan Kent, 449–512. New York: Columbia University Press.
Blakely, Robert L., and Bettina Detweiler-Blakely
   1989   The Impact of European Diseases in the Sixteenth-Century Southeast: A Case Study. *Midcontinental Journal of Archaeology* 14:62–89.
Brown, Alan
   1967   *The Aboriginal Population of the Santa Barbara Channel.* Archaeological Survey Report no. 69. Berkeley: University of California Archaeological Research Facility.
Cook, Sherburne F.
   1943   The Conflict between the California Indian and White Civilization I: The Indian versus the Spanish Mission. *Ibero-Americana* 21:1–194.
   1978   Historical Demography. In *California,* edited by Robert F. Heizer, 91–98. *Handbook of North American Indians,* vol. 8, William C. Sturtevant, general editor. Washington, D.C.: Smithsonian Institution.
Cook, Sherburne F., and Woodrow Borah
   1979   Mission Registers as Sources of Vital Statistics: Eight Missions of Northern

California. In *Essays in Population History: Mexico and California,* vol. 3, by Sherburne F. Cook and Woodrow Borah, 171–311. Berkeley: University of California Press.

Creamer, Winifred

1990   The Study of Prehistoric Demography in the Northern Rio Grande Valley, A.D. 1450–1680. Paper presented at the 59th Annual Meeting of the American Association of Physical Anthropologists, Miami.

1992   Developing Complexity in the American Southwest: A Model for the Rio Grande Valley. Paper presented at the 57th Annual Meeting of the Society for American Archaeology, Pittsburgh.

Crosby, Alfred W., Jr.

1976   Virgin Soil Epidemics as a Factor in the Aboriginal Depopulation in America. *William and Mary Quarterly* 33:289–99.

Dobyns, Henry F.

1966   Estimating Aboriginal American Population 1: An Appraisal of Techniques with a New Hemispheric Estimate. *Current Anthropology* 7:395–416.

1983   *Their Number Become Thinned: Native American Population Dynamics in Eastern North America.* Knoxville: University of Tennessee Press.

1989   Native Historic Epidemiology in the Greater Southwest. *American Anthropologist* 91(1):171–74.

1991   New Native World: Links between Demographic and Cultural Changes. In *Columbian Consequences,* vol. 3: *The Spanish Borderlands in Pan-American Perspective,* edited by David Hurst Thomas, 541–59. Washington, D.C.: Smithsonian Institution.

Dunnell, Robert C.

1991   Methodological Impacts of Catastrophic Depopulation on American Archaeology and Ethnology. In *Columbian Consequences,* vol. 3: *The Spanish Borderlands in Pan-American Perspective,* edited by David Hurst Thomas, 561–80. Washington, D.C.: Smithsonian Institution.

Ewers, John C.

1973   The Influence of Epidemics on the Indian Populations and Cultures of Texas. *Plains Anthropologist* 18(59):104–15.

Griffen, William B.

1969   *Culture Change and Shifting Populations in Central Northern Mexico.* Anthropological Papers no. 13. Tucson: University of Arizona Press.

1981   Some Problems in the Analysis of the Native Indian Population of Northern Nueva Vizcaya during the Spanish Colonial Period. In *Themes of Indigenous Acculturation in Northwest Mexico,* edited by T. B. Hinton and P. C. Weigand, 50–53. Tucson: University of Arizona Press.

Hann, John H.

1986   Demographic Patterns and Changes in Mid Seventeenth Century Timucua and Apalachee. *Florida Historical Quarterly* 64(4):371–92.

1988   *Apalachee: The Land Between the Rivers.* Gainesville: University Press of
        Florida.

Harris, Marvin
    1991   Depopulation and Cultural Evolution: A Cultural Materialist Perspective. In
            Columbian Consequences, vol. 3: *The Spanish Borderlands in Pan-American
            Perspective,* edited by David Hurst Thomas, 581–86. Washington, D.C.:
            Smithsonian Institution.

Harvey, Herbert R.
    1967   Population of the Cahuilla Indians: Decline and Its Causes. *Eugenics Quar-
            terly* 14:185–98.

Henige, David
    1986   Primary Source by Primary Source? On the Role of Epidemics in New World
            Depopulation. *Ethnohistory* 33(3):293–312.

Hillier, Bill, and Julienne Hanson
    1984   *The Social Logic of Space.* Cambridge: Cambridge University Press.

Hodder, Ian
    1987   The Meaning of Discard: Ash and Domestic Space in Baringo. In *Method and
            Theory for Activity Area Research,* edited by Susan Kent, 424–48. New York:
            Columbia University Press.

Hurtado, Albert
    1988   *Indian Survival on the California Frontier.* New Haven, Conn.: Yale Univer-
            sity Press.

Jackson, Robert
    1983   Disease and Demographic Patterns at Santa Cruz Mission, Alta California.
            Journal of California and Great Basin Anthropology 5:33–57.
    1985   Demographic Change in Northwestern New Spain. *The Americas* 41(4):462–
            79.

Johansson, S. Ryan
    1982   The Demographic History of the Native Peoples of North America: A Selec-
            tive Bibliography. *Yearbook of Physical Anthropology* 25:133–52.

Kealhofer, Lisa, and Stephen Epstein
    1990   Introduction: Choice and Pattern in Material Systems. Paper presented at the
            89th Annual Meeting of the American Anthropological Association, New Or-
            leans.

Kramer, Carol
    1982   *Village Ethnoarchaeology: Rural Iran in Archaeological Perspective.* New York:
            Academic Press.

Krech, Shepard
    1978   Disease, Starvation, and Northern Athapaskan Social Organization. *Ameri-
            can Ethnologist* 5(4):710–32.
    1983   The Influence of Disease and the Fur Trade on Arctic Drainage Lowlands Dene,
            1800–1850. *Journal of Anthropological Research* 39(1):123–46.

Kroeber, Alfred L.
  1925   *Handbook of the Indians of California.* Washington, D.C.: U.S. Government Printing Office.
Larsen, Clark Spencer, and George R. Milner, eds.
  1994   *In the Wake of Contact: Biological Responses to Conquest.* New York: Wiley-Liss.
Lycett, Mark T.
  1989   Spanish Contact and Pueblo Organization: Long-Term Implications of European Colonial Expansion in the Rio Grande Valley, New Mexico. In *Columbian Consequences,* vol. 1: *Archaeological and Historical Perspectives on the Spanish Borderlands West,* edited by David Hurst Thomas, 115–25. Washington, D.C.: Smithsonian Institution.
McGlade, James
  1995   Archaeology and the Ecodynamics of Human-Modified Landscapes. *Antiquity* 69:113–32.
McGuire, Randall H., and Maria Elisa Villalpando
  1989   Prehistory and the Making of History in Sonora. In *Columbian Consequences,* vol. 1: *Archaeological and Historical Perspectives on the Spanish Borderlands West,* edited by David Hurst Thomas, 159–77. Washington, D.C.: Smithsonian Institution.
Milanich, Jerald T.
  1990   The European Entrada into La Florida: An Overview. In *Columbian Consequences,* vol. 2: *Archaeological and Historical Perspectives on the Spanish Borderlands East,* edited by David Hurst Thomas, 3–29. Washington, D.C.: Smithsonian Institution.
Perttula, Timothy K.
  1991   European Contact and Its Effects on Aboriginal Caddoan Populations between A.D. 1520 and A.D. 1680. In *Columbian Consequences,* vol. 3: *The Spanish Borderlands in Pan-American Perspective,* edited by David Hurst Thomas, 501–18. Washington, D.C.: Smithsonian Institution.
  1992   *"The Caddo Nation."* Austin: University of Texas Press.
Ramenofsky, Ann F.
  1987   *Vectors of Death: The Archaeology of European Contact.* Albuquerque: University of New Mexico Press.
  1990   Loss of Innocence: Explanations of Differential Persistence in the Sixteenth-Century Southeast. In *Columbian Consequences,* vol. 2: *Archaeological and Historical Perspectives on the Spanish Borderlands East,* edited by David Hurst Thomas, 31–48. Washington, D.C.: Smithsonian Institution.
  1991   Historical Science and Contact Period Studies. In *Columbian Consequences,* vol. 3: *The Spanish Borderlands in Pan-American Perspective,* edited by David Hurst Thomas, 437–52. Washington, D.C.: Smithsonian Institution.

Redman, Charles L.
  1991   Distinguished Lecture in Archaeology: In Defense of the Seventies. *American Anthropologist* 93(2):295–307.

Reff, Daniel T.
  1987   The Introduction of Smallpox in the Greater Southwest. *American Anthropologist* 89(4):704–8.
  1989   Disease Episodes and the Historical Record: A Reply to Dobyns. *American Anthropologist* 91(1):174–75.
  1991   Anthropological Analysis of Exploration Texts. *American Anthropologist* 93(3):636–55.

Snow, Dean R.
  1995   Microchronology and Demographic Evidence Relating to the Size of Pre-Columbian North American Indian Populations. *Science* 268:1601–4.

Stannard, David E.
  1991   The Consequences of Contact: Toward an Interdisciplinary Theory of Native Responses to Biological and Cultural Invasion. In *Columbian Consequences,* vol. 3: *The Spanish Borderlands in Pan-American Perspective,* edited by David Hurst Thomas, 519–39. Washington, D.C.: Smithsonian Institution.

Steward, Julian
  1938   *Basin-Plateau Aboriginal Socio-Political Groups.* Bureau of American Ethnology Bulletin 120. Washington, D.C.: U.S. Government Printing Office.
  1955   *Theory of Culture Change.* Urbana: University of Illinois Press.

Stewart, Omer C.
  1941   Culture Element Distributions, XIV: Northern Paiute. *University of California Anthropological Records* 41(3):361–446.

Thomas, David Hurst
  1989   Columbian Consequences: The Spanish Borderlands in Cubist Perspective. In *Columbian Consequences,* vol. 1: *Archaeological and Historical Perspectives on the Spanish Borderlands West,* edited by David Hurst Thomas, 1–14. Washington, D.C.: Smithsonian Institution.
  1991   Foreword. In *Columbian Consequences,* vol. 3: *The Spanish Borderlands in Pan-American Perspective,* edited by David Hurst Thomas, xv–xxii. Washington, D.C.: Smithsonian Institution.

Thornton, Russell
  1987   *American Indian Holocaust and Survival: A Population History since 1492.* Norman: University of Oklahoma Press.

Thornton, Russell, Tim Miller, and Jonathan Warren
  1991   American Indian Population Recovery Following Smallpox Epidemics. *American Anthropologist* 93(1):28–45.

Upham, Steadman
  1986   Smallpox and Climate in the American Southwest. *American Anthropologist* 88:115–28.

1987   Understanding the Disease History of the Southwest: A Reply to Reff. *American Anthropologist* 89:708–10.

Verano, John W., and Douglas H. Ubelaker, eds.
1992   *Disease and Demography in the Americas.* Washington, D.C.: Smithsonian Institution.

Walker, Phillip L., and John R. Johnson
1992   Effects of Contact on the Chumash Indians. In *Disease and Demography in the Americas,* edited by John W. Verano and Douglas H. Ubelaker, 127–39. Washington, D.C.: Smithsonian Institution.

Walker, Phillip L., Patricia Lambert, and Michael J. DeNiro
1989   The Effects of European Contact on the Health of Alta California Indians. In *Columbian Consequences,* vol. 1: *Archaeological and Historical Perspectives on the Spanish Borderlands West,* edited by David Hurst Thomas, 349–64. Washington, D.C.: Smithsonian Institution.

Zubrow, Ezra
1990   The Depopulation of Native America. *Antiquity* 64:754–65.

CONTRIBUTORS

Brenda J. Baker is senior scientist in bioarchaeology for the Anthropological Survey at the New York State Museum in Albany.

Mark C. Griffin is assistant professor of anthropology at Moorhead State University, Moorhead, Minnesota.

M. Cassandra Hill is osteologist for the New York African Burial Ground Research Project at Howard University.

Jay K. Johnson is professor of anthropology and associate director for the Center for Archaeological Research at the University of Mississippi.

Lisa Kealhofer is visiting assistant professor of anthropology at the College of William and Mary.

Clark Spencer Larsen is professor of anthropology at the University of North Carolina.

Geoffrey R. Lehmann is zone archeologist for the U.S. Forest Service at Kisatchie National Forest in Alexandria, Louisiana.

Elizabeth Miller is director of the Physical Anthropology Lab in the Office of Repatriation at the National Museum of Natural History, Smithsonian Institution.

George R. Milner is associate professor of anthropology and museum curator at Pennsylvania State University.

Ann M. Palkovich is associate professor of anthropology at George Mason University.

Christopher B. Ruff is professor of cell biology and anatomy at the Johns Hopkins University School of Medicine.

Ann L. W. Stodder is consulting bioarchaeologist for Paul H. Rosendahl, Ph.D., Inc., in Hilo, Hawaii.

Index

Page numbers in italics refer to illustrations.

Creamer, Winifred, 75, 151, 211
cremations. *See* burials
cribra orbitalia, 62, 126, 131, 132, 134, 135,
138, 158, *159*. *See also* porotic
hyperostosis
CRM (contract archaeology), 61, 71–72, 210
cross-sectional geometric properties, 96,
100–114, 117, 118, 203
Curren, Caleb B., 49
cybernetics, 27

data sets, 7, 15,16, 180–82, 190, 210, 217
de la Vega, Garcilaso, 38, 46
de León, Ponce, 99
de Niza, Fray Marcos, 148, 149
de Prada, Fray Juan, 188
de Soto, Hernando, 22, 29, 30, 38–40, 48–51,
199, 203
de Vargas, Diego, 188
deer, 44, 48, 47
demographic: change, 2, 9, 56, 57, 61, 64, 65,
67, 74, 103, 180, 184, 209–17; collapse, xi,
1, 2, 4–9, 16, 56–58, 60, 62–64, 71, 74, 75,
77, 95, 178, 181, 191, 198–200, 209–17;
data, 8, 22, 71, 77; decline, xi, 2, 16, 56, 66,
67, 71, 73, 75, 76, 167, 186, 209–17 (*see
also* depopulation); disruption, 150, 151,
166; models, 180; paradigm, 2; reconstruction, 1, 57, 60, 63–65, 180, 186–89, 209–
17; recovery, 4–6, 56, 68, 74, 75;
reorganization, 191; response, 184; trends,
199. *See also* population
Denevan, William, 3, 76
de Niro, Michael J., 71
dental: abscesses, 126, 127, 131, 133–37, 139,
154, 155; anomalies, 23, 24; bifurcated
roots, 23; calculus deposits, 23; caries, 23,
109, 111, 126, 127, 131, 133–36, 139, 154,
155; enamel hypolasia (linear enamel
hypoplasia), 25, 60, 126, 127, 131, 132,
134–36, 139, 155–57; plaque, 136, 137;
pathology, 23, 25, 131–40, 154–57, 203;
wear (occlusal wear, attrition), 132, 133–
35, 137, 140, 154, 203
depopulation, 1–9, 16, 31, 49, 56, 57, 63, 73–
78, 94, 95, 126, 150, 151, 167, 177–92,
200, 201, 209, 211–17. *See also* demographic decline

DeRousseau, C. Jean, 102
developmental arrest, 154, 155, 157, 158,
166, 183
deviation-amplification process, 28
diachronic: analysis, 96, 103, 214; change, 7,
57, 60, 75, 153; investigations, 6, 93, 187,
190
diarrhea, 139
Dickel, David N., 62
diet, 28–31, 67–69, 95, 103, 109, 110, 112,
113, 118, 126, 128, 130, 132, 133, 136,
137, 140, 149, 154, 158, 160, 182, 185,
189–191, 212; marine diet, 70, 98, 109,
128
disease, 5, 15, 28, 31, 49, 56–58, 60, 62–69,
73–75, 93, 95, 126–28, 138, 140, 141, 148,
150, 151,153, 160, 164, 166, 168, 177–82,
186, 188, 191, 192, 198–202, 204, 205,
209, 213–16
Dobyns, Henry F., 2, 3, 60, 62, 65, 73, 150,
189, 200, 201, 209, 215, 216
Dolores, Colo., skeletal infection at, 161
Drake, Sir Francis, 65
drought, 149, 150, 164, 167, 185
Dunnell, Robert C., 216
Durant's Bend, 20
Dyar phase, 50
dysentery, 68, 69

Early Horizon period, 59, 70
Eastern Pueblos, 153–54, 167, 184–92, 211
Eastern Woodlands Period, 199, 201
English, 46, 98, 140
entradas, 22, 39, 48, 50, 148–49. *See also*
Coronado; de Soto; de Niza
environment, 3, 8, 9, 15–16, 28, 30, 39, 49,
57, 67, 68, 73, 127–28, 150, 179, 181, 184,
186, 191–92, 209
epidemics, xi, 1–5, 8, 9, 49, 51, 56, 57, 63, 64,
67, 68, 74–77, 93–95, 109, 149–51, 160,
164, 167, 168, 179, 185, 186, 188, 189,
191, 192, 200–2, 209–11, 213, 214, 216.
See also pandemics
epidemiological: change, 180; context, 183;
data, 94; effects, 179; evidence, 192;
impact, 180; insult, 183; models, 2, 9, 75,
180; response, 184
ethnoarchaeology, 216